Praise for Engaged Knowledge Management

"Exactly what's needed to breathe new life into a field now dying for lack of a practical, results-oriented perspective. Desouza and Awazu show us how to capture the essence of good management – knowledge – while actively *engaged* in the nitty-gritty of complex organizations. You will be engaged by this book." — **William E. Halal**, *Professor of Management, George Washington University; Co-Director, Institute for Knowledge and Innovation; author of **The Infinite Resource*** (1999)

"Desouza and Awazu uncover the subtlety of knowledge management programs. They identify the salient elements required to create sustainable knowledge-based organizations. Organizations that are engaged with the realities of managing knowledge will be successful in the marketplace, those that don't have much to lose." — **Akira Ishikawa**, *Director, Knowledge Management Society of Japan: President, Crises Management Society of Japan; Honorary President, Corporate Accounting Society of Japan; former Dean and Professor Emeritus, Graduate School of International Politics, Economics and Communication, Aoyama Gakuin University, Tokyo, Japan*

"The field of Knowledge Management, like knowledge itself, is in a constant state of flux. While many claim that the KM market is 'mature' and, as such, should require little attention to its continued health and growth, Desouza and Awazu recognize that KM cannot be viewed as having one linear life cycle, but that it must be revisited – even reinvented – periodically. The authors provide a theoretical framework grounded in the context of their work that will help organizations examine KM strategies in light of the real-time, dynamic nature of information today. With a particular focus on capturing and using customer knowledge to aid both the objectives of an organization and the user experience, *Engaged Knowledge Management* provides insights and strategies that will reinvigorate the KM community." — **Michelle Manafy**, *Editor, **EContent Magazine** and the **Intranet: Enterprise Strategies & Solutions Newsletter***

"Knowledge management is a field that has been surrounded by a lot of technology hype, and has been the center for a number of books in recent years. What I like about this book is the broad view on knowledge management, discussing some of the problems many companies see about knowledge management systems, and seeing knowledge management in relation to process improvement. The rich and colorful examples make it a truly engaging book." — **Torgeir Dingsøyr**, *Research Scientist, SINTEF Telecom and Informatics Research Foundation, Norway; co-author, **Process Improvement in Practice: A Handbook for IT Companies*** (2004)

"*Engaged Knowledge Management* is a significant contribution because it unearths the missing links in knowledge management and offers solutions to make it work. With 'knowledge' as the currency of the new economy, many companies jumped on the bandwagon and launched knowledge management programs. I meet many executives who are quick to add, 'We have a knowledge management initiative, too,' only to expose their frustrations hidden beneath their faces. This book distills the wisdom they and their knowledge managers need. Desouza and Awazu offer a robust meta-framework for knowledge management connected with the realities of the business. Contextual alignment, adaptation and customization, when supported by the three capabilities of 'segmentation,' 'destruction' and 'protection,' hold the key to a successful KM program. This book offers both the know-how and show-how to make knowledge management pay-off and how to give a competitive edge to corporations." — **Deependra Moitra**, *Associate Vice President and General Manager (Research), Infosys Technologies Limited, India*

"This book takes an unusual approach to KM, which is a positive treat. It exhibits a good understanding of the business world, which makes it realistic and pragmatic – even a bit too pragmatic for my taste, but by way of contrast this is appreciated. It recognizes both the up and down sides of KM and its interactions with organizations in a wide sense. It hinges on the 'responsibilities to take care of' in KM implementations in a crisp, down-to-earth way, without overlooking relevant issues such as that of trust. It is also a wise piece in that it doesn't forget about related experiences that are nice complements – for example, references to Decision Support Systems, or to the classical subject of 'problem finding'; in this it makes a useful integrative contribution. Thus, the book is worth reading. Easy to follow arguments and examples, pragmatic and at the same time conceptually solid enough, and not reinventing basic wheels. It will fill a gap in the KM world." — **Rafael Andreu**, *Professor of Information Systems and General Management, IESE Business School, Spain*

"Finally a book on knowledge management that is aware of what it really takes to bring about enterprise-wide change. *Engaged Knowledge Management* is pithily written, without hype, deference to fads or unrealistic focus on single solutions. If you're an experienced KM practitioner who has implemented some of the common practices – perhaps with mixed results – then you will benefit most from this book. It doesn't offer simple answers, but it will stimulate you to consider issues broadly and work out the answers for yourself. At the end, you'll have a greater awareness of how to mature your organization's approach into a balanced, realistic KM program." — **Sam Marshall**, *Knowledge Management Specialist, Unilever*

"Whether you are a long-standing practitioner or a recent convert to the KM world, this book introduces new concepts required for KM success, interwoven very effectively with KM foundational concepts. The result is a very practicable model for assessing, planning and implementing a program to ensure consistent, actionable results. Engagement is a major success factor and herein lie very powerful mechanisms for engaging all types of organizations in effective KM practices." — **Randy Hale**, *Global Program Manager, Internal Portal Services, Information Management + Collaboration + Taxonomy/Metadata, Sun Microsystems*

"*Engaged Knowledge Management* recognizes the importance of institutional knowledge capital and uses a systematic approach to identify keys issues, challenges and potential areas where corporations can boost bottom lines. In today's competitive business environments where customers are increasingly having more options in products, services and providers, managing customer information and data across the enterprise to derive opportunities for cross selling opportunities represents the most challenging problem facing senior business and IT executives. Knowledge capital in my view is probably one of the most underutilized assets at the majority of multinational institutions, while information sharing across business segments also represents the most sustainable products and services differentiators for companies seeking a competitive advantage in attracting and retaining loyal customers through improved customer satisfaction." — **Donald J. Raphael**, *Vice President, Technology Strategy and Implementation Services, Enterprise Architecture-Technology Research, Bank of America, USA*

"This book talks about every aspect that we had successes in and more. From initial set up of KM program to its capabilities, to engagements throughout various management levels, and to interactions between people and technology. . . . I highly recommend this book for everyone to read." — **Kiho Sohn**, *Site Leader for Knowledge Management, Boeing Canoga Park, USA*

"Knowledge management is at cross-roads today. One of the challenges of KM is how to overcome 'information overload' irrespective of the sector. With an excitement to share knowledge, people in KM tend to 'overload' the customers resulting in losing the customers. In this book, the authors discuss how various players, organizations, technologies, and customers need to be 'engaged' in KM. Documented with recent literature in the field of KM, this book addresses the practical applications of KM in a wide variety of organizational environments. It is an essential reader for all those who want to 'engage' continually in KM irrespective of the nature of organization." — **Raja Rajasekaran**, *Agricultural Information Scientist/ Intranet Information Manager, Monsanto Company*

"Knowledge management has become a must in modern management. Drawing on their broad consulting experience and sound research, Desouza and Awazu provide many new ideas on how to excel in managing your knowledge assets. In this book the authors show that knowledge management is more than a buzzword. In an easy to read way, engaged knowledge management covers the most important aspects of the topic. This book can be recommended to everybody who wants to improve the firm's efficiency and the effectiveness of its operations by creating new knowledge and re-using existing knowledge about customers, markets, processes, etc." — **Kurt Matzler**, *Department of Marketing and International Management, University of Klagenfurt, Austria*

"This book combines excellent insight with practical application. It is well suitable both to the management thinker and the knowledge practitioner who faces the challenge of managing tomorrow's knowledge-based organization." — **George Tovstiga**, *Visiting Professor, Henley Management College, and Arthur D. Little Ltd, Switzerland*

"*Engaged Knowledge Management* will be one of the most important books in your library. It is a wonderful compendium of the critical issues related to knowledge management and will clearly be labeled as a 'must have' for all academics and practitioners who work in this field. The text starts with a clear discussion on who should be responsible for KM including the roles of various C-level executives as it relates to all processes including ones that don't have much coverage in the extant literature such as knowledge destruction, and my personal favorite, knowledge protection. Other chapters cover global and customer issues as well as the critical debate on incentives for knowledge sharing. The final messages discuss technology and KM's future. All in all, the book is comprehensive and well written. A fine reference for the KM novice and expert." — **Nick Bontis**, *Associate Professor, DeGroote Business School, McMaster University; Director, Institute for Intellectual Capital Research, Canada; Associate Editor,* **Journal of Intellectual Capital***; co-author,* **The Strategic Management of Intellectual Capital and Organizational Knowledge** *(2002)*

"This is a very easy book to read and through the various aspects of each subject, the different facets of each application and the multitude of real life examples, one actually gets a total picture of this fascinating subject that knowledge management is – whether you are a researcher or a practitioner." — **Rony Dayan**, *Chief Knowledge Officer, Israel Aircraft Industries, Israel*

"As knowledge management matures as a discipline, our understanding of it is becoming more complex and multifaceted. In their book, Desouza and Awazu are leading this charge to greater understanding by expanding the scope of the knowledge management literature. Drawing on ideas from complex systems theory and social networking, they provide a succinct and informative overview, moving knowledge management from an abstract theory waiting to be applied to a more concrete understanding of how KM needs to play out and evolve in real life. Covering a wide range of topics, from globalization, engaging external constituencies, and incentives to knowledge sharing, this book provides both the new practitioner and the seasoned veteran with a new look at some of the critical topics in the field." — **H. Frank Cervone**, *Assistant University Librarian for Information Technology, Northwestern University, USA*

Engaged Knowledge Management

Engagement with New Realities

Kevin C. Desouza and Yukika Awazu

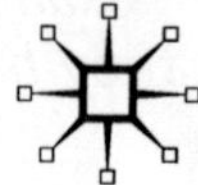

First published 2005 by
PALGRAVE MACMILLAN
Houndmills, Basingstoke, Hampshire RG21 6XS and
175 Fifth Avenue, New York, N.Y. 10010
Companies and representatives throughout the world

PALGRAVE MACMILLAN is the global academic imprint of the Palgrave Macmillan division of St. Martin's Press, LLC and of Palgrave Macmillan Ltd. Macmillan® is a registered trademark in the United States, United Kingdom and other countries. Palgrave is a registered trademark in the European Union and other countries.

ISBN-13: 978–1–4039–4510–5 hardback
ISBN-10: 1–4039–4510–1 hardback

This book is printed on paper suitable for recycling and made from fully managed and sustained forest sources.

A catalogue record for this book is available from the British Library.

Library of Congress Cataloging-in-Publication Data
Desouza, Kevin C., 1979–
    Engaged knowledge management : engagement with new realities /
    Kevin C. Desouza and Yukika Awazu.
        p.   cm.
    Includes bibliographical references and index.
    ISBN 1–4039–4510–1
    1. Knowledge management.   2. Organizational effectiveness.
    3. Commitment (Psychology)   I. Awazu, Yukika, 1970–   II. Title.
    HD30.2.D468 2005
    658.4'038—dc22   2004066391

10   9   8   7   6   5   4   3   2   1
14   13   12   11   10   09   08   07   06   05

Transferred to digital printing in 2006.

We dedicate this work to our parents. They have shown by example what it means to be engaged and through sacrifices they have provided us with opportunities to read, learn, and think.

Contents

List of Tables and Figures

Preface

Writing a book is a journey. On every journey, there is a start and a sometimes elusive end that often turns into yet another new start. Although this book has been a long and sometimes tiring journey, it has also been a fruitful and most rewarding one. Whenever I finish a book, I like to take some time to refresh my thoughts and recharge my mind by taking a road trip to a tranquil destination a short drive from my present home city of Chicago. Once I arrive where I'm going, I typically enjoy some good food and wine, admire the beautiful scenery and sometimes catch a movie or a play if I'm lucky. When I return, I feel a new sense of energy and excitement, and am prepared to deal with the challenges and obstacles that await me.

Why am I telling you this? Because a road trip in October of 2003 was anything but relaxing! For this I thank my fellow researcher and colleague, Yukika Awazu. She, like me, having just completed a research project, wanted to take a short break around the same time that I did, so we hit the road one weekend. We began by discussing our recent investigations into various aspects of managing knowledge in organizations. We talked about lessons learned from past projects and brainstormed new and areas for future investigation. During our discussion, as we jotted down the names of various projects, Yukika remarked, "A compilation of these project insights would make a nice book."

My first reaction to that statement was hardly positive. Having just finished writing two books, I wanted a break before starting on a third. However, as Yukika worked diligently with me to put this text together over the next few months, I was quickly convinced that the time to begin book three was the present. Yukika's enthusiasm, her willingness to learn (and teach), to lead (and follow), and her interest in helping me organize and manage the know-how and insights we have accumulated from our past research projects, have all made this book a reality.

Our goal here is simple but salient – to re-architect current practice in organizations to permit them to build engaged knowledge management programs. Knowledge management has been a buzzword since the early 1990s. Many organizations have invested millions (if not billions) of dollars to help them better manage knowledge, their most vital resource. We have traversed a long path since the first days of knowledge management efforts in organizations, and we think it time to revamp the state of the discipline now that so much has been learned in the last ten years. Re-architecting calls for building a knowledge management program that is *engaged*.

Most organizations have been able to achieve a few of the intended benefits of knowledge management, but many benefits still remain elusive. One reason for this is that the strategic, people-oriented and technology-oriented aspects of knowledge management need to be fine-tuned for better engagement with the realities of the current business environment. To provide one example, until very recently much effort was expended on the intricacies of how to capture, store and distribute knowledge within the enterprise. These are salient capabilities that play a pivotal role in the initial stages of a knowledge management program. Still, while their significance does not diminish as the knowledge management program grows, the increased prominence of three other capabilities needs to be discussed: segmentation, destruction, and protection. Unless a knowledge management program encompasses these capabilities, it will not be in tune, or *engaged*, with the current realities of an organization's workings. Similarly, an effective knowledge management program needs to be engaged with the intricacies of functioning in a global, distributed, and dynamic marketplace. Existing knowledge management systems, the technology artifacts, also need to be redesigned. In our research, we have uncovered several reasons why such systems are abandoned by employees, and can summarize our findings as poor engagement with the needs of employees. In this book, will discuss the pragmatics of re-architecting knowledge management in organizations.

In the process, we hope to shed some light on how organizations can redesign current knowledge management approaches to achieve some of the still-elusive benefits. These insights have been deduced from researching and consulting with over fifty organizations ranging from traditional *Fortune* 100s to lesser-known, small-to-medium-sized enterprises. They range from private institutions to governmental and academic organizations. These organizations are quite varied in terms of geographic location; we have studied knowledge management initiatives on every continent except Antarctica!

This book is written primarily for three audiences. First and foremost, we are speaking to knowledge managers and senior executives. For you, we provide actionable thoughts and insights that can be implemented by your organizations. Since no insight will work exactly as taught in every organization, we advise you to consider the peculiarities of your organizational setting prior to implementing the ideas presented here. Second, we would like to attract the attention of architects, developers, and programmers – in essence, the creators of knowledge management systems. For you, we offer ways to design better systems. We provide guidelines on how to devise dynamic systems that adapt to their environments, rather than traditional static systems. Last, but by no means least, we speak to the curious minds of academics. Both accomplished researchers and upcoming scholars can benefit from the book in several ways, as it provides new insights that can be put through rigorous research examination. We hope that such examination will lend further insights that advance the field of knowledge management. The book also provides an effective training tool for students in graduate business programs, as all current and future managers will be knowledge managers in some form. To this end, an appreciation of the concepts presented here will prove enormously beneficial.

We hope you enjoy reading our text; it was certainly our pleasure to write it. Every reader will have to decide individually how to prioritize, experiment with and implement the ideas presented here. We welcome your inquiries and ask that you drop us a line (or two!) to share your ideas, suggestions and criticisms of the text. By engaging with you, our readers, we will learn from your experiences and better manage our own knowledge.

KEVIN C. DESOUZA

Chicago   YUKIKA AWAZU

Acknowledgements

Book-writing is a daunting task without the support, encouragement, and counsel of great people. This page and those that will follow would not have seen the light of day were it not for some outstanding individuals.

We would first like to acknowledge our professors and mentors in academia. They were instrumental in helping us appropriately channel our energy throughout the pursuit of our academic and scholarly inquiries. We thank them for their tireless support, words of wisdom, and intellectual stimulation. They taught us that knowledge is most valuable when it is shared and instilled in many rather than hoarded by a select few. Both of us have had the pleasure of learning from these distinguished scholars and will forever treasure their generosity of time and intellect. We especially thank two great professors, George Kraft and Chiaki Nishiyama, for their tireless support, dedication, and words of wisdom.

This text is the outcome of years of interaction with a number of distinguished colleagues. These include both our fellow researchers and our contacts at the organizations that provided us with valuable data on numerous aspects of their companies' knowledge management practices. They have all challenged us to think differently and to question our underlying assumptions. They practice the art of knowledge management on a daily basis. Many of the chapters in this text resulted from joint research investigations with these esteemed colleagues, and we thank them here for sharing their ideas and allowing us to partake in their scholarly investigations. We would like particularly to thank Roberto Evaristo, Thomas Davenport, Robert J. Thomas, Jeffery Raider, Mark Nissen, Torgeir Dingsøyr, Ganesh Kumar Vanapalli, Amrit Tiwana, Tobin Hensgen, Mark Power, John Mehling, Carlo Bonifazi, Richard Wang, Anthony Lausin, Raymond Hackney, and Yun Wan. Kevin would also like to thank Nicola Sequeira for the interesting conversations during his visit to Boston in November 2004. Yukika would like to thank Kaori Sato for her continuous encouragement and Clare Danes for her support. We would like to thank Stephen Rutt and Jacky Kippenberger, from Palgrave, who saw the value of the manuscript and gave us the opportunity to publish our work.

Finally, we have been fortunate to have the support of innumerable personal sources of influence. We profusely thank our friends for their understanding during this project, as well as our families, who understood the need for this book and supported it from inception to completion.

Kevin C. Desouza
Yukika Awazu

1
Introduction

Often the most difficult part of writing is coming up with a title. Choosing the title for this book was far from straightforward. The last five years have seen a surge in the publication of books on knowledge management, so, we wanted a title that would stand out from the crowd and differentiate the content that we present in this book from other works. We wrestled with more than thirty potential titles before deciding on *Engaged Knowledge Management*, which best articulates the essence of this book. This chapter introduces our title concept and, we hope, will entice the reader to learn more about the field.

The term *engagement* has different meanings depending on its context. We most commonly hear the word when we say that two people are *engaged to be married*. This condition normally means that they are seriously committed to each other's wellbeing, have mutual romantic feelings, understand each other's behavior well enough to accept one another, and are planning a happy future together. For a marriage to be successful, the two parties must be seriously interested in each other. They must be able to understand how each complements the other. Ideally, there will be areas to complement and areas where the two's skills overlap. They must enjoy spending time together, seeking advice from each other, playing together, and even working hard together. They must have a common dream that guides their actions. Unless most or all of these conditions are met, chances are that the two parties will eventually go their separate ways.

We can analyze the term *engagement* using a process view. Early on, as the two people get to know each other, one can expect some bumps in the road. After all, this is the stage when each is exposing his or her character; and one hopes that, through trial and error, both will work out their differences and stay the course. Ultimately, if things go well, comes marriage, when each makes a commitment to stay the course "until death do us part."

The ideal relationship between an organization and its knowledge management program should mirror the pattern of "courtship," "engagement", and "marriage" that occurs in romantic love, and, to a degree, this already has begun to take shape. After all, we have observed knowledge management activities in organizations for quite some time. The field of knowledge management has its roots in the works of philosophers who spent much effort probing the epistemological issues of knowledge. Friedrich August von Hayek and Peter Drucker were the first to introduce the concept of knowledge workers in the context of economics and business respectively. Following them, a large body of literature developed that examined various aspects of knowledge management through the varied lenses of economics, strategic management, information systems, organizational behavior, human resource management, and operations management. In short, we saw the early days of courtship in the mid 1990s. Knowledge management was the cool business fad of the day, and almost every organization was jumping on the bandwagon. Money was being invested to court the concept and improve companies from Tokyo to Palo Alto.

The early 2000s saw the crash of the dot-com bubble. Since spending was being cut all over, the first thing to be tossed out was that which managers perceived as unnecessary or extraneous, and unfortunately, many saw knowledge management programs under this heading. Chief knowledge officers, knowledge repositories, and water-cooler conversations were suddenly out, and all at once everyone was asked to do more with less. The focus of organizations was to optimize areas that they knew were successful, and cut spending on high-risk or uncertain areas. Unfortunately, this thinking had soon reached it ceiling, as innovations were stifled and new sources of wealth creation were not surfacing. Hence, recently (we would say since the middle of 2002), organizations have begun slowly revamping spending in areas that were cut. One of the fascinating items with knowledge management is that it has the potential to help an organization succeed in goal attainment in terms of efficiency and effectiveness, and also in foresight and innovations. If conducted properly, knowledge management can help an organization improve the efficiency and effectiveness of its operations by re-using the existing know-how to prevent reinvention and wasteful consumption of resources. The resources that are saved from waste can then be put to good use, especially in the context of new knowledge creations which one hopes will lead both to innovations and to their commercialization.

As the pendulum swings back in favor of knowledge management today, companies have realized that they must leverage what they know to the best of their ability and embrace this essential component of successful businesses. The courtship with the discipline has been reignited, and knowledge management spending, to judge by our recent conversations with executives, is once again seeing a rise. Still, we have one major concern: even though the interest in knowledge management has received widespread attention, organizations have failed thus far to *engage* themselves adequately in the intricacies of managing their knowledge. They have yet to *commit* to the field and fully incorporate it into their work. In failing to do so, "bad marriages" between companies and their knowledge management programs have sprung up everywhere like dandelions. When this happens, knowledge management does not deliver what organizations want.

Engaged knowledge management

In this book, we discuss several themes from our research which are in need of attention in order to foster *engaged knowledge management* in business. We take as our starting point the conviction that an organization must seriously engage itself with the concept for a relationship to prove meaningful, and that failure to do so will render any attempt counterproductive. We are not here to convince anyone that knowledge management is imperative for them to survive in today's marketplace. This is an established fact that has been expounded upon to great lengths by scholars and practitioners alike. Rather, we hope to help the reader to leverage what they have, to fill in the gaps, and to draw attention to seemingly unconnected components – essentially, to build a knowledge management program that is *engaged* with the reader's own organization and the realities of the environment it operates in.

Webster's New Collegiate Dictionary offers several definitions for *engaged: being involved in an activity; pledged to be married; involved, especially in a hostile manner;* and *being in gear.*[1] Let us turn to each of these meanings one by one to see how each is relevant to our mission in this book. First, an organization must obviously be *involved* in the concept of knowledge management to have any relationship with it. In order to do this, it must be sensitive to the different types of knowledge in its midst and the different capabilities needed to leverage the knowledge, as well as have dedicated personnel at the strategic level who are interested and invested in knowledge management. Conducting knowledge management in a haphazard manner is not an option. Every aspect of the organization must appreciate and engage itself with knowledge management – then, and only then, can optimal results be achieved. Being involved calls for an organization to realize that knowledge management cannot be viewed as a commodity simply to be purchased, like for example a printer or a copier; knowledge needs to be managed with care and needs to be channeled appropriately within and around the organization to be of strategic value. As we will posit in a later chapter, most organizations do not appropriately involve themselves in the calibration of knowledge management systems (KMSs). Most organizations take a deterministic, top-down approach to system calibration and then assume that employees will embrace them and use them for economic ends. This is a futile exercise, however. A better approach is to give users the opportunity to customize, personalize, and innovate with their KMSs; such involvement in the knowledge management process is more likely to lead to optimal results.

To extend our metaphor further, a knowledge management program must also be *married* with the reality in which the organization operates. Today, we operate in a global and ever-changing world. Our modern workforce is virtual, distributed, dynamic, and loosely connected. Organizations also engage in similar kinds of relationships with other organizations. For example, all of us are aware of the prominence of offshore outsourcing relationships, which are much like having temporary or contingent workers coupled with virtual workers. Strategic alliances and mergers and acquisitions deals are also on the rise. Moreover, the unit of work is now the project. Projects have moved from single locations to multiple ones as satellite offices and telecommuting have flourished. Unless an organization's knowledge management efforts can deal with these issues and function under these dynamics, a firm will fail to achieve its goals. These realities call for an organization to monitor its knowledge management processes and tweak them to embrace the new realities; failure to do so will make such programs obsolete and a mismatch.

Organizational knowledge management activities also need to be *engaged in a hostile manner* – with force and with intent – with their respective businesses. Although rising in acclaim, knowledge management is still a relative afterthought in the principles of business administration, and is seldom incorporated into the work practices of employees. In fact, most employees report dismal results when they attempt to engage themselves with knowledge management systems. Many find such systems wanting in their ability to provide requisite knowledge. Moreover, many employees view knowledge management as an *option*, seeing no direct consequences, either positive or negative, of engaging oneself in knowledge management. As a result, the organization as a whole suffers. On the whole, employees today would rather hoard their knowledge than share it with their peers. The effects of economic downturn, job insecurity, and rightsizing all add to this fear of knowledge sharing. Moreover, incentives are seldom provided to employees who share their knowledge. This should not be so. Employees should be encouraged to apply the principles of knowledge management to better the goals of the organization and should not focus only on individual objectives. Incentives must be provided for employees who to their knowledge and in so doing foster innovation.

Returning to our extended metaphor, the above concerns could be said to indicate a knowledge management program that is *not in gear* and unable to move an organization in the right direction. Being out of gear obviously hinders and may actually cause more harm than good. This book is about re-engaging the organization with knowledge management and putting it back in gear. We must re-architect current knowledge management programs to make them more cognizant of and *engaged* with new realities faced by organizations. Failure to do so will almost surely lead to the demise of the organization and result in grave consequences to society at large. The reader may care to think about when they might shift gears when driving a car.

A driver changes gear as new realities are faced, for instance a stop light, a curve, or a clear road ahead to speed. In all instances, failure to appropriately change gears will compromise the health of the automobile (the organization) as internal damage will occur to engine and other parts, or in the worst cases to both the automobile and the driver (the manager), namely a crash. Knowledge management initiatives need to be looked upon in a similar manner. In this book, we hope to provide an overview of some of the lessons learnt from conducting, observing, and researching knowledge management initiatives in several organizations. These lessons have helped us uncover salient themes that have not been debated thoroughly in the extant literature, and also have the possibility to put knowledge management in the right gear.

Organization of the book

In the next chapter we begin by looking at how best to control knowledge management initiatives in organizations. In essence, who should be responsible for engaging knowledge management within organizations? Should direction come only from top-ranking officers, or should individuals be allowed to decide how they would like to conduct knowledge management? Our answer: both. For some types of knowledge, the agenda for its management will need to be controlled tightly, whereas for others a more liberal and emergent approach is optimal. In addition, for certain types of knowledge management processes like knowledge creation a decentralized control mechanism will be better suited, whereas for others, such as knowledge commercialization, a centralized approach will be successful. The focus of this chapter will be to demonstrate that an organization must actively be engaged in the management of tensions between centralized and decentralized management approaches, and also be cognizant of how and when to chose the right strategy in a given context.

Chapter 3 will address the missing capabilities of knowledge management. Much attention has been paid in the literature to concepts of creation, integration, distribution, and application of knowledge. While all of these are essential components of the knowledge management process, three capabilities – segmentation, destruction, and protection – often get overlooked. As an organization's knowledge management agenda blossoms, we will surely see an influx of knowledge in repositories and also heavy traffic in terms of knowledge flows between employees and KMSs. Unless we are able to segment out knowledge and knowledge flows in terms of what is important and what is of utmost importance, we will suffer from overload. Important knowledge will not be acknowledged or acted upon, and this may lead to delayed or absent action on the part of the organization. Moreover, over time, we must replace old knowledge with new. If we don't, it will be difficult to keep the organization up to date, since individuals will hold on to old practices and resist change. Protection capabilities are important to ensure that the hard-earned knowledge of the organization is not compromised through acts of theft, espionage, or disasters. Knowledge possessed by an organization must be rare in the marketplace, else it will not be a sources of sustained competitive advantages. Unless segmentation, destruction, and protection capabilities are incorporated, we will not have a program that is *engaged* with the reality of dealing with a growing knowledge management agenda.

Chapter 4, "The Knowledge Chiefs," examines the intricacies of three "C-level" executives who are charged with managing various aspects of knowledge management. Here we look at how chief knowledge officers, chief learning officers, chief privacy officers, and chief security officers engage the knowledge management agenda. We also explore how the three chiefs can work together and complement one another's skills to build an optimal knowledge management agenda. We must have symbiotic engagement of three disciplines of knowledge, learning, and security in order for knowledge assets to be optimally leveraged. The goal of the chiefs is to work in coordination with one another and the other C-level executives to ensure that an organization's knowledge programs are in gear and are keeping pace with new realities as and when they emerge.

Chapter 5 will explore strategic aspects of managing knowledge in a distributed and global world. Distributed natures can be found in the concepts of how work is conducted, for instance in the case of virtual teams, the use of knowledge workers who have distributed and varying organizational affiliations, as is the case in the hiring of contingent workers, and also in the conduct of projects that are distributed. Effective and efficient knowledge management is important to ensure that we have appropriate coordination, collaboration, and communication across the distributed entities so that we can align them towards the attainment of overall organizational goals.

In Chapter 6, we will look at how to engage knowledge *around* the enterprise. In particular, we will discuss knowledge management within the context of strategic alliances. We will elaborate on how to manage knowledge when entering into relationships with an external party. External sources must be tapped into for knowledge that is not available within the organization. We look at issues an organization must contend with when entering into an alliance with an external party. We survey the range of alliances from simple licensing agreements to complex merger and acquisition deals, and the underlying knowledge management issues.

Chapter 7 will next elaborate on the concept of customer knowledge management. It is imperative for any business, regardless of size and scope, to manage customer knowledge in order to survive and excel in the current marketplace. As customers need to be empowered with tools and techniques to manage knowledge, we see them as a vital component of the knowledge management agenda. Customers must be engaged with the knowledge management efforts of an organization in a holistic and lively manner. Here we tell how.

Chapter 8 will discuss the concept of incentives. How do we promote knowledge management in organizations? We believe that the best way is to pay people for their knowledge, and to this end we discuss the concept of the knowledge market. We will consider the various factors that determine the success of a knowledge bazaar and whether an organization should set one up. Consider the relatively simple example of a retail store in which salespeople are paid on commission. If we want personnel to share their knowledge (strategies for making a sale, customer pitch techniques, and the like) but reward them on the basis of commissions calculated on individual sales, are they likely to share their knowledge? Of course not, as there is no incentive to share those techniques that allow each individual to one-up his co-workers. But if we change the reward system to one that is group-based, where for example commissions are calculated based on the sales record of the whole team, we can then expect them to share their insights, as the salary of one now depends on the success of the group.

Chapter 9 deals with the technology aspects of knowledge management, specifically with the interactions between people and technology. Currently, most KMSs are disengaged from the reality of how employees actually use them. We examine and question these barriers to the effective use of knowledge management systems and the concept of user innovation with KMSs. We have tracked how users engage with KMSs over the course of time, from their initial use to super-user status. The chapter will highlight the cycle of innovation that we uncovered, as well as its governing dynamics. In addition, we will discuss the issues of "context" and "distributedness" and why one should pay close attention to these in the design of KMSs.

Chapter 10 concludes the book by looking at the future of engaged knowledge management. We discuss how a knowledge management agenda can benefit from incorporating the expertise of diverse groups in the organization. Currently, knowledge management systems (KMS) such as intranets, electronic yellow pages, and agendas have made headways into almost all organizations. Yet they are seldom accepted or used optimally by employees. A key reason for this is that they are designed by the IT folks! The users of such systems are seldom the IT folks, but rather the accountants, financial analysts, production engineers, marketing managers, human resource professionals, and lawyers. While the input of these users may be solicited during the design of the KMS, these individuals are not really "engaged" in the process, and a poorly designed, underutilized system results. Engaged knowledge management brings the customer fully into the design process. It is our firm belief that all agents (employees) of the organization must be engaged and be allowed to be engaged with knowledge management and that, thus, they will be more involved with this important activity, which in turn will benefit the entire organization.

2
Engaging Tensions of Knowledge Management Control

Any proficient activity calls for balance, which normally entails striking the right median between extremes. As they say, 'All work and no play makes Jack a dull boy,' or 'Don't overdo things.' Management needs to strike the right balance when it comes to deciding how best to control resources, processes, and assets under its purview. Managing knowledge management programs is no different, and entails a judicious balance in managing the tensions of centralization and decentralization.

Of the many definitions of the term 'tension', the following most closely captures our connotation of it in this chapter: "balance maintained in an artistic work between opposing forces or elements."[1] This definition is apt for two reasons. First, the term 'artistic work' accurately describes the process of constructing a knowledge-based organization, or re-architecting an existing organization into one that is more knowledge-centric. In addition, breaking down the term 'artistic work' into 'art' + 'work' helps bring out a primary tension: knowledge management is both an art and work. The *art* element has to do with having imagination and vision about what a knowledge-based organization should look like, identifying its attributes and its dimensions, and examining how each component of the organization fits into the overall architecture. The *work* element has to do with constructing the vision. One might think of work as the job of transforming the architect's plan, a logical design, into a physical reality like a building or a piece of machinery. Unless one can strike the right balance between the art and the work product, there will be disconnects, leading to a poorly created knowledge organization. Two common disconnects are (1) when the art conceptualization is excellent but is followed by poor work, and (2) when the art conceptualization is poor but is followed by excellent work. In the first instance, we have a good design on paper but it is implemented poorly; in the second case, we have an unimaginative design that is implemented correctly. To promote *art*, we must allow for creative work through decentralization and looseness in control. Conversely, to facilitate *work* we must strive to control the process of engineering, for which we require centralization and tight control dynamics.

The second item of interest in the definition of 'balance' is the concept of 'opposing forces'. Tensions that we describe in this chapter can best be characterized as opposing answers to important governance questions such as: Does an organization exercise tight control over its knowledge management process or does it allow it to be conducted loosely? Should an organization choose centralization over decentralization? Should order be achieved through top-down or bottom-up directive mechanisms? Questions such as these are important and must be considered when embarking on a knowledge management program. We will focus on them in this chapter.

Managing a knowledge management program is no easy feat. While there are many reasons for this, we will concentrate on a single aspect: how to best control and command the knowledge programs of the organization. We feel that executives face an unusual surge of tensions in this area, all of which can be reduced to one of control dichotomies.

At the fundamental level, executives think they must choose between centralized or decentralized approaches to control. Centralized approaches to control can be characterized by tight structure. Decision rights are normally restricted to one individual or a select few. Order is therefore imposed in a top-down fashion through directives from top management, or from senior personnel with decision rights. These individuals normally determine what is permitted, how the organization should conduct work, and how order is ensured and governed. Decentralized approaches are the opposite; here decision rights are available to individuals across all hierarchical levels of the organization. Order emerges mostly from a bottom-up direction, rather than being imposed in the top-down mode. This is because individuals have the right to act on information and knowledge to make decisions – decisions that affect not only their own work but also their surroundings, such as their team or their department. As we expand the concept of surroundings and the number of decision-makers, order emerges from these actions at the lower level. The question becomes: 'When should one choose a centralized mechanism for knowledge management versus a decentralized one?' The answer lies in three aspects: the type of *knowledge process*, the type of *knowledge workers*, and the type of *knowledge* we are seeking to manage (see Figure 2.1).

Type of knowledge process: knowledge creation versus knowledge commercialization

Knowledge management can be viewed as a two-phased approach. The first deals mainly with the *creation* of knowledge. This phase represents knowledge generation, and consists of knowledge sharing, storage, transfer, and application, all geared towards the generation of new knowledge. One might consider this akin to the act of invention. In order to invent, we must be able to go through the knowledge creation cycle many times and, hopefully, obtain

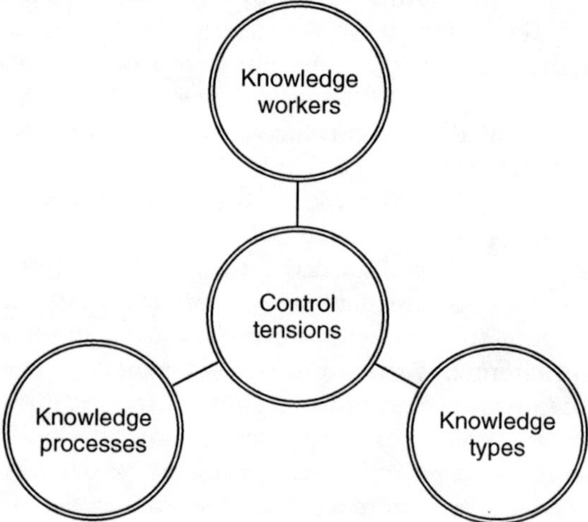

Figure 2.1   Knowledge management control tensions.

new knowledge with each cycle. The second phase of knowledge management is the *commercialization* of knowledge. This is where we would like to transform the invention into an innovation. The differences between an invention and an innovation are not inconsequential.[2] Innovations are commercialized inventions that call for taking inventions to the market and being successful at transforming them to realize economic ends. Knowledge creation and knowledge commercialization feed into one another. New knowledge created will, hopefully, lead to new inventions that should inform future commercialization processes. Likewise, commercialization of knowledge should lead to discovery of weaknesses in products and services, which should serve to inform future knowledge creation activities.

Each of the two processes requires different governance approaches. Knowledge creation calls for a fluid space – one that can promote creativity, rich exchange of insights, debates and dialogue, and also nurtures new ideas. As an example, consider some of the research and development labs: these are spaces where each scientist operates, for the most part, autonomously. Scientists share knowledge voluntarily, because the sharing will benefit each other's inquiries and experiments. Order is not imposed on them, but emerges from their mutual interaction. Take the case of scientific communities: in these spaces, norms and best practices emerge as knowledge is shared, dialogues are conducted, and debates surface. We can even assert that order emerges out of evolutionary cycles. Best practices are shared, these get debated and new best practices emerge. Some practices are refuted, others get refined, and new practices emerge with the strong ones surviving over time. Bottom-up order is the dominant style of operations.

To foster knowledge creation, management must ensure that they operate at a distance, and do not impose on creative cycles or actions. Management should not be involved with resolving disputes and the emergence of norms; these should be left to the knowledge workers. Self-governance and self-organization are important strategies to appreciate here. Often, management feels that if they are not directly involved in a project or participating actively, they are not doing their job. This is not so; management needs to act as a catalyst here, by promoting the creative environments, providing resources for knowledge creation to occur, and also seeking new ways to enhance the work processes of the knowledge workers. Decision rights, however, cannot reside exclusively with the managers but must be delegated to the knowledge workers on site. The best analogy we can provide to help managers envision their role in the knowledge creation space is that of a funding agency. Management is the provider of funding for interesting projects. Each knowledge worker has the right to collaborate with fellow workers or work independently and put together a proposal for funding. In compiling a proposal, the knowledge workers have the burden of clearly articulating why the project is important to the organization, how it contributes to strategic objectives, what the deliverables are, when these will be delivered, and how they build upon the existing knowledge stock of the organization, and so on. This is significant, as the knowledge workers are putting in place metrics against which they think they should be measured. For instance, if the project says a deliverable will be handed in on a particular date, and this does not occur, only the knowledge workers can be held accountable, since they put the proposal together.

Management must take a portfolio approach and try to balance out investment in the various endeavors and ensure that the most interesting and important projects are funded in a timely manner. Ultimately, through the rules of evolution, only the strong will survive in this approach. Knowledge workers who continually under-achieve and do not deliver on their promises will not be respected by their peers, and hence will be involved in fewer proposals and initiatives, this eventually resulting in their exit from the organization. On the other hand, those who are successful will ascend in the ranks, lure other workers to take on joint engagements, and, one hopes, eventually produce better management of organizational resources.

Allowing order to emerge has another interesting benefit: the emergence of core competencies. In due course, the organization will learn to distinguish areas that are popular and successful from areas that are not. It can then plan on how to better leverage the successful areas for organizational ends. Additionally, it can help address issues in non- successful areas, if the exercise benefits the organization. In the final analysis, we must remember that management can easily destroy knowledge creation by trying to micromanage the process and seeking to control rather than direct knowledge creation efforts. The successful management approach is one that seeks to provide direction without direct imposition and interference with creative cycles.

Let us now contrast the requirements for knowledge creation with those for knowledge commercialization. We are now concerned with what it takes to turn an invention – the outcome of a successful knowledge creation exercise – into an innovation. Innovations can be internal or external to the organization. For example, a group may invent a best practice such as a knowledge process, and then seek to commercialize it in the organization by proliferating its acceptance and adoption. Similarly, the R&D lab may develop a product enhancement that needs to be commercialized for the external market. Interestingly, many of the 'rules' for successfully transforming inventions into innovations are similar, regardless of internal or external focus. This is because, in both cases, the invention must be taken from its 'original' space and transplanted into a 'foreign' one.

Successful knowledge commercialization occurs when an organization has a systematic process.[3] An architecture that is efficiently and effectively managed needs to be in place to take the invention and transform it into an innovation. Consider the analogy of a manufacturing plant whose goal is to transform a logical idea into an innovative product by marketing it appropriately, producing it efficiently and effectively, dispatching it to the end-consumers, and having provisions to take in feedback from the consumers on usage issues. Successful manufacturers have an optimized, repeatable, well-defined, and tightly controlled process for commercializing inventions. To ensure success, such organizations must forgo decentralization for centralization to ensure that the process can be better controlled and order can be more definite and static.

Let us look at the management of the human resource function of an organization. What would happen if, every time we needed to hire someone, we reinvented the recruiting process? The organization would be engaged in an ineffective and wasteful usage of corporate resources. The process of recruiting, for the most part, is fairly straightforward, and needs to be managed by exerting centralized control. The very purpose of human resource divisions in organizations is to represent centralization in functions. Without this, each person will be left to their own devices when recruiting, which will result in duplication of effort, lack of coordination, and a disorganized reality for the organization to contend with. Centralization of functions ensures that we have one entity responsible for conducting actions within a domain rather than having them conducted in a dispersed and haphazard manner. In addition to centralization of the function, we also centralize decision-making rights. The goal is to have a coordinated and unified effort on management matters.

Commercializing knowledge calls for similar dynamics. We must put knowledge created, that is inventions, through a well-regulated and systematic process. This process must continually be refined as we learn how to improve the aspects of knowledge commercialization. Centralized management of the process is important to ensure appropriate control. As is suggested by the theories of transaction cost economics, it is better to be vertically aligned and hierarchically structured when one is engaging in transactions that are repetitive and frequent, and where organizations need to reduce uncertainty associated with outcomes.[4] As argued by Ronald Coase, the Nobel laureate economist, one reason why organizations exist is to increase the efficiency of conducting transactions. Commercializing knowledge can be considered akin to conducting transactions where efficiency is critical. Creating knowledge can be considered as a more ad-hoc process, since serendipity plays a vital role in determining whether knowledge will be generated. Consequently, the process of knowledge creation is amorphous to allow for creative thought. Consider this example: when an organization is making routine purchases there is not much uncertainty associated with the process or the outcomes, because there is a fixed protocol to follow. This is what knowledge commercialization is about. On the other hand, knowledge creation is much like going to the market and seeing what turns up. Spontaneous order is created, and knowledge emerges when creative thoughts collide, making it very difficult to predict events. Hence, unlike knowledge commercialization, it is harder to manage knowledge creation from a top-down perspective.

There are many cases of organizations that are successful at inventing but poor at innovating. Xerox is one such organization that has been plagued by failures to profit from its own inventions. The researchers at PARC, Xerox's research hub, have been responsible for some of the most critical inventions in many fields, especially computing. For instance, it was the PARC researchers who devised the GUI, yet it was Apple which was successful in commercializing it to inform personal computer monitor designs. One of the reasons for this innovation failure was lack of recognition for the different engagement rules for knowledge creation versus knowledge commercialization.

Organizations that are successful at creating and commercializing knowledge normally impose the two necessary but different control regimens essential for success. Consider the example of knowledge creation and commercialization in the defense departments of various countries. Knowledge creation is relegated to research labs that are funded by defense. These centers assemble researchers of the highest caliber and give them space, resources, and time to come up with inventions. Most of these centers, such as the US Army Research Laboratories or the US Office of Naval Research, work on the basis of grant funding. Researchers – the knowledge workers – seek funding for their projects by demonstrating how they contribute to the various agendas of the agencies. Researchers here not only engage locally with other scientists but also collaborate with academicians and private sector enterprises as required, to get access to knowledge and improve their chances of inventing successfully. The knowledge commercialization side of the organization is handled by the armed forces, which operate in a top-down fashion. Once innovations are accepted and introduced to the organization, they are pushed down hierarchical ranks via directives. There is very little ambiguity in this process, as soldiers get their orders and are expected to follow them. Order-based procedures result in efficiency in the flow of information and the acceptance of innovations in a timely manner, thereby promoting effective knowledge commercialization.

It is interesting to note that both sides, the research and the armed units, work in synergy with one another. The armed services implement the knowledge invented by the researchers, and in doing so inform the researchers on where to direct future knowledge creation so as to better their chances of victory in engagements. This results in the needed inventions being calibrated, that will, it is hoped, be more successfully adopted by the armed services, since it helps them achieve their military goals. Success can be linked to the fact that the knowledge creation and knowledge commercialization units are managed using different principles and are allowed to be successful by recognizing the differences in decentralized and centralized control regimens.

Types of knowledge workers: standard versus radical

Knowledge workers in organizations range in types and specializations. We will discuss the concept of segmentation of knowledge assets and resources at greater length in the next chapter. For now, we will focus on a simple dichotomy – those who perform standardized tasks versus those who work innovatively and are radical in their use of knowledge. Both types of workers use knowledge, but the different ways they use it requires corresponding differences in management mechanisms.

Knowledge workers who apply knowledge in a standardized manner are normally engaged in routine tasks. These tasks can be monitored, regulated, and controlled since they are predictable in design. Success measures can also be easily calibrated. Consider the example of customer call center operators. These knowledge workers are bound by routine procedures that govern how they answer a call and resolve customer queries. Success measures to manage such workers are based on time-and-motion studies of, for example, how quickly the call was resolved, if the customer needed to call back, and so on. Knowledge workers who are engaged in standardized tasks are better suited for centralized management controls, since here performance needs to be monitored against well-defined objectives, and also requires less skill in the independent application of knowledge. Therefore, decision rights on knowledge should be controlled and their application restricted.

Radical knowledge workers are those who work with knowledge in unconventional ways. First, the knowledge workers in these domains can be considered high-end knowledge workers.[5] They know their work better than anyone else, and hence are best suited to devise protocols on how to manage their work processes. Second, since these workers thrive in creative and loose environments, they do not do well under the imposition of external pressures. Third, since the work performed by these individuals is non-routine, it is not suitable for a tailored style of management. Time-and-motion studies are not suitable for these workers, as there is no single way to judge the quality of their work. Decentralization is the best approach to ensure optimal knowledge creation.

Organizations cannot order people to innovate, but must actively seek out inventions and nurture them into innovations. In our experience, only a select few knowledge workers take the time, effort, and risks involved in conducting innovations. These individuals are normally considered radical knowledge workers, as they seldom follow the *status quo* and do not mind spending the time or effort to build a viable alternative. When such radical knowledge workers are successful, they are given glamorous rewards; when they fail, they are derided and ridiculed. The history of innovation tells us that the radical knowledge workers will fail more often than succeed. Failure, however, is not a bad thing. New knowledge is often discovered during a failed experiment. Ask any radical knowledge worker of the times they failed on an experiment in knowledge creation and they will probably mouth an echo of Albert Einstein's famous words, "I haven't failed, I just found 100,000 ways that don't work."

High-end knowledge workers are best managed in decentralized forms. For instance, consider the recent surge in open-source software development efforts.[6] The unique characteristics of the open-source approach distinguish it from existing commercial software development practices. Participants in open-source are globally and virtually distributed, and usually never meet face to face. These geographically distributed participants successfully coordinate software development without traditional mechanisms such as design processes, schedules, and so on. Compared with the traditional approach, the open-source system makes the development of high-quality software strikingly faster and cheaper. Today, there is growing interest in open source among government departments and business firms. For example, the NSA (National Security Agency) in the USA has funded a private company to develop a variant of Linux, and some European governments encourage use and development of open-source software.[7]

The fundamental concept behind open source is quite simple: the evolution of software occurs because users can read, redistribute, and modify the source code. There are several requirements for open-source development. First, source code must be available to any user. This accessibility drives fast innovation, since it allows users to engage in real-time updates and corrections. Since source code is not available in traditional software component development, programmers usually experience difficulty when fixing bugs, which hinders and complicates the development process. Unlike traditional development protocols that retain source code licensed under restrictive conditions, open-source systems make source code available to other firms, allowing programmers to easily modify programs. Such access is essential for programs to evolve.

Second, software knowledge must be redistributable. A user in an open-source system is given full rights to reproduce and redistribute the software without incurring any costs. This privilege allows users to see open-source software as something for the public good, since a user's consumption of the software in no way reduces another's opportunity to use it. In traditional software development, proprietary code is seen as a source of power, as it represents an instantiation of the producer's tacit knowledge. This on its own is not bad, but when the source of power prevents the flow of knowledge it impairs the rate and quality of innovation.

Third, the software license must not discriminate against any age, group, or field of endeavor. Diversity is encouraged, since it is considered to contribute to the software development process. Also, open-source communities do not exclude commercial users. In traditional software development, access to source code is strictly restricted because source code is considered a competitive advantage that cannot be disclosed to everybody.

Fourth, software must be modifiable, and derived works permitted. This versatility encourages programmers to 'just try' programs, and is important for speedy and high-quality software development. Traditional software development, in contrast, does not allow programmers to modify or understand programs, which makes development slower. Moreover, traditional software is distributed only in executable format; the natural language code is seldom if ever shared. Traditional software development is therefore restrictive and, for the most part, counterproductive in terms of promoting innovation. Knowledge assets, such as code, blueprints, system charts, and system know-how are seldom freely shared and developed on, resulting in less than optimal products and services.

In most organizations today, access and ownership to knowledge is viewed as a source of power. Therefore, this power is seldom shared openly or parted with. Most of it is made available on a restricted, need-to-know basis, so that a few individuals control much of the organization's know-how. In much the same way, most commercial vendors provide only object or binary software code. However, participants in open-source networks share the source code, which not only allows for rapid improvements to the source code, but is also a key determinant of openness in the community.

Communities play an important role in open source. Individuals care about the reputation obtained from their peers. This concern can deter individuals from producing lower-quality works. Such peer-level horizontal monitoring differs from the vertical monitoring within the boss–subordinate hierarchy, because decision-making does not have a top-down approach. Rather, it is a bottom-up approach, where a peer-voting scheme is implemented to seek fair process results and consensus. Self-governance schemes enable more open participation, as the end users and programmers implement order within the practice, rather than relying on an 'outsider', such as management, to impose it.

High-end knowledge workers are managed by peers, seldom by management, and in cases where they are so managed, conflicts usually arise. Consequently, the organization must ensure that it can decentralize the management of high-end knowledge workers to communities. As in the case of open-source movements, the community ensures the rules of member participation: what is accepted behavior and what is not, how to monitor performance, and other details. We can see a prominence of self- governance rather than directive or top-down management.

The final issue in terms of tensions deals with how best to evaluate the efforts of knowledge workers. On one hand, we have process-based measures of control. These involve measuring a knowledge worker's performance against a set of outlined procedures. As long as all the steps are followed, the knowledge worker has acted in an appropriate manner. Such measures are apt for dealing with knowledge workers who perform standardized tasks. The other measure of performance calls for output-based evaluations. Here, instead of specifying a process to be followed, the knowledge worker is allowed to be resourceful, and is judged on their final output. This measure is apt when workers are required to think creatively about how best to achieve objectives and do not require micromanagement. Workers who need to be managed under the output-based performance measure are high-end knowledge workers such as doctors, scientists, researchers, writers, and poets. Process-based and output-based measures are at two extremes and we can have balances between them. We see these balances in most organizations, such as when most employees are required to adhere to certain process-based protocols, such as sending emails, or work etiquette requirements and where output-based measures are used in their performance evaluations to measure success or failure in terms of objective achievements.

Type of knowledge: public versus private knowledge

Organizations are laden with different types of knowledge that need to be managed differently in terms of centralization and decentralization. One distinction that can be used from the organizational perspective is between public and private knowledge. Public knowledge represents information that is made available to all members of the organization. This knowledge includes organizational procedures, products, services, and other necessities needed to perform work. No organization can exist without some level of public knowledge, also called common knowledge. Public knowledge can be seen as the integrating mechanism that binds the various constituents of the organization. For example, consider the process of how a cappuccino is brewed by Starbucks franchisees. If the baristas at the various franchisees did not share common knowledge about the process, each would serve a slightly different version of the beverage. Moreover, Starbucks would find it difficult to move knowledge workers from one location to another, as the various franchisees would have different routines in place. This would be problematic for effective and efficient operations, and would result in the essence of the franchisee-based business being lost. Similarly, customer service representatives of the organization must share common knowledge of how to manage grievances so that there is a unified method for interacting with customers. Management of common knowledge – or public knowledge in the context of the organization – is the focus of many knowledge management books, including this one. Such management, especially when it is put to use, is handled through decentralized mechanisms. Public knowledge is allowed to flow loosely within the organization, and can be freely used by its various members. Decentralized regimes are apt when we do not suspect workers will need extensive supervision, and when the knowledge that is in use is innocuous, that is sharing it would cause no harm.

In contrast, private knowledge is information that is closely held by an entity and not made common to the public. In the context of organizations, we are concerned with knowledge that is private to the organization and not available to the general marketplace or the organization's industry. As an example, consider the case of the formula to make Coca Cola. This represents the organization's private knowledge and is the source of its competitive advantage. This knowledge is of high value and could cost the company dearly were it to be leaked or otherwise misplaced. We must point out that in this discussion we are not concerned with private knowledge held by employees. Each employee holds private knowledge such as their own unique expertise and experience. Employees value this knowledge because it enables them to compete successfully with other knowledge workers, and in many cases is the basis for their remuneration. We will discuss this knowledge in Chapter 8 on knowledge markets, where we will elaborate upon the issues and dynamics associated with getting employees to share their private knowledge.

Managing knowledge that is highly private to the organization is best handled via centralized rather than decentralized mechanisms. Opportunism – which may be defined as devious conduct – must be controlled to ensure that the value of private knowledge is maintained.[8] The use of centralized mechanisms will help preserve the proprietary nature of knowledge, because they can exercise strict limitations on access to the knowledge, how it is used, and who has decision rights on it. These limitations are difficult to achieve in decentralized regimes where it is difficult to monitor all who interact with the knowledge and how it is used. Knowledge that is confidential or sensitive should be available on a need-to-know basis.[9] Many organizations have secure locations where they conduct knowledge management activities on highly sensitive know-how. These facilities can be physical (such as a separate office building), or logical (such as secure spaces on corporate intranets that a select group of knowledge workers is privy to). We will devote most of the next chapter to the issue of protecting knowledge assets from theft and destruction. For now, it is important to note that decentralization works well for knowledge that is innocuous and public to all organizational members, whereas centralized regimes are necessary to ensure that private knowledge remains so.

Conclusion

Managing tensions between centralized and decentralized management approaches is salient to building successful knowledge management programs. Choosing the right management strategy depends on the type of knowledge, knowledge worker, and knowledge process in question. Each knowledge management program is different and hence unique, and must be carefully examined before choosing a management approach. When it is essential to monitor the knowledge, knowledge process, and knowledge worker, a centralized management approach should be taken; when the opposite is true, management should be more decentralized.

Rather than viewing centralization and decentralization as extremes, we suggest that organizations should be engaged with the two realities and embrace them as warranted by environmental circumstances. We have suggested several possible strategies. First: encourage the use of decentralized management for knowledge creation, while employing a centralized regime for knowledge commercialization. Second: manage high-end knowledge workers through communities of peers to foster decentralized approaches, while managing knowledge workers who apply knowledge in a standardized manner through centralized approaches. Third: use a centralized approach to manage knowledge of a sensitive nature and a decentralized one for common knowledge.

When organizations are first formed, there are a lot of informalities in how knowledge is generated and transferred. Formal mechanisms eventually replace informalities to enable efficient work and economies of scale. As organizations mature, they tend to favor formalized and centralized procedures over decentralized ones – this may be appropriate for most organizational operations where efficiency is important. However, it is not suitable for knowledge creation. Organizations need to tread the fine line of balancing what is important for current efficiencies against how best to motivate resources to innovate for a successful future. This is what many have referred to as the *ambidextrous* organization. Adroit balancing between centralization and decentralization management approaches is critical to achieving this objective.

3
Engaging with Missing Knowledge Management Capabilities

Successful knowledge management in a competitive business environment requires an organization to possess certain capabilities. In particular, the organization must be able to create, transfer, store, retrieve, and apply knowledge. Traditionally, an organization can claim capability in knowledge management if it can execute these activities with rigor, clarity, effectiveness, and efficiency. Any book about knowledge management – including this one – will devote a great deal of time to discussing topics associated with the five major capabilities, and this devotion is entirely justified. Creating knowledge is a significant aspect of any knowledge management program. If an organization cannot create knowledge by examining data and pieces of information and by harvesting information from the expertise of its agents, there will be nothing to manage. Once the knowledge is created, the next logical steps are to transfer, store, and retrieve it. Without these three components, it will be difficult for an organization to ensure knowledge generated in one sector of the organization or at a single, unique time is transferred to another sector and available for future use. It will also be difficult for the organization to ensure that agents who require particular knowledge are able to retrieve and apply it efficiently and effectively. Unless an organization can demonstrate competency in these five activities, its knowledge management program is incomplete and likely flawed. Often an organization excels at one activity and is hopeless in another. For example, if an organization has a sophisticated storage mechanism in place, but fails to generate or create knowledge, the storage mechanism is useless – they will have no knowledge to store! Such imbalance among the five capabilities will cause serious problems for any organization in the future.

Yet the importance of having and maintaining balance among the five capabilities of knowledge management is not contested. In fact, the importance of these capabilities is well established and over-analyzed. Nearly every knowledge management article, report, or book, discusses one or all of them. Yet almost no piece of literature spends adequate time investigating the three capabilities missing from most knowledge management programs. This chapter

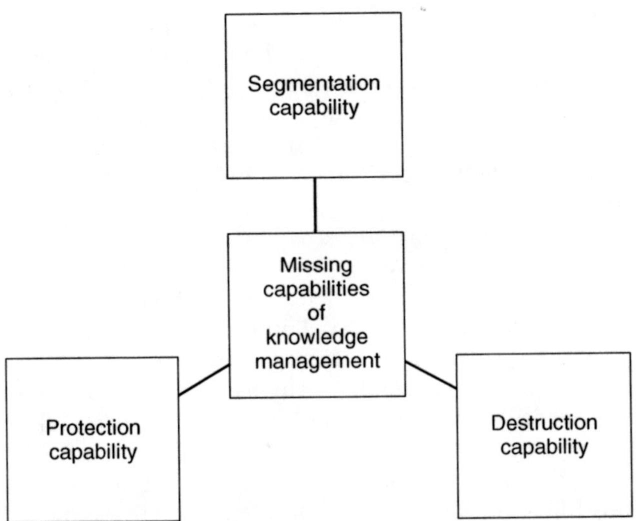

Figure 3.1   Missing capabilities of knowledge management.

discusses these missing capabilities that require management and scholarly attention: segmentation, destruction, and protection (see Figure 3.1). These three capabilities complement and augment their peer capabilities and furthermore, if an organization neglects them, the benefits of their knowledge management program will be limited. Our research and consulting experience has enabled us to identify leaders and laggards in knowledge management by how well they attend to these missing capabilities. Most organizations have some competency in the five established capabilities, yet few consider the impact of the missing ones. Organizations that consider the missing capabilities have witnessed significantly improved knowledge management programs compared with when the capabilities were missing from their agenda.

What are capabilities?

There is an extensive literature discussing capabilities in strategic management, economics, and organizational behavior. Yet, the wealth of literature does not provide clear answers to the basic questions of knowledge management. We could not find a single integrative definition of organizational capabilities. So, rather than providing a review of the existing literature, we will instead explain our concept of *capability*. This concept follows most closely the work of the renowned strategic management and economics scholar David Teece.[1] Consider an organization as a collection of resources and capabilities. Resources in the form of assets are static and represent any entity in the possession or control of the organization: physical machinery, land, labor, capital, and expertise. Capabilities are the routines or processes that use or leverage assets. For example, a farmer can use a piece of machinery to prepare the soil. Using the machinery to impact the value of the soil is a capability. Similarly, if a software engineer can put his knowledge to use and create a technology artifact, he has a capability in knowledge application. Capabilities are dynamic and are applied to assets. An organization must have a collection of capabilities it can deploy to extract value from its assets. Capabilities put assets to work.

Yet simply possessing capabilities is not enough; competitive success demands mature capabilities. Mature capabilities are experienced, rigorous, highly effective and efficient. This maturity is what makes capabilities highly valuable. Many children in Western Europe or the Middle East aspire to becoming great football players. Playing football demands a certain set of capabilities: ball control skills, stamina, physical maneuvering skills, strong leg muscles, and knowledge of the game. If a youngster possesses all the capabilities required to play football and can even fare well on the field, it doesn't necessarily mean that he will play for a high-caliber club like Manchester United or Real Madrid. Playing for a world-class football club at that level demands that an athlete demonstrate a high level of maturity in their football capabilities. It is not sufficient just to have capabilities, one must excel in them. Certainly, having capabilities is better than *not* possessing them and yet, in a competitive environment, merely possessing capabilities is not sufficient. Some organizations have mature product development capabilities but poor marketing capabilities; others may face the opposite situation. Maturity in one capability is of limited value, especially if all the other capabilities are poor or weak. For instance, it is of little value to have an excellent marketing capability but poor capabilities in product development, research and development, or customer service. Capabilities mature with time, experience, and the the accumulation of knowledge. Athletes improve by training, watching tapes of previous games to uncover strengths and weaknesses, playing matches, and learning from their its peers. Like an athlete, an organization must constantly improve each of its capabilities by infusing them with timely knowledge and by learning from its past deployments.

The nature of capabilities possessed by an organization differentiates it from others in the environment. Dell, for instance, has a mature supply chain management capability. This capability helps it differentiate itself from its competitors, and moreover it makes for the underlying value proposition of Dell Computers. Dell is known for not carrying an inventory and for making computers to order in a timely and effective manner. Similarly, McDonald's is known for its capability in preparing low-cost meals in a timely manner. Why does Dell lead in customized computer production, and why has McDonald's retained its position as the fast-food leader? The answer lies in the organizations' ability to manage knowledge in and around their capabilities. McDonald's operates on a franchise model. In order to do so, they must be successful in transferring their fast-food expertise from headquarters to the new locations. In addition, they must be able to learn from the local operations of franchises and transfer such knowledge to the other locations. McDonald's must be able to conduct a variety of knowledge management activities effectively and efficiently, and their proficiency with knowledge transfer activities makes the overall corporation more successful. Success in conducting knowledge management can have a positive effective on the maturity of other organizational capabilities.

Segmentation capability

To *segment* is to separate out or to classify into. Consider management approaches for traditional assets – physical machinery for example. It is rare to find organizations managing physical machinery haphazardly. We seldom see photocopiers lying idle, printers on the floor, fax machines stored with cleaning equipment, or desks hanging from the ceiling. Structured management approaches are more common when it comes to caring for physical equipment. Management will first segment equipment into its designated classes: office furniture, computer peripherals, and so on. Each piece of equipment is inventoried and tagged, and then put into use for a specific organizational purpose. When it comes to maintaining the equipment, management normally follows a prescribed plan, in which the equipment is evaluated for usefulness and obsolescence and, based on that observation, management decides whether to conduct routine maintenance or replace the machine. In the final analysis, an organization can account for its physical equipment, assign values to it, and manage the fluctuation in equipment inventory.

Now consider how knowledge assets are managed in organizations. In most organizations, it is common to have a "knowledge jungle." Knowledge resides in the organization haphazardly and is scattered in multiple parts of the organization. Moreover, no one can separate organizational knowledge from junk. In the beginning of the knowledge management revolution, the major issue was simply getting people to contribute to knowledge management systems (KMSs). Currently, organizations deal with a more specific problem in getting people to contribute only knowledge that has organizational value. Most organizations embrace a comprehensive approach to knowledge management, valuing everything from how to fix to a broken copier to how to win the next consulting engagement, resulting in the "Wild-West syndrome," in which an organization is overloaded with so-called knowledge and managing it is time-consuming and not especially productive. The mismanagement of tacit knowledge – knowledge that resides exclusively in the minds of employees – is a more damaging problem. Many organizations lack an appropriate framework in which to identify the employees who possess important knowledge. What makes these knowledgeable employees tick? How is their knowledge engaged, and who represents the truly valuable and knowledgeable employees?

The consequence of a haphazard approach to organizational knowledge assets is that management efforts have poor results because an organization will not be able to divert resources to knowledge assets of significance. It would be a mistake and a waste of resources to manage pencils with the same vigor and effort as computer systems. Unless the organization can differentiate between a computer and a pencil, in terms of value and significance, it will not be able to manage the resources appropriately. Obviously, trying to execute the same management attention for pencils and computer is futile and will result in wasted resources and lack of attention to the more critical asset – in this case, computers.

An organization's ability to segment their knowledge assets is an important capability. Not all knowledge assets are alike in nature, value proposition, and significance. Unless an organization has the capability to segment knowledge assets, management efforts will not be focused appropriately. There are several steps in the segmentation process. First, we must segment by *type*. Segmentation by type is grouping knowledge assets by their genres or categories. This is the simplest type of segmentation and common in almost all organizations. In most KMSs, knowledge assets are grouped by categories like marketing, finance, and engineering. Classification into sub-classes and even smaller sub-classes of sub-classes is typical. For example, the engineering category can contain the sub-classes of product design, testing modules, software code, and quality control documentations. In addition to segmenting knowledge by genres, we segment by other features such as format: text document, spreadsheet, presentation, or graphic. Explicit knowledge can also be segmented by a variety of other classifications including date, author, and source of expertise.

Segmenting tacit knowledge occurs naturally in organizations. In organizations, employees with specific expertise are commonly assigned related job roles and in related teams or departments. Tacit knowledge is susceptible to the same types of classification experienced with knowledge artifacts, and usually results in specialization with departments or teams. A member of a software engineering team, for example, would have knowledge of information systems, and yet each member of the team likely brings a specific and unique expertise to it.

Segmentation by genres or other features of the knowledge artifact or expertise, in the case of tacit knowledge, is the first step in creating a fruitful management agenda. Doing so provides a sense of organization and control. Another benefit of segmentation is that now we can begin to process knowledge artifacts within their classes and discover higher-order knowledge assets. For instance, if a bookstore groups knowledge artifacts by genre, they can analyze the knowledge represented in these classes to determine emerging patterns, trends, or peculiarities. The segmentation process also allows us to engage in cross-class operations. We can make associations between knowledge about books on foreign affairs and business management. Analyzing knowledge across classes of knowledge artifacts illustrates patterns and relationships between groups. In analyzing knowledge about gangs in law enforcement, authorities must inter-relate knowledge on individuals committing crimes with how individual crimes relate to the context of the collected gang and, even further, must correlate the data with other crimes and gangs to get a bigger picture of inter-gang cooperation and rivalries. We must remember that knowledge, both tacit and explicit, can be used for multiple purposes. As such, segmentation may call for us to have two types of processing strategies for knowledge artifacts. We can have a set of predefined routines that are easy to specify a priori and can be reused time and time again. In addition, we can also have ad-hocplug-and-play rules that are used to process knowledge artifacts across the classes. It is difficult to envision every possible use of a particular knowledge artifact a priori, hence having the ability to plug-and-play is important. Knowledge objects may also change classes or categories as they are produced or are in stages of work-in-process. For instance, if we combine knowledge objects created by John and Mary then we must store the resultant knowledge in a new category. For instance, we can use the name of the team (John and Mary Team), or we can store it by the name of the person who conducted the integration of the knowledge object. Classes of knowledge objects are hence seldom static in nature and need to be flexible to appreciate change and dynamism.

Once the basic segmentation is complete, knowledge must be segmented according to value. This is the *neglected* dimension of the segmentation capability. We suggest that knowledge managers take a step back and truly question what comprises organizational knowledge. To this end, consider adopting the resource-based view of the firm.[2] The resource-based view of the firm provides a lens through which to examine and isolate the resources in the organization's collection that can lead to sustained competitive advantages. Particularly valuable resources are those that are rare, heterogeneous, immobile, and non-substitutable. Primarily, is the resource valuable? Unless the resource has some valuable proposition, it is of no use to the organization. Once the resource is determined to be valuable, assess if it is rare in comparison with those possessed by competing firms. In particular, is the resource heterogeneous and immobile? Unless a firm possesses a resource scarce in the industry, the resource will not provide sustained competitive advantage. Immobility also provides a salient resource test. Unless a resource is immobile, other firms in the industry can easily acquire it. Mobile resources can provide only a temporary competitive advantage. The final question is whether the resource has substitutes. If it does, then its value proposition is impaired, since there are other resource candidates if needed. However, if the resource of interest has no perfect or close substitutes, than the resource can be considered as highly significant and valuable.

The resource-based view can be applied to segmenting knowledge assets in organizations. Managers must determine the value of the knowledge based on these characterizations. Most knowledge objects will meet the conditions of being valuable; however, only certain knowledge resources will be able to meet the condition of being a rarity. Consider a software engineering firm. While every piece of code written has some "value," is it unique? Moreover, the knowledge processed by each software engineer is certainly valuable, although only a small portion of that knowledge is truly rare. Most of the engineer's knowledge complements and overlaps the knowledge of other software engineers. While almost all knowledge provides value in assisting in the completion of routine tasks, knowledge objects that meet the condition of uniqueness are normally of high value. First, these knowledge objects are missed in the organization when they are taken out of play or lost. For instance, when an expert leaves an organization gaps or holes in the knowledge structure emerge. Second, these knowledge objects owing to their uniqueness can lead a firm to develop competencies that might not be available to competitors. The conditions of non-imitation and non-substitutability are critical because knowledge that cannot be imitated easily by other members of the organization or by external organizations is truly valuable, as it is not easy to replace it. Knowledge that is unique and difficult to replace gives any organization a competitive advantage. Knowledge that does not aid in strategic advantages must still be managed but is not an organizational differentiator.

Segmenting expertise by value is equally appropriate. Not all knowledgeable workers are alike and treating them as such will result in a failed management approach. Some employees work in a highly autonomous way and are highly skilled; they often know their work in great detail. Others are highly skilled, yet their work is more dependent on an external party like a boss or supervisor. A hospital nurse, for example, is certainly a knowledge worker, yet a nurse's schedule and work practices are likely dictated by a doctor and/or the hospital. By comparison, an artist knows best how to create a masterpiece and will work independently to meet the need of the client. Other types of knowledge workers are not highly skilled, yet they know how to follow knowledge-based procedures and perform tasks. The most common example for this class of workers is call center personnel. Incoming calls are handled based according to a predefined routine that dictates the opening greeting, method of problem resolution, problem reporting, and other intricacies. The role of the worker is to follow these knowledge-based routines and complete the call in an effective and efficient manner. Each type of knowledge worker needs to be managed differently and offers different value propositions to the organization. For example, if an organization has an apt knowledge base on which to draw and has a mature call handling procedure, the knowledge worker who takes the call can be substituted easily. Any individual with basic speaking skills and simple etiquette should be able to follow the procedures outlined in the call manual. If an organization does not have a truly mature and valuable call manual (the knowledge asset), the skills of the call takers must be evaluated more individually and in comparison with one another. Without a call manual, the organization is at the mercy of the experienced call takers since these individuals will have the necessary expertise required to complete a call optimally. Segmenting knowledge workers by the value propositions they offer allows an organization to focus their management and incentive practices, in for instance choosing between centralized versus decentralized control mechanisms (see Chapter 2). It would be a shame for an organization to lose a knowledge worker whose skills are rare, valuable, non-imitable, and non-substitutable in the organization. Losing such an employee to faulty management practices leads to gaps in an organization's knowledge structure and will impact business outcomes.

Segmenting knowledge within the organization leads to a better-focused management agenda. Knowledge that does not meet the conditions of a valuable resource should not be the focus of management efforts. Knowledge assets that meet the basic condition of being valuable should be managed in a limited fashion since the return on such assets is minimal. Critical organizational resources are those that cannot be imitated or substituted with ease. These must be the focus of knowledge management efforts since they have the potential to truly deliver corporate value. Segmenting knowledge helps address the cost-benefit issue, since it helps to focus organizational resources on the most critical knowledge assets.

Destruction capability

In an effort to create a greater quantity of competitive resources, organizations focus primarily on generating and storing knowledge. While this may be true for traditional resources like land, labor, and capital, it is not necessarily true for knowledge. Excessive knowledge about products, processes, and practices can have negative consequences for organizations.[3]

When it comes to explicit knowledge artifacts residing in KMSs, problems can occur in terms of knowledge overload where there are multiple versions of the same knowledge on different aspects of products and services. Excessive knowledge results in inefficient knowledge retrieval. In several software engineering organizations with whom we've worked, KMSs are laden with multiple versions of the same knowledge object. The same knowledge is encapsulated in multiple files. The end result is that people abandon such systems, as the cost of finding the most recent, current, comprehensive, and accurate knowledge artifact is too high. Ultimately, if no one uses the KMSs, they are a cost for the organization and will not be a viable means for fostering effective knowledge management.

In the tacit realm, unless old and irrelevant knowledge is purged in a timely fashion, organizational change becomes difficult, resulting in several problems. Routines and practices become institutionalized, which makes future change and creative problem-solving impossible. As such, the organization will make only incremental and minor improvements on this past knowledge without much hope for seeing opportunities and seizing the future of the marketplace. Polaroid made this mistake in the advent of digital imaging and Swiss watchmakers lost ground to the leaner and more agile Japanese competitors. Strategies that work today may not work tomorrow or the day after tomorrow; knowledge relevant today may be irrelevant tomorrow. It is in the organization's best interests to keep a watchful eye on new opportunities and business practices in the marketplace and make relevant and necessary changes to stay competitive.

Necessity is the mother of invention, and within an organization relying too much on the past stifles the motivation for creative thought. Organizations often try to answer questions on the basis of existing knowledge resources. As a result, problem definition is based solely on available solutions. Arrogant organizations, with high levels of pride and self-confidence, get blindsided by new threats since they are typically reluctant to switch strategies in a timely manner. Abandoning old routines in favor of new ones is certainly risky. The role of every manager is to manage risk. Executives, especially those locked into benefit packages or close to retirement, resist change because of the potential for failure. Furthermore, executives often equate strategic failure with personal failure. As a result, they continue following historic paths since these are easier to justify and do not require risk-taking behavior. When executives and managers continue to follow failing courses of action, even in the face of negative feedback, their actions are an "escalation of commitment."

Individuals are less likely to solicit or investigate new knowledge that goes against their current view. It is easier to view current success in the light of a chosen strategy rather than as a result of unforeseen external factors. This management tendency makes exchanging an existing strategy for a better one difficult. Why make a change when we are getting satisfactory results? Organizational inertia stems from this behavior and an organization cannot change its behavior effectively and quickly. All organizations have strengths and their strategies reflect these strengths. Economics dictate that an organization should invest maximum resources in its strengths to maximize returns. However, in doing so, the organization fails to devote adequate attention to seeking out new practices and strategies that may question their current strength or complement it by enhancing its potency. Over time, an organization's strengths become obsolete and common in the marketplace, thereby losing the potential to provide competitive advantages, and if the organization has no secondary or fall-back strategy the organization will fail. Organizations also resist the destruction of old knowledge because of the investment sunk in that knowledge, "We have already invested in it, so we should follow through on it." There is a cost associated with creating new knowledge, and often an organization may not have the resources available to cover the initial cost. Organizations are reluctant to destroy knowledge in which they have invested so much time and money in favor of an untried and potentially costly new strategy.

In most cases, past knowledge has limited value for future organizational efforts. Organizations operate in a dynamic and fiercely competitive environment. Their knowledge, much like computer hardware, has a high rate of depreciation. While important, lessons learned from past endeavors are helpful yet they need to be qualified. While helpful in an operational sense, much of yesterday's knowledge has little bearing on designing the future. Designing or charting the future demands new and uninhibited creativity. Unless the old knowledge is purged or challenged, no one will question its existence or validity. Over time, myths become standard corporate knowledge because no one questions them. This practice is dangerous to the future of an organization. Systematic destruction of knowledge must be a component of knowledge management efforts in organizations. Knowledge managers must institutionalize the destruction capabilities. The term "destruction" is not used casually. While most organizations have the capabilities to purge old and outdated knowledge, they do not engage in destruction. Even within organizations that do engage in mechanical destruction of knowledge artifacts in their KMSs, practices based on those knowledge assets continue to prevail. An organization's destruction capability must include both the act of purging explicit knowledge and modifying or updating practices and procedures based on tacit knowledge. Personnel can be designated to review knowledge in systems and purge or archive old knowledge in a timely fashion. The use of automated technologies can also be useful in conducting knowledge reviews and destruction. Training and development programs are vital aspects of the destruction capability and, as such, should not be overlooked since they infuse the organization with new knowledge. It is important that an organization use a test of *existence* to check whether practices are based on knowledge or on myths. Often current practices in organizations are outcomes of myths. A myth is all that survives of knowledge that may have been valuable at one time, but now no longer exists in the organization, though practices based on it may still be prevalent. Such practices need to be identified, tackled, and revised in order to have a viable destruction capability.

Protection capability

Why do we need to protect organizational knowledge? Conventional wisdom states that the value of knowledge increases when it is shared. This is both true and false. This chapter – and this book – discusses the topic of "organizational knowledge." Organizational knowledge needs to be shared and protected. It needs to be shared with the right agents within and without the organization and, by the same token, must be protected from an organization's competitors. In today's tough economic times and under fierce competitive pressures, protecting organizational knowledge has become increasingly important.[4]

An asset's value is determined by its economic results and its scarcity in the marketplace. The current literature on knowledge management has focused exclusively on the former issue – leveraging knowledge to improve effectiveness, efficiency, and organizational innovation. As noted earlier, unless an organization's asset is rare and competitors have difficultly imitating it, the asset has limited competitive value. An organization can capitalize on its assets if these assets are scarce in the marketplace and if the process of leveraging the assets is also scarce.

Knowledge possessed by an organization must be protected and made scarce to the external world for an organization to remain competitive. To recall an example given earlier, the Coca-Cola formula remains one of the mostly closely guarded trade secrets. If the Coca-Cola Company made this knowledge public, it's unlikely the organization would earn any profits from the sale of Coke. The reason is simple: competitors would take advantage of such knowledge and dramatically undermine Coca-Cola's profits. Knowledge must be proprietary to the organization and not common knowledge in the marketplace. If we knew how the CIA gathers intelligence on threats, the value the CIA offers to the US government would be significantly diminished. Shared knowledge alone is no guarantee of destroyed value, but knowledge and expertise is an incredibly damaging combination. If we knew not only how the CIA gathers intelligence, but could duplicate their processes and functions, then we could extinguish the entire value of the CIA. Knowledge resources are the source of competitive advantages for organizations, and unless we have apt security measures in place we risk losing them to acts of theft, misuse, espionage, and disaster.

Securing knowledge assets is even more important given the current economic, social, and political conditions. Political tensions such as are caused by an increase in terrorist activities call attention to improved security practices in organizations. Terrorist organizations have targeted business enterprises and will continue to do so, as the ripple effect of such damage has wide-ranging impacts for the local economy, for the country, and even for its trading partners. With the current rise in alliances between organizations, the need for knowledge security takes on increased prominence. Organizations have accepted that they must hone their core competencies and forge alliances to secure their non-core needs.[5] Alliances demand that organizations share and rely on a business partner's knowledge (the whole of Chapter 6 is devoted to knowledge management in alliances). An organization must ensure not only that its internal controls and security protocols are functioning, but also ensure that its business partners have adequate security protocols in place. Remember, nobody is better than their weakest link.

Ultimately, the sophistication, ubiquity, and pervasive nature of technology can be a factor that compromises an organization's knowledge security. There are multiple devices in common use for knowledge communication and sharing – office phones, email, personal digital assistants, laptop computers, personal computers, and so on. We work and communicate in multiple environments and, as such, use these devices in multiple settings. The use of heterogeneous devices in a wide range of heterogeneous environments makes securing knowledge exponentially difficult. With the increase in hacking, sniffing, spoofing, spamming, spyware, worms, viruses, and other nuisances that intercept, harm, sabotage, and destroy electronic networks, digital communications are increasingly at risk. Moreover, heterogeneous environments demand additional efforts to ensure that knowledge assets are secured that multiple devices and that the operating parameters of multiple platforms are secure. Consider the statistics of fraud and theft published in a recent edition of *CSO* magazine (see www.csoonline.com for more information). The article reported that a typical business loses 6 percent of its annual revenue to occupational fraud. In the US biotech industry, this amounts to $12 billion. In all fraud cases exceeding $1 million, 18 percent were uncovered by accident. In organizations with anonymous fraud reporting procedures, the median loss from incidents was $56,500 and, in those that lacked an anonymous reporting mechanism, the median loss was $135,300. Even more interesting, the percentage of fraud not reported to law enforcement agencies increased from 24.6 percent in 2002 to 31.1percent in 2004!

Lastly, one must remember that confining the protection of knowledge assets to getting copyrights and patents is not sufficient. Patents and copyrights make certain only that the owner of a knowledge asset is known. A company must be able to ensure that no one violates its copyright statements and that knowledge indeed remains secure. Most high-profile organizations like Nike or Coca-Cola take great care to ensure their trademarks are not used by individuals or other organizations without appropriate permission. However, even companies with the strictest protocols in place have difficulty enforcing their patents and copyrights in the global corporate environment. Copyright laws that are favorable to a company in one location may not be so in another. Patents and copyrights also have limited lives and must be renewed and updated. Hence, the goal of the organization is to ensure appropriate diligence in initially securing their knowledge assets rather than scrambling to protect them when it is too late.

Securing knowledge is a strategic imperative for organizations, yet it is not easy to accomplish. Organizations are still grappling with information security issues and securing knowledge is even more difficult, tedious, and cumbersome than securing information. Why?

Information is a product and because it is a product, securing it demands that it is tagged, stored in a secured location, accessed by authorized personnel, and transmitted over secure communication lines to designated recipients. Securing information requires the same activities as securing any raw material or product. Knowledge is more than a product; it is fluid, dynamic, and more mobile than information. Unlike information, knowledge is not easy to capture since it resides in the minds of employees, is embedded in work processes, and is captured in product and service offerings. Moreover, unlike information, knowledge is in a continuous state of flux. Knowledge changes its state when it is exchanged between individuals and entities; moreover, knowledge is represented in actions. For instance, the analysis of customer purchasing behavior produces knowledge about customer behavior in combination with the context, experiences, and expertise applied to that behavior. If two individuals are presented with the same customer information, they will draw different conclusions, and if the two engage in a dialogue, then their knowledge about customer behavior will combine and increase. Owing to its changing nature, knowledge is difficult to pin down and capture.

So, how do you go about securing knowledge assets?[6] First, conduct an organizational knowledge audit. You must identify and place value on knowledge before you can begin to secure it. The knowledge audit must be systematic and holistic and include these key issues: identification of knowledge assets; identifying knowledge asset creators, owners, hoarders, distributors, and users; valuing knowledge assets; assessing threats to the knowledge assets and to the personnel interaction with the assets; and assessing the implications of knowledge assets to the competencies and competitive advantages of the organization.

Once knowledge assets are identified, we must understand the governing dynamics of how they are employed. This will demand a thorough analysis of the various organizational actors that interact with the given knowledge asset. Determining the value of knowledge assets is difficult, yet worthwhile – even crucial. While all organizational knowledge is valuable, an organization must determine: Is the knowledge asset in question rare? Can it be substituted? Can our competitors imitate and duplicate the knowledge asset? Answering these questions will determine the true value of an organization's knowledge assets. For instance, if a knowledge asset is easily imitable by our competitors, then we must either increase the difficulty of imitation, thus using the high cost to deter competitors from doing so, or we must create alternative knowledge assets that are more difficult to imitate. Once we ascertain the value of our knowledge assets, we must enumerate the threats to that asset. It is essential to be absolutely clear about the significance of the threat. The significance of the threat and the associated value of the knowledge asset determine the managerial intervention necessary to secure the asset. If the significance of the threat is high but the value of the knowledge asset is low, economics dictate that an organization should not expend an inappropriately high amount of energy and resources protecting that knowledge. The final important part of any thorough knowledge audit is to link the knowledge assets possessed by the organization with the organization's overall mission, competitive strategies, and core capabilities. This step is critical to determining and segmenting knowledge on the basis of its contribution to the core of the enterprise. The knowledge audit is a critical first step in building the foundation for a successful knowledge security program.

Using the knowledge audit as a background, we must dig deeper into knowledge vulnerabilities. In the second part of the knowledge audit, we uncovered the people who own, create, store, distribute, and apply knowledge. Now, we must determine how vulnerable the organization is should these people leave or misuse their knowledge. For instance, if one of our chief innovation scientists left the organization, would he take knowledge not documented or available to anyone else in organization? If so, we would have a problem, since his departure could halt a significant amount of current research. Moreover, what happens to the organization if the individuals who distribute knowledge have a grievance with the organization and go on strike? What if the email computer systems are damaged by a hacker or a virus? How will these situations effect the organization's overall health? Assessing vulnerabilities is never easy since it requires an organization to swallow its pride and face its weaknesses. Difficult though this can be, you can be certain your adversaries are enumerating your weaknesses to discover how they exploit them for competitive advantage.

After determining the vulnerabilities of your knowledge assets, you must decide on a security strategy. At this point, the processes required to secure knowledge deviate from those used to secure information. If you have knowledge assets that, if compromised, could make the corporation vulnerable, you must choose to either protect or duplicate them. If the knowledge is stored in organizational practices and processes – for example, in a secret process that helps you build better products – you will choose a strategy of protection. To enact this strategy, you will need to make sure that you have the appropriate patents, copyrights, trademarks, and other legal protections. You will also have to make sure that access to such knowledge is limited. Remember, getting a patent or trademark will call for disclosure of the knowledge, so make sure that you understand all the legal ramifications. In some cases, disclosing the knowledge to a patent or copyright office may not be the best alternative. If the knowledge assets reside in the minds of select employees, you must conduct a strategy of duplication. You must create "knowledge backups." The experts (or knowledge creators and/or owners) should be asked to train and mold apprentices. In this way, we create duplicate knowledge repositories. Moreover, as these experts train the apprentices, the apprentices will learn the art of creating the knowledge and will eventually make their way along the learning curves required in pursuit of competency using the knowledge. This knowledge can be protected by asking experts to document their knowledge in "knowledge captures."

Documenting their knowledge will require the experts to externalize and express their expertise, and this is difficult for most people to do. Experts often fear that externalizing their knowledge will make them less valuable to their organization. However, externalizing the knowledge could be one way to perceive the experts. Externalizing knowledge requires an organization to recognize the depth of an individual's expertise. If novices in the organization are able to advance and learn on the basis of an expert's knowledge, the expert must be rewarded and assured that he will not be replaced by the novice.

Training is the next important step in knowledge protection. Private sector organizations would benefit from imitating their counterparts in the defense and intelligence sectors (DIS) of the government. All DIS organizations have strict training and indoctrination programs. Once candidates pass the initial screening tests, a rigorous training program is commissioned. It is during this training process that candidates are taught the organization's mission and their individual roles and responsibilities. Knowledge is transferred to the candidates via in-class instructions and field-based simulations and physical exercises. Training regiments seek to mold the individual's character into one that meets the ideal characteristics of members of the organization. One of the most important aspects of training, especially in the armed services, is indoctrination with the code of conduct. Because these organizations are command-and-control-based and strictly hierarchical, it is essential to new members to be acquainted with the right processes and procedures. For instance, in the armed services, there are entire training modules explaining the "code of conduct." The use of conduct codes is as old as war itself. Thus the Roman legions adhered to a code whereby if a man fell asleep while he was supposed to be on watch in a time of war, he could expect to be stoned to death. In feudal Japan, the code of the Samurai specified that a warrior was not to approach his opponent using stealth. He was to declare himself openly before engaging the enemy. As French notes, "[T]he code of the warrior defines not only how he should interact with his own warrior comrades, but also how he should treat other members of his society, his enemies, and the people he conquers."[7] The code not only demands the highest standards of conduct, but also specifies how to use the knowledge provided in its intended manner. Failure to use the knowledge in its true spirit could lead to serious consequences and repercussions. A code is useful primarily because it details organizational protection and allegiance. For an individual to defect to a rival and leak knowledge is a serious crime.

In addition to the code of conduct, trainees at DIS organizations learn by being thrown into simulated real-life situations. Thus a soldier cadet might be involved in a simulated battle and a trainee intelligence agent might be captured by pretend adversaries. By engaging in simulations, members learn how to conduct themselves in situations that are less than ideal, involve stress and fatigue, and exact high emotional tolls. Their conduct is put to the test and then hardened to deal with adverse conditions. Hence, it is rare for DIS members to leak knowledge of their missions, agencies, or nations to their captors. In private sector organizations, simulation-based training can be ideal for teaching employees how best to secure the organization's knowledge by playing through an array of scenarios.

DIS agencies also follow a model in which individuals are given "general knowledge" first, and only after competency has been displayed and vetted by the organization is an individual then given more "specialized knowledge." When an individual joins an air force, they spend their initial time learning the basics of a command-and-control regiment, physical conditioning, and the fundamentals of avionics. This general knowledge is not unique to any given air force; whether somebody wants to fly in the US Air Force or the Royal Air Force, this knowledge is fundamental. Only after competency is achieved in the general-knowledge area and the organization is assured of the trainee's commitment to the organizational mission does the organization impart "specialized knowledge." Specialized knowledge can be defined as highly sensitive nuggets of insight that require security clearance to gain access (see the next point). To summarize, the training programs teach an organizational member what is acceptable behavior in using the organization's knowledge and it is this training that helps an organization protect against theft from and misuse of the knowledge by insiders.

Knowledge can be protected by carefully setting access controls and permissions. Another key characteristic of managing the people aspect of security in DIS organizations is the concept of security clearances. DIS organizational members have a "status;" this can be a rank status (private, lieutenant, captain, general, admiral, and so on) and/or a security clearance status (confidential, secret, and top secret). A rank status identifies what information and knowledge is pertinent to an individual's function in the field. It is acquired, in that all enlisted personnel must follow a predefined process that governs how their ranks will change on the basis of their time in the service, skill development, and performance. No one entering the armed services should be given the rank of general or admiral on their first day; this is acquired over time, with effort and experience. DIS organizations have clear guidelines that articulate the roles, responsibilities, access, privileges, and accountability for each rank. Rank status is earned, but the organization awards security clearance. Security clearance is also awarded on the basis of job function. More specifically, the informational access requirements of a job function govern the security clearance. In order to acquire a security clearance, individuals must complete a rather lengthy information sheet which the organization uses to conduct a thorough background investigation. Background investigations evaluate the history of the applicant five to ten years back: criminal history, financial records, past employment, and travels. In addition, investigators conduct interviews with friends, coworkers, educators, and neighbors. To obtain top secret clearance, applicants are put through a security interview – the main aim being to determine if the individual can keep classified materials in confidence. Each security clearance is evaluated regularly and failure to adhere to prescribed codes of conduct and the misuse of authority could result in its revocation. A security clearance is also required of each DIS business partner such as a contractor, researcher, or consultant before they are made privy to sensitive knowledge. These individuals must apply for security clearances with the government and are put through the same security and scrutiny as regular DIS employees.

The security clearance is an apt way of investigating an agent who interacts with sensitive knowledge and is an excellent way of ensuring that only an authorized individual has access to knowledge.

To assure knowledge protection, you must monitor your own organization. All DIS organizations have counterintelligence (CI) teams whose job is to catch culprits who steal, misuse, or vandalize knowledge. CI teams monitor activities to ensure that only authorized processes, activities, and behaviors are conducted. These teams operate independently of other organizational functions and also in continuum. They are not reactive and do not merely come into existence after a breach has occurred; their value is specifically linked to their ability to preempt a threat from materializing. Having CI teams serves as a deterrent to those who would otherwise contemplate conducting a security breach in two ways. First, the presence of CI within the DIS means that DIS members know their actions are being monitored. Second, when breaches do occur, the CI teams can quickly intervene to mitigate the losses and learn from these efforts to improve their capabilities. In recent times, the cases of Aldrich Ames (CIA) and Robert Hanssen (FBI) have been a testament to the value of CI within an organization. CI investigations range in scope and gravity, and they can be used to alert a DIS employee that they are doing something wrong, knowingly or unknowingly. If the matter is not serious, the employee can be counseled and asked to return to work. It is important for an organization to sense and act on signals of impending failures before they materialize, since case studies have shown that perpetrators of insider crimes are more likely to start out slowly by trying to cause a small amount of damage before causing a major catastrophe. CI investigations can be of grave magnitude when an employee is the subject of a heated investigation. In most cases, CI investigators do not let the employee know that they are being monitored. Valuable knowledge can be gained by monitoring the suspected individuals carefully and secretly. CI operations can be and are conducted on an agency's business partners to ensure that knowledge and information are used appropriately. CI teams work closely with the agency's security personnel to ensure that lessons learnt from operations can be used to bolster organizational security practices. To summarize, CI initiatives monitor how authorized individuals utilize knowledge and information in pursuit of their task assignments and, as such, can provide a wealth of valuable and rare knowledge.

Finally, it is important that organizations take great care to ensure that knowledge is protected in work designs, processes, and practices. One way of doing this is to disaggregate or divide a process into manageable pieces. Each piece can be handled by a group of employees who are not connected to the groups that work on other pieces. In this situation, no one knows the whole picture. The organization should have a process for linking the various components in an optimal way and preserving the integrity and secrecy of the process. This is a common practice in the defense departments. Defense departments routinely solicit external contractors. Each contractor may work on a part of the system, but no contractor will have access to the complete system blueprint. The blueprint will reside with the defense department, which will integrate and combine the various components.

Securing knowledge assets is going to be an imperative as we move through the future. The Appendix to this book contains two commentaries that further explore the concept of knowledge protection (see p. 211).

Missing capabilities and known capabilities

The missing capabilities outlined here complement the other capabilities required to conduct knowledge management. The segmentation capability provides an organization with a clearer appreciation of its current knowledge assets and how they relate to one another. After segmentation, the organization can expend the necessary energy creating the right kinds of knowledge artifacts – those with the highest value proposition. The process of segmentation will also enhance the success of knowledge transfer because the organization will be more aware of its domain weaknesses and knowledge deficiencies. Tacit knowledge and expertise can be moved from areas of high concentration to deficient areas. Moreover, the organization can begin training employees on knowledge that is highly valuable and that is a source of competitive advantages, so it will better meet goals and objectives. Knowledge storage can also gain from the segmentation capability since knowledge assets are best stored based on their value. Organizations can separate high-value knowledge assets from those that offer only minimal value. Finally, knowledge of the highest value can be applied in a centralized fashion to exert maximum control – as discussed in Chapter 2. The destruction capability allows an organization to stay current and to generate new knowledge through a continued examination of existing knowledge assets. It also helps the organization keep its knowledge repositories current and, in doing so, fosters the transfer of current knowledge between organizational parties. The capability to apply current knowledge to business problems provides an organization with an advantage over others possessing only historical and outdated knowledge. The protection capability will be of paramount interest as we move through a future that is likely to be both tremulous and hostile. Generating, storing, and applying knowledge are costly endeavors, and so an organization must protect its investment in knowledge assets from unauthorized usage and unscrupulous individuals. Highly sensitive knowledge must be protected from its inception, while in storage, and during application. Segmenting knowledge will provide a way to identify valuable knowledge and protect it. Knowledge transfer and application mechanisms also need to be secured so that competitors do not discover how to construct or recreate a firm's knowledge and erode its value and rarity.

The sophistication of knowledge management capabilities in organizations will vary. Some will have sophisticated and optimized knowledge capabilities that are routinely inspected, improved upon, and revised as needed. Others will have less than ideal capabilities that are outdated and obsolete, as they have not kept up with changes in the environment. Many will fall in between these two extremes. A clear indicator of a mature and sophisticated knowledge program is the care and attention given to the missing capabilities, and how well these are integrated with the traditional knowledge management capabilities.

Conclusion

In this chapter, we have discussed the three missing capabilities of knowledge management and have shown their relationship to the traditional knowledge management capabilities. We have argued that a viable knowledge management program should have an appreciation of the missing capabilities. Including the missing capabilities helps an organization to have a more engaged knowledge management program on several fronts. By using the segmentation capability, an organization can be better engaged and in line with the realities of its current knowledge stocks. The organization can better appreciate the knowledge inventory it possesses and understand the knowledge assets with high value. It can best expend efforts and resources and manage them adequately. The destruction capability ensures that an organization has a current and useful knowledge base. As we have argued, knowledge assets are subject to depreciation like any other assets. Choosing not to destroy outdated knowledge can lead to the demise of an organization's competitive position. If an organization refuses to embrace innovations in a timely fashion, it can lead to competitive takeovers. Not destroying knowledge in a timely manner can lead to organizational inertia, and inertia has no place in the current marketplace and competitive environment. Finally, having adequate protection measures – the protection capability – ensures that an organization is cognizant of the threat of knowledge being leaked to competitors and of insiders using knowledge maliciously. Not protecting the most critical resource, organizational knowledge, shows poor management and sloppiness and can cost an organization dearly. An organization must engage its security protocols and incentive structures to ensure that knowledge is used effectively and appropriately within its bounds for goal attainment. As stated in the introduction, the nature of their respective capabilities can help differentiate one organization from another. The missing capabilities differentiate a successful knowledge management program from one that is incomplete and wanting. Put another way, missing capabilities distinguish an *engaged* knowledge management program from a knowledge management program that is simply basic.

4

Engaging the Knowledge Chiefs

While almost all organizations recognize that knowledge management is essential for organizational success, only a select few ones put their money where their mouth is. It is not uncommon to find organizations managing knowledge unsystematically; often this lack of a knowledge management program can be attributed to lack of appropriate accountability and reporting mechanisms. Absence of senior personnel to lead efforts is one reason for a lack of accountability and credibility in organizational initiatives.

In this chapter, we will describe these strategic players who are responsible for ensuring that an organization has a clear, cohesive, and integrated approach to the management of knowledge. We will focus our energies on four types of chief – the chief knowledge officer (CKO), the chief learning officer (CLO), the chief privacy officer (CPO), and the chief security officer (CSO). We are not going to discuss the position of chief information officer (CIO) in this chapter, despite this chief's influence on an organization's knowledge management agenda; there is an abundance of literature that has already examined the role, responsibilities, and success factors of the CIO position.[1] The chiefs that will be the focus of this chapter must work in conjunction with the CIO to realize knowledge management goals. Today we cannot envision an organization without a CIO, and tomorrow we will not be able to envision a successful organization without the knowledge chiefs.

Why have knowledge chiefs?

Imagine what would happen to an organization without a chief financial officer (CFO). Who would be responsible for cash flow issues? What about issues of interest rates and corporate loans? How about asset purchases and stock equity programs? Financial chaos is certain without a CFO. The CFO ensures the financial matters of the organization are handled with care, vision, and clarity. The successful CFO will integrate financial matters within the organization and ensure consistency, effectiveness, and efficiency in the discharge of financial transactions. In addition, the CFO will serve as the link to the chief executive officer (CEO) and other C-level executives on financial matters. In doing so, the CFO acts as the bridge connecting financial issues to other organizational functions such as marketing, production, operations, and information technology. Connections must be made at the strategic level of the enterprise's operations. A CFO must consult with the chief operating officer (COO) on issues of asset purchases and disposal; similarly, the CFO must work with the CEO to ensure that the strategic objectives of the organization are being met. The success of the CFO position depends on the competency of the incumbent and how much respect the CFO is accorded by other senior-level members of the organization.

The knowledge chiefs are critical for the very same reasons that organizations need a CFO, a chief operating officer (COO), or even a chief executive officer (CEO). Each of the knowledge chiefs must be responsible for integrating matters within their domain and for connecting these issues to other strategic events in the organization. For example, a CSO must ensure that the security of knowledge assets, resources, and processes is handled effectively and efficiently. The CSO must also be able to connect security issues with issues in finance, marketing, and human resources. For example, the CSO must be able to advise the human resource department on the significance of and proper procedures for employee background checks.

None of the chiefs proposed in this chapter should operate apart from other strategic players within the organization. Linking these chiefs to other departments and senior-level managers is absolutely necessary for success. In September 2002, the US Department of Defense asked JetBlue, a commercial passenger airline, for their passenger list. The list requested contained information on over 5 million passengers. The privacy policy of JetBlue clearly stated that passenger information would *never* be shared with external parties. Despite this policy, the list made its way to the Department of Defense. Today, JetBlue contends with a number of class-action lawsuits by disgruntled passengers. How did this happen? The Department of Defense contacted the marketing group of the organization for the data. The marketing department did not check with the IT group before providing the data. Had the marketing group consulted with IT – the group responsible for overseeing security and privacy issues – they could have averted this disastrous outcome. It would have taken a five-minute conversation between the CIO and the chief marketing officer. In any situation like this one, having a CPO who is in direct charge of privacy issues will prove valuable to the organization. The CPO will make the final decision about privacy matters and serve as the link to the external world on such issues.

Knowledge chiefs are responsible for various strategic aspects of an organization's knowledge management agenda. The chiefs integrate knowledge management *within* their domains: privacy, security, learning and knowledge, and also *across* the various domains of the organization – for integrating knowledge management activities with those of financial planning or

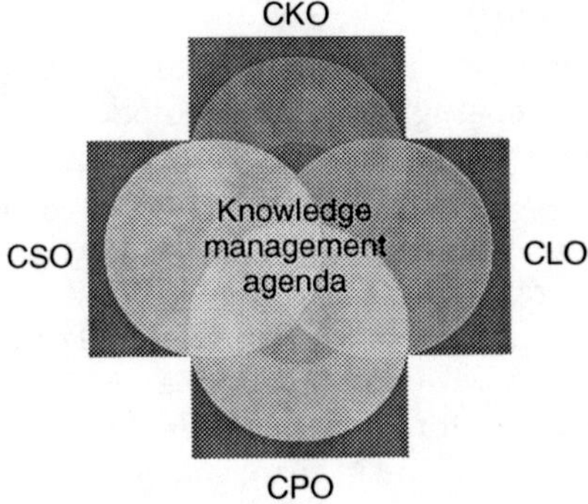

Figure 4.1   The knowledge chiefs.

marketing. We can examine the chief's contribution by looking at knowledge management from the perspective of both resources and processes. As discussed in Chapter 3, the resource discourse – which stems from the literature on strategic management – demands an organization to assess and segment their knowledge on the characteristics of rareness, value, non-inimitability, and non-substitutability. If organizational knowledge has these characteristics, it will help maintain the firm's competitive advantages. The process perspective traditionally segments knowledge management into a series of distinct activities ranging from acquisition and creation, through storage, transfer, and distribution, to application. In addition to the traditional activities, we must account for the missing capabilities of segmentation, destruction, and protection. As will be made clear in the next few pages, the knowledge chiefs play distinct, yet interrelated, roles in managing the process and resource issues of knowledge management agendas (see Figure 4.1).

The knowledge chiefs

We will begin by profiling each of the chiefs. In doing so, we will discuss the typical background of each, the industries or sectors in which they are popular, and their primary areas of focus. In this chapter, we profile the "typical" chief. We have spent significant energy, effort, and resources investigating the characteristics and peculiarities of the chiefs and have come to realize that every chief is different and that these differences can be significant. A CKO in the manufacturing sector will have roles and functions very different from those of his counterpart in the consulting industry. Hence we do not want to give the impression that all chiefs are alike and are cast in the same mold. Instead, we discuss similarities or commonalities that we discovered from talking to Chiefs, even after accounting for their unique peculiarities and challenges.

The chief knowledge officer

CKO positions are popular in the management consulting and technology sectors. This is not surprising, since the lifeblood of any service organization is their ability to leverage knowledge. For example, a consulting company must be able to reuse its expertise efficiently to operate in a cost-effective manner and innovate effectively. If the company fails to reuse knowledge effectively and generate new knowledge efficiently, it risks going out of business. Knowledge generated by one individual or team within the organization must be shared with the rest of the organization for all to benefit from the insights and use it to generate more knowledge revenue.

Almost all CKOs have a blend of management and technical competencies. These competencies were acquired by academic training and on-the-job experiences. Any CKO that had a strong technical background usually spent several years gaining management experience before becoming a CKO. The management-trained professional who likely spent time gaining technical competency was less common. Management-trained professionals did occasionally gain technical knowledge by completing certificate programs and/or short courses at academic institutions. A handful of organizations hired former academicians, usually professors in the area of strategic management and information systems, for the role of the CKO. To our dismay and surprise, out of the 23 CKOs we interviewed, only one was listed as part of their organization's core executive group, at the same level as the CFO, COO, and CIO. The remaining CKOs were supervised by either the CIO or the chief human resource officer, sometimes called the chief talent officer.

Most CKOs focus on four areas – (1) leveraging the technical infrastructure to better manage the transfer and flow of explicit knowledge assets; (2) fostering and developing social mechanisms to enable the exchange of tacit expertise and skills; (3) managing the flow of knowledge between an organization and its business partners; and (4) making knowledge management an integral part of the organizational culture, routines, processes, and daily work. We detail each of these activities, although, because this book is about knowledge management, our coverage of the intricacies of the CKO position will be scant. We will focus only on highlighting their critical tasks here and will cover the concepts in greater detail in other chapters.

Leveraging the technical infrastructure typically involves developing repositories for storing explicit knowledge artifacts – repositories that house software code, business plans, consulting documents, sales material, and marketing presentations – and developing a communication infrastructure to connect employees of the organization and engage them in dialogues. This is commonly handled via the development of internet-based tools such as chat rooms, emails, and short message service (SMS) systems. The role of the CKO is analogous to that of an architect. The CKO sets the designs, determines the needs, calibrates the relationships between various system components, and then turns the plan over to the CIO – the developer – to build. In order to be successful, the CKO must have a good grasp of the technological and behavioral issues involved in setting up knowledge management systems and repositories (this is addressed in Chapter 9). CKOs must have broad knowledge that gives them visionary perspectives on the architecture of the organization and how to foster knowledge flows.

No CKO can rely entirely on technology-based mechanisms to get a knowledge management program running. After all, knowledge management is a human endeavor and can be supported only by technology. Therefore, every CKO must demonstrate a high degree of competency in leveraging social mechanisms for fostering knowledge management. While there are many intricacies to this task – from addressing issues of knowledge transfer (see Chapter 5 on distributed knowledge management) to developing economic incentives for rewarding knowledge sharing behaviors (see Chapter 8 on knowledge markets) – the biggest challenge is the management of knowledge hoarders and gatekeepers. Every organization has knowledge hoarders, individuals who are repositories of knowledge but who resist sharing it with the rest of the organization. Knowledge gatekeepers, on the other hand, are individuals who act as stoppers or checks for knowledge movement between two or more entities. A social network for knowledge sharing will perform miserably if such individuals are not managed effectively.

Knowledge hoarders

Knowledge hoarders are normally domain experts. These individuals have gained their knowledge over time, through experience, and have designated organizational statuses based on such knowledge; as such, they are reluctant to share their expertise for several reasons. They feel that sharing such knowledge will compromise their current organizational status – possibly lower it. It may also be difficult for them to communicate with novices because they have such extensive knowledge of that area. Many experts experience their knowledge tacitly, and articulating it is not easy. Knowledge sharing also requires a significant time investment and many experts are reluctant to participate because such a commitment pulls them away from their primary work tasks. In one software organization, an expert commented:

> For every hour that I spend teaching someone a programming scheme or sequence...the organization pays dearly...I can be much more productive solving the problems for which I command my high salary...knowledge sharing is not for me...I do not want to cheat the organization in terms of lost time...there is no guarantee that I can even impart such know-how to my peer.

It's clear that there are a variety of reasons why experts resist involvement in knowledge sharing exercises, and yet an organization must find ways to address these concerns and make experts feel more comfortable and competent in knowledge sharing.

A CKO has several options. He can consider developing knowledge markets where knowledge can be bought and sold in organizations. The organization could provide experts with "time away from their work" during which the experts could be asked to get involved in training programs and to learn communication skills. Most experts are excellent knowledge managers; they simply lack the skills to impart knowledge to non-experts. The organization could take active steps to help experts improve their communication skills. Finally, experts need to be rewarded on the time and effort they spend training their peers. Seldom do organizations reward their employees, especially experts, for their soft achievements. Experts should be evaluated on their success in knowledge sharing, and an organization must make knowledge sharing a mandatory component of their experts' jobs. If an organization has an expert who does not share his knowledge and applies it individually then the organization gains only minimally. In the face of an adamant knowledge hoarder, an organization may have more success terminating the contract of the expert in favor of quick-study novices or reasonably skilled individuals who can appreciate the importance of knowledge sharing.

Knowledge gatekeepers

Knowledge gatekeepers are normally middle managers, project leaders, team leaders, and others who act as a connection between one logical entity and another. A team manager acts as a bridge between the team and the external units of the organization. Knowledge entering and exiting a group usually passes through these individuals. In one consulting company we interviewed, an individual was given the title of knowledge manager. She was responsible for knowledge management activities of her department, and described her role as follows:

> I am the gatekeeper...the checkpoint for knowledge...Knowledge that is to be stored in our [knowledge management] system must be submitted to me...I check to see if the knowledge nugget is valuable, new, unique, and then approve it...Once approved, I store it in the system and announce it to the team...external teams need to get my permission to access knowledge nuggets stored on our system...this is to ensure they have the appropriate training to use the knowledge in its intended manner.

Gatekeepers, depending on how they are managed, can be assets or liabilities to knowledge management programs.

The advantage of a gatekeeper is that they can help a local unit, such as a team or department, to avoid knowledge and information overload. By screening relevant knowledge before it is made available to the group, they can prevent useless, irrelevant, and low-quality knowledge from distracting the group. They can scan for new knowledge nuggets that would be valuable to the team and bring them into the group's work practices. A gatekeeper can also ensure consistency in knowledge repositories by acting as the checkpoint for those repositories. They can also maintain the KMSs. However, a gatekeeper can be a bottleneck that impedes the flow of knowledge by stopping it, delaying it, and even preventing it from reaching the group. This problem is usually related to the gatekeeper's workload. If they are overburdened with work, chances are high that knowledge transfer will be impeded since there will be delays in getting knowledge into the group and, consequently, into the external environment. Moreover, knowledge management systems may also begin to decay owing to the absence of necessary maintenance efforts.

The CKO must first identify the knowledge gatekeepers – both formally and informally appointed.[2] There are several techniques and tools – such as social network analysis – available to identify gatekeepers.[3] We will not cover these techniques in this book, but highly recommend *The Hidden Power of Social Networks*, by Robert Cross and Andrew Parker.[4] Once the gatekeeper is identified, a CKO must monitor how well he performs knowledge management. Is the gatekeeper overburdened? Is he able to transfer knowledge effectively? Such an analysis will help the CKO better manage the gatekeeper. When gatekeepers are stressed for resources and time, the CKO can intervene and help manage the flow of knowledge better by lowering the gatekeeper's burden – perhaps by adding a secondary gatekeeper. However, when a gatekeeper is deliberately impeding the flow of knowledge for political reasons, the CKO must intervene and provide incentives that can entice the appropriate behavior in the gatekeeper; if this fails, the CKO must work to remove the gatekeeper from the position and find a suitable replacement.

In the context of managing knowledge flow between an organization and the external world, the goal of the CKO is to view the organization in the context of an "extended enterprise" and manage knowledge flows in outsourcing, strategic alliances, mergers, and acquisitions (Chapter 6 discusses these issues in depth). In addition, the CKO is responsible for managing knowledge flows between the organization and the customer. Customers represent a viable and sometimes most salient source of external knowledge for the organization. Unless the CKO can actively manage knowledge flows between the organization and its customers, and use customer knowledge to improve organizational practices, there is a high probability the organization will fail. (Chapter 7 is dedicated exclusively to the concept of customer knowledge management.)

The concept of knowledge management must be engrained in the organization, and getting an organization to recognize the inherent significance of knowledge management is a twofold strategy. First, all sectors of the organization must be involved in the concept of knowledge management. (Chapter 10 discusses this issue in depth.) Second, the organization's social capital must be improved.[5] Social capital

> is the sum of the actual and potential resources embedded within, available through, and derived from the network of relationships possessed by an individual or social unit. Social capital, thus, comprises both the network and the assets that may be mobilized through that network.[6]

Social capital is salient for effective knowledge management, since it provides the foundation for effective knowledge exchange, work collaborations, and the calibration of innovations. There are three components that comprise the construct of social capital.

First, the structural dimension refers to the architecture in place that facilitates sharing information and knowledge. The structural element comprises the knowledge networks and the configuration of the network linking entities. An organization has high structural capital when its network ties are strong and there is connectivity between all entities of the organization. Second, the relational dimension deals with the issue of trust between entities. Trust emerges from relationships and trust informs how relationships function. In an organization, expectations and obligations lead to the development of a collective trust, which acts as an organizational asset. Collective trust enhances effective knowledge transfer and enables the smooth coordination and cooperation of work practices. Third, the cognitive dimension represents the shared meaning and understanding of the purpose, motivation, and scope of the network. As entities interact, they exchange meaning and inform perspective, and these interactions lead to the emergence of collective meaning within the organization. In addition, repeated interactions reinforce the network's identity and goals.

The CKO plays a vital role in building the organization's social capital. The CKO works in conjunction with the CIO to ensure that an appropriate technical architecture is in place for knowledge sharing. In addition, by working with knowledge hoarders and gatekeepers to improve their knowledge sharing capabilities, the CKO helps build better informal knowledge sharing networks. These acts contribute to the structural dimension. To build the relational dimension, the CKO must focus on improving the organization's collective trust. Building trust among organizational members is not always easy. An organization can build trust by providing incentives and disincentives. Incentives include rewards for knowledge sharing, open communications, efforts expended to improve coordination, and movement away from individualistic work models to group- or team-based models. Disincentives include penalties for undesirable behavior; this may include reprimands for those who prevent knowledge sharing, limiting promotion within the organization for those who hoard knowledge, and so on. The CKO will experience a challenge in building trust "across the organization." Trust normally exists between individuals who work in close proximity; individuals tend to trust other members of their group. The challenge is to develop trust *between* groups. To do this, the CKO must frame knowledge management efforts in the context of the *organizational mission*. This will enable the organization to build both the relational and cognitive dimensions of social capital. By focusing the attention of individuals on the *organization*, rather than on their local work units, the CKO can encourage the development of inter-group trust. For example, if individuals realize, and are reminded on a constant basis, that their work has broader implications for the survival of the organization at large, then they may start to pay more attention to requests from outside groups. To this end, all chiefs should constantly remind employees of the organizational mission.

The chief learning officer

CLO positions are common in the technology and service sectors for two reasons. First, these industries experience constant change. Changes include the introduction of new products and services, delivery methods, product development mechanisms, and changes in business ideologies. In the technology sector, trends in technology deployment constantly capture the attention of executives. If technology or electronic retailers fail to keep their employees' skills current, they risk losing business since customer queries will not be answered effectively, while in some cases the customer may possess more knowledge than the seller. The second reason for the popularity of CLO positions in these fields is that both sectors experience high employee turnover, especially from employees interacting directly with customers. In the hospitality industry, hotels experience a nearly 100 percent turnover of their receptionist/concierge staff and this high turnover exacts a price from the organization. It must recruit new employees and have adequate training mechanisms in pace to help new hires to get accustomed with the organizational practices that will enable them to operate effectively.

Like their CKO counterparts, CLOs are highly educated and, in some cases, even outshine CKOs. Most CLOs possess doctorates, with areas of concentration in organizational psychology, human resources, or public administration. Organizations draw a significant number of their CLOs from academia. This academic experience means that a vast majority of CLOs have published articles, conference papers, and books. This quality is truly unique and, as such, should warrant appreciation. CLOs who are able to blend academic and business knowledge have an advantage over executives with competency in just one area. These CLOs consider themselves either *consulting academicians* or *academic consultants*, since their practices and scope moves between academic and practical inquires. This ability to flow between academia and the private sector is an important asset because it brings an advantage to an organization over those who are mere consultants or academicians.

Most CLOs have their professional career origins in one of three areas – education, technology, or organizational behavior. CLOs with a background in education have experience in training and development, human capital development, and e-learning strategies. More tech-savvy CLOs have spent their time leveraging technology in educational settings – such as schools and colleges – and some of their experience includes deploying web-based courses, managing course infrastructure like video and voice classes over the Internet. CLOs with a background in organizational behavior have experience in the areas of human resource planning, leadership training, and organizational consultants. Unlike CKOs, most CLOs are hired externally – an organization almost always picks a person from outside it to lead learning efforts. Moreover, almost half of the CLO positions we examined were listed as part of the core executive team of the organization. This is a pleasant finding and demonstrates the seriousness of the role played by learning initiatives in the organization's future.

CLOs focus their energies on managing the learning agenda of the organization and the capabilities of the organization's workforce. Managing the learning agenda involves choosing the right training method, learning platform, and classes; preparing a mechanism to scheduling training, and encouraging employees to switch from traditional classroom training to web-based training. Managing the capabilities of the workforce includes assessing each employee's knowledge, determining if additional training is required to increase an employee's competency, determining if the training can be completed internally or externally, and insuring the employee actually receives the training. When assessing the capabilities of the workforce, the CLO must also determine if currently present expertise can be transferred to a place of need in the organization.

The learning regiments

Managing an organization's learning agenda is a significant undertaking and maintaining or creating a viable training program is a must. For some organizations, training programs are the key selling point for recruiting talented individuals. Why do most MBAs in the USA aspire to work for a large consulting firm like McKinsey, Bain, Accenture, or the Boston Consulting Group? Economically speaking, they could earn comparable salaries working for other institutions, but other organizations would be unlikely to provide them with the same level of training and knowledge infusion. Similarly, organizations such as the defense departments (Navy, Air Force, Marines, Coast Guards, and Army) must be able to "sell" their learning and training abilities. Many of their recruits join immediately following high school, and thus, the organization advertises itself as a viable way to get the training necessary in their careers and private lives. High school students normally look at the defense forces as a way to get sufficient training and serve their time, to get funding for attending colleges and universities. Therefore it is important that these organizations live up to the expectations of providing adequate training, learning, and knowledge-enhancing mechanisms.

There are several kinds of training options a CLO can employ – classroom training, web-based training, satellite-based or video-based classes, computer-based training, and so on. A CLO must consider the advantages and disadvantages of each training style. For example, classroom training is apt when we require economies of scale – when an organization must train several individuals on a specific topic. A particular advantage of classroom training is that the individual pupil can interact with the knowledge source, the trainer. Its disadvantage is that it the requires the learner to be away from work. Computer-based training, such as classes on a CD-ROM, has the advantage of being portable; a learner can use it wherever and whenever they have a computer. However, the drawback is that the individual is learning from a CD rather than directly from a human knowledge source. Hence, the learning process fails to provide the opportunity for the feedback and interaction that enhances the learning situation. Computer-based training is appropriate when an organization must train employees in areas where they have the prescribed background knowledge. Employees can learn better using computer-based-training if they can link it to pre-existing knowledge. Conversely, computer-based training works poorly if an employee is seeking to gain knowledge in a novel arena. For example, asking an administrative assistant to learn computer programming from a CD is unreasonable. For novel areas, individuals need to have access to human experts who can guide them through the learning process.

Regardless of the training method, the CLO determines the strategic direction of the learning agenda and manages it effectively. Learning in an organization can be expensive primarily because of its currently existing ad-hoc style. In one particular organization, eight employees scheduled a class from an external vendor. Each employee did so independently and the organization compensated them for the expense and missed an opportunity to seize corporate discounts; in this case, close to 32 percent of the cost would have been saved but no one suspected the same class was of interest to several employees. In a large organization especially, training costs can rise very quickly if the organization does not integrate training needs. An example of a success story is, JCPenney's use of the OneTouch knowledge system to deliver interactive training to satellite classrooms in nearly all of its store locations. Training programs last no longer than two hours and the students get live, interactive training that includes pretests and post-class testing. This helps the CLO to analyze how much learning has occurred because of the programs. Since implementing the learning program in 1996, JCPenney has saved $1 million every year owing to reductions in travel costs and other expenses, such as printing, warehousing, and mailing training programs. The company has also been able to increase employee participation in training programs and to train more consistently.[7] Another success story is found in the US Navy learning initiatives. The US Navy's online learning portal enables the user to determine their learning needs on the basis of the five-vector model. The five vectors are areas of interest for any naval personnel and are professional development, personal development, leadership, certifications and qualifications, and performance. The portal helps personnel to determine knowledge and learning paths based on what professional track they would like to pursue.

The chief privacy officer

CPO positions are flourishing in the financial, marketing/advertising, and healthcare sectors. This proliferation is not a coincidence, since data management and information is heavily regulated in these industries. Like the other two chiefs, the typical CPO is highly educated. Almost all the CPOs we studied had postgraduate degrees and some possessed doctorates. The academic backgrounds of those with a masters degree include healthcare, business, and computer science. At the doctorate level, the vast majority of the CPOs had earned a juris doctorate (JD) with areas of focus in patent and privacy litigation.

A majority of the CPOs had a primary background directly related to privacy issues. They worked on privacy, from the perspective of either technology or non-technology. CPOs with a background in technology-related privacy issues had been network administrators, network security specialists, and systems engineers. CPOs from the non-technology perspective held positions in legal-related backgrounds, such as intellectual property law and electronic commerce regulations. Legislation is the reason stated for making some CPOs part of the organization's core management team. For example, the arrival of HIPAA (Health Insurance Portability and Accountability Act) legislation in the USA (1996) means that most health-care organizations who have appointed a CPO have made them part of the senior executive team. In most other industries, CPOs were typically outside the core executive team, but did report to a member of the executive team such as the CEO, president, or COO.

The CPO provides aid to other executives in addressing privacy issues related to their tasks. For example, a CIO can consult a CPO before building the next IT solution to ensure that the integrity of customer data is maintained and that the new solution adheres to privacy standards; a CPO leads efforts to make privacy controls and protocols more pervasive and ubiquitous throughout the organization. CPOs are typically involved in the development of a new business deal, especially in the business-to-business (B2B) sector, where data and information exchanges are involved. A CPO serves as the organization's public relations (PR) person on privacy-related issues. As such, the CPO must be an excellent communicator between the organization and external audiences. Their main task is to increase public awareness regarding the organization's commitment to online privacy. The CPO also works closely with government and legislative bodies and industry leaders to shape privacy standards and regulations that guide the organization's present and future. A CPO must lead the charge in developing a sound privacy management agenda. Microsoft offers a good example of a privacy agenda, with a policy built on five principles. The first of these is *notice* – they are committed to giving customers disclosure about who is collecting information, what is being collected, and for what purpose. The second is *choice* – giving customers the choice of what information they would they like to share. The third is *access* – giving customers access to the systems that store the information collected so that they keep it updated and maintain it accurately. The fourth is *security* – ensuring data protection activities so that customer information is not compromised by acts of theft, sabotage, or disaster. The final principle is *enforcement* – creating policies and procedures that will hold the organization responsible and encouraging strict adherence. While articulation of a privacy policy is the important first step, this must be followed by definite actions.

The chief security officer

Among the knowledge chiefs, the CSO has made the most recent debut. Most organizations have introduced the position of the CSO because of a number of external events such as an increase in global terrorism, a rise in industrial espionage activities, a heightened awareness of the pervasive and ubiquitous nature of computing, and the increasingly distributed nature of organizations. The job of the CSO is easy to understand: it is to secure corporate expertise from unscrupulous individuals and external sabotage. The CSO is the primary person who ensures the organization has adequate knowledge protection capabilities. The reasons for the installation of a CSO are the same as those presented earlier for calling attention to the missing capability of knowledge protection.

Most CSOs have backgrounds rich in security matters. Some have held positions in law enforcement agencies, some have worked on cases of electronic crimes and industrial theft, and some have backgrounds in the armed services complemented by managerial experience. In contrast with the other chiefs, most CSOs do not have advanced degrees, but their rich experience in security compensates for this lack. CSOs focus primarily on securing products, processes, and people.

The CSO must work closely with the organization's HR department to ensure adequate controls are in place to investigate new employees and how new employees are performing with organizational knowledge. For the CSO to successfully prevent unscrupulous individuals from joining the organization, background checks and employee surveillance processes must be institutionalized. Although background checks will help eliminate some untrustworthy individuals, employee surveillance is an absolute must. It is naive to assume that existing employees will always keep the organization's best interests in mind. It is a well-known fact that most organizational crimes are perpetrated by insiders. Employees typically begin by violating small rules and then move to larger and more significant violations. The CSO must nip this behavior in the bud. If small violations occur, the employee can be counseled and warned; moreover, organizational loss at this stage will be minimal. On the other hand, if the organization waits until the employee causes significant damage, then the CSO's role in the incident will be limited to damage control.

Successful processes are salient sources of competitive advantage and must be protected carefully. Adequate security procedures must be in place to ensure that only authorized individuals enter sensitive areas or are privy to sensitive material. To protect knowledge products, the CSO works in conjunction with the CIO and the CKO to ensure KMSs and communication channels are secure. The CSO must be sure to stay abreast of new technology, of situations within the organization that allow outsiders access to the organization's technology resources, and of changes to the information architecture, since these issues affect protection measures. The Appendix (p. 211) contains two commentaries that explore security issues in further detail.

Critical success factors

This section will describe key success factors facing the chiefs. While some of these factors may be more pertinent to a particular class of knowledge chiefs – for example, the CKOs – they are nonetheless relevant to the success of every knowledge chief.

Creating and managing a knowledge inventory

All chiefs must focus on managing the knowledge inventory (KI) of the organization. The KI may be defined as the collection of knowledge assets and links within the organization. Knowledge assets represent the explicit knowledge documents and the human knowledge workers, while the knowledge links represent employee connections to sources of knowledge external to the organization. The KI serves as a template from which each chief can manage the knowledge of the organization. The chiefs, by definition, focus on different areas of the KI.

For the CKO, the KI provides a portrait of knowledge that resides in the organization. Using this, the CKO can develop strategies to leverage knowledge by mobilizing it from one location to another. The CLO can use the KI to get a sense of skills possessed by each employee, how current those skills are, and what areas of learning need to be enhanced. The CPO and CSO will most likely use the KI to learn if knowledge is being adequately protected from the external world and used in the intended manner – if the organization is adhering to various privacy standards, for example.

Without a KI, the knowledge management efforts of each knowledge chief will be haphazard and fragmented. For example, consider the organizational benefits of an adequately managed KI. The chiefs might examine the KI and discover that knowledge was thinly spread across the organization, with the various sectors lacking common knowledge, each sector having knowledge in specialized areas alone. Common knowledge is knowledge shared by all members of the organization and is a critical determinant of an organization's groups' ability to make sense and communicate with one another. After deducing this from the KI, the CKO and CLO could adequately deploy a job rotation program that would enable employees to become acquainted with other areas of the organization. Job rotation can be a viable learning and knowledge infusion mechanism. A job rotation program gives employees a chance to rotate among various positions in the organization and, in the process, gather rich experiences from the various sectors. It affords employees the opportunity to gain an appreciation for the wide array of business lines in which an organization may be involved and, in some cases, even allows employees to explore operations in various geographical sites. Often, employees are afforded this opportunity during their initial tenure with the organization because it helps them decide on the position or role they would like to pursue within the organization. Job rotation allows employees to acquire not only a wide range of domain expertise and/or knowledge but also social knowledge and connections with new knowledge sources that help them communicate.

The CSO, in conjunction with the CKO, can use the KI to deduce areas with a high risk of knowledge loss. In some cases, future knowledge losses could be owing to lack of adequate personnel with a requisite skill. Knowledge may be housed in the heads of a select few employees and the organization can be left vulnerable if they leave (see the next point). In this case, the CSO can work with the CKO and the CLO to train more employees in the skill so as to mitigate future issues.

The KI must be maintained and kept current. An outdated KI is irrelevant and useless. The KI should reflect the fact of an employee gaining a skill, moving from one project to the next, learning a trade, taking a class, or even having a knowledge need or area of future interest. Any organization can develop an intranet-based tool to act as the organization's KI. Employees should be provided access to the KI so that they can see who have the requisite skills and who are experts in a domain. Finding and transferring knowledge is also enhanced with a well-managed KI. A current and accurate KI benefits the organization and its employees.

Knowledge workers need expertise to succeed in their jobs. If they do not receive a constant flush of new ideas, skills, and experiences, their jobs may be at risk from automation or standardization. If knowledge workers engage in routine activities in a regular fashion, they are vulnerable to automation via computer-based systems. Tax accountants, at one time, could command a sizable hourly fee to aid individuals and organizations in filing tax returns. Today, this is not the case. Current software packages like Turbo Tax help individuals prepare their own tax returns in a more efficient and effective manner and cost much less than contracting a tax accountant. The advent of software for tax preparation led to a major shift in the accounting industry. Many "tax service" firms closed their doors. Among those that did survive, business from tax services took a dramatic hit, forcing these organizations to refocus and rethink how their expertise could provide services of a higher value. They had to learn how to better equip themselves to provide more in-depth knowledge of accounting and the tax practices than that which could be automated. Using the KI, the chiefs can manage the currency of organizational knowledge and identify trends. In forecasting a change, the KI can help determine how best to update the skills base of the organization.

A current and accurate KI is also important in determining if knowledge workers do not improve the quality, quantity, depth, and breadth of their knowledge; if they do not improve their knowledge base, they risk stagnating their position with the organization. Not allowing a position or skill set to stagnate is the best way to fight competition and outsourcing. If someone cannot demonstrate why they are uniquely qualified to do their job, why should anyone pay them a premium for it when it can be outsourced to someone else for a much lower wage? They should not. Simple economics will dictate that an organization has limited resources and unlimited wants. As such, the organization must economize its resource consumption, and the first way to economize is always to remove slack in resources. In difficult economic times, the first thing organizations ask is: How can we do more with less? This almost always leads to downsizing or outsourcing premium workers. If each worker has access to the KI, they can turn to areas of high growth, see who has the skills, and try to learn new talents. Doing so will help them move to better positions and keep their skill levels current.

Managing knowledge loss

Managing worker mobility and the associated knowledge loss that occurs is seldom an easy task. Workers may exit the organization for internal or external reasons. Internal factors are often self-motivated: retirement, new job opportunities, or moving to a new location. External factors are those factors outside the employee's control: job loss owing to downsizing, termination of contract, closing of work locations, and death. Knowledge loss occurs regardless of the situation.

Michael, a software engineer, lost his job in 2001 soon after the collapse of the dot-com bubble. He had been with the company since 1998 and was a dedicated worker. He worked on a specialized component of the organization's information system architecture. After relieving Michael of his job, the HR manager called him at home and asked him to return to work! She told him that they had not realized the value of his skills and that they had made a mistake in firing him. After considering the situation, Michael realized what had happened. In 1998, Caroline trained him to work on the specialized component of the information system architecture. Upon completion of his training, Caroline left the organization. Between 1998 and 2001, Michael had trained only one other person on the specificities of his work and the trainee left the organization in 2000. Hence, when the organization fired Michael, they did not realize that he was the only one who knew the work. Furthermore, there was no documentation of this knowledge in the organization. As a result, work on one of the ongoing projects would be compromised and the company would fail to deliver their proposed product – resulting in a loss of brand name, legal consequences, and loss of revenue.

Claudia had her personal bank accounts with a prestigious financial institution in Western Europe. owing to the volume of her transactions and her significant financial assets, the bank provided her with a personal banker – Jason. Jason managed the accounts of 5 to 10 of the bank's high-value customers. His job included helping these clients attain their financial objectives in the most effective, efficient, and pleasant manner. One fine day, Jason never showed up to work! The last time we checked he was still not accounted for and the police had a missing persons case open on him. Three weeks after Jason's disappearance, the bank called Claudia to tell her about the event. It was too late. Claudia had been frustrated that her numerous messages on Jason's mobile phone had gone unanswered, and had had several financial matters jeopardized by the bank's sluggish behavior in informing her about such a serious matter. She instantly closed her account and moved it to a competing institution.

These cases are not exceptions or uncommon. Such situations happen all the time, though the magnitude of outcomes resulting from poor management of knowledge loss can vary. In the first case, the knowledge loss can be blamed on sloppy organizational governance, while in the second the organization was to blame for the poor management of the knowledge loss after it occurred – the organization did not cause the knowledge loss, but fared poorly in managing it.

Knowledge loss is a serious issue for organizations and demands diligence from the knowledge chiefs. From our experience with organizations, we can suggest some of the best ways to manage knowledge loss. First, as mentioned earlier, every organization should have a knowledge inventory and manage it effectively. Using the KI, the organization should track the movement of expertise in and out of the organization. It is essential that when an employee leaves the organization should deduct their knowledge from the KI. The CSO must get involved to make sure that the employee is aware of restrictions on sharing organizational knowledge with the external world.

In most companies, employees sign agreements where they agree not to disclose organizational knowledge to competitors, or use their expertise for personal gain. If the KI is managed appropriately then there will be other individuals with the knowledge skills of the outgoing employee. The organization should put training programs into motion that will help transfer some of the scarce knowledge to other employees, and in so doing maintain adequate levels of the knowledge in the KI.

In cases, where the organization has not been careful in managing the KI, the employee should be enticed not to leave the organization without training other employees. This is not always possible, as when the employee dies. Therefore, an organization should be prepared and anticipate potential areas of knowledge loss that could be avoided. In the cases where it is possible for the employee to stay a few extra days and train another employee, organizations should encourage the widespread and accepted Japanese custom of *hikitsugi*. This routine stresses that an exiting employee must make every effort to make the incoming employee's job transition a smooth one by passing on necessary training, tools, and assets. An employee does so by imparting tacit insights and by also making practices and procedures explicit. Hikitsugi is helpful, especially when the exiting employee is taking significant expertise away from the company. For example, if a salesperson who handles a highly valued client leaves the company, the chances are high that knowledge will exit the organization too. What is lost here will be not the basic knowledge of sales or marketing, but more intimate and tacit expertise like the preferences of the client, when to pitch a sale, their favorite place for business lunches, and so on. These details can make or break a business relationship. Any relevant party outside the organization will feel disfranchised if they must reiterate all this knowledge to the new salesperson and may move their account to stay with their original salesperson in their new company or may move it to a new organization entirely. The knowledge possessed by the departed salesperson was what made the client's transactions with the organization smooth and comfortable. This knowledge needs to be passed on to the next employee who will need to manage the account. Without it, they are likely to fail in managing the relationship.

Managing knowledge loss is a critical issue for organizations, and when it comes to effectively preventing knowledge loss it is better to be proactive than reactive. Trying to manage knowledge loss as an employee is walking out the door is not an effective way to prevent knowledge from leaving the organization.

Perception management

Managing perception is vital to the respect, credibility, and resources received at the strategic levels. It is essential that a chief takes great care in managing how he is perceived by his peers, the other chiefs, the rest of the organization, and the employees at large. A chief not perceived favorably will be unsuccessful in meeting his goals. The chiefs we discuss in this chapter can learn from the trials of the CIO.

Many CIOs had initially to earn the respect of their peers. It was not uncommon to find CIOs treated as "techies" who were never invited to contribute to the strategic matters of the organization. Those days are long gone, and today CIOs are considered important strategic players. We can say with certainty that all organizations have a CIO, in some shape or form, on their executive team. CIOs have been successful in changing their perceived focus from operational to strategic. In addition, they have been able to improve the respect and credibility for the work they perform and manage. The traditional view of the information technology department as a cost center is long gone. Organizations today recognize the strategic role information technology departments play in maintaining competitiveness in the market-place. To make the transition from an operational to a strategic player, CIOs focused on a number of areas.

CIOs changed the perception of themselves as innovators to one of organizational consultants and change agents.[8] In doing so, they focused on the value-added approach, that is: "How can I add extra value to the organizational work using information technology?". This worked well and the other chiefs began to see the contribution of the CIO to organizational goal attainment. Efforts in IT could be tied to benefits and gains achieved. Most of the knowledge chiefs, especially the CKOs and CLOs with whom we spoke, mistakenly strive to be constant innovators. They try to develop novel methodologies, either technologically or organizationally, to engage knowledge management in the organization. We posit that the drive towards innovation, while worthwhile in its own right, can be a root cause for the demise of the CKO. Innovation is productive if someone has the proper resources at their disposal. However, in the current marketplace where resources are scarce, the chiefs must consider such drives as an unaffordable luxury. Any chief should strive to assume the role of a consultant for the various sectors of their organization. If performed properly, their role as consultant should add value to the firm by optimizing the movement of knowledge in projects. This will result in shortened project life-cycles and the effective delivery of value to customers. Moreover, the chiefs must induce change in the organization through a gradual process rather than through radical approaches. Radical approaches are harder to execute and can be disastrous if they fail. A chief should instead serve as a change agent, working with other business partners and devising change programs at a gradual pace by winning support of the people whose jobs or tasks need to be changed.

An important aspect of perception management is how close the chief works with the CEO. Support from the CEO, both formally and informally, can truly foster the agenda of the chief. Support from the CEO will translate into endorsement of the chief's policies and, if it is used effectively, the support can be a viable way for the chief to engage in change management.

The CEO must be convinced at all times that the knowledge chiefs are contributing positively to the organization. When the CEO is not forthcoming with support, there is a high probability that the knowledge chief will come under increased scrutiny from his peers and that requisite programs and policies will experience poor implementation. It is best if we think of support from the CEO as one of a project sponsor towards a pet project. Pet projects survive and have room to grow, mainly through the diligent work of the project sponsor. The project sponsor expends the effort and energy justifying the project, getting support for the initiative, charting the project's course, and managing emergencies associated with the project as they arise. Since many of a chief's projects are, by necessity, in infancy, the CEO is the ultimate project sponsor for such efforts. If the CEO is convinced of the need and benefits of the project, there is a high probability that it will be successful.

One of the best examples of CEO sponsorship for knowledge management efforts can be found in Jack Welch's transformation of General Electric from a traditional manufacturing house to a knowledge-based organization. GE's current success in the marketplace can be attributed to Welch's vision of the benefits that knowledge management would bring the organization. Welch articulated his vision of the knowledge-based organization as comprising two characteristics: boundarylessness and a learning culture. He encouraged knowledge sharing across GE's multiple business units and made it a point to engage the company in what he considered "the art of continual learning." GE is one the largest companies in the world, both in its size and in the breadth of products and services offered. As such, the success of GE, as Welch conceptualized, relied heavily on the ability to move knowledge across the various business lines, products, and services. In addition, unless GE could learn and adapt its practices on a near-constant basis, they would lose ground to competitors. Welch endorsed, led, and energized the knowledge management effort at GE. One of the outcomes of his vision was the creation of Support Central, a knowledge management portal. Support Central serves as the organization's knowledge center. It provides employees with 24-hour access to both knowledge repositories and contact information for topic experts. Employees can access a wide range of knowledge nuggets created by other employees and by GE's business partners, contractors, vendors, and suppliers. Today, there are 165,000 registered users of Support Central and these users span more than 1300 communities or work-groups.

Imagine trying to lead a knowledge management effort at GE without the support of the CEO. It would be a disaster, not because the chief was not brilliant, but because of the sheer size, complexity, diversity, and distributed nature of the organization. The CEO, the principal chief, is the single source of integration and has the capability to unite the various corners of the organization and rally them behind a cause. The knowledge chiefs must be cognizant of this reality and must use the CEO to further their agendas.

A select few CEOs write weekly emails or leave phone-mail messages with all employees of the organization to discuss their thoughts and experiences of the week, as well as the lessons learned from interactions with customers, and even to share practical pointers to be incorporated into daily work routines. These emails help focus the energy of the organization on managing knowledge effectively and also bind each employee's work to the organizational mission.

Harp on the organizational mission

The knowledge chiefs are employees of their organizations. They work to contribute to the mission, objectives, and goal achievements of their organization. In seems appropriate that they, along with the other employees, would be able to articulate the mission and core values of their organization. During our research and consulting, we were surprised to find that on average only 10 percent of all employees in an organization can articulate their organization's mission and values. Among the knowledge chiefs interviewed, only 60 percent could state with any degree of clarity the core mission and values of their organization. This finding is significant and warrants immediate attention by management.

Employees, at all levels, combine to make up the organization. The essence of the term *organization* is often lost. To be organized is to "to form into a coherent unity or functioning whole," or "to arrange by systematic planning and united effort." The mission statement and the core values of the organization are the foundation on which it is created. These are the two items that should bind the constituents of the organization. The mission is what the organization strives to achieve by respecting and abiding by its core values. Unless employees have an intrinsic understanding of these objects (mission and values), the essence of organization will be lost. This is especially pivotal for large organizations. As organizations grow, they specialize and diversify. As a result, we see specialized groups emerge. Specialization helps the local groups focus on their competencies and this results in the efficient accomplishment of tasks. However, this also places a burden on the organization to efficiently coordinate disparate groups and align them to meet its larger goals and objectives. Lack of appreciation for the mission and core values of the organization will hamper coordination efforts and result in several other problems.

It is difficult for an organization to meet the challenges of the external world if it has internal conflicts and issues that demand attention and resources. Internal conflicts can be attributed to lack of focus on the mission and core values of the organization, which creates factions or sub-groups within it. A faction is different from a department. A department works in a cohesive and interdependent manner with other departments to meet the organization's goals. Factions however are groups fundamentally driven to promote and advance their local goal without regard for overall organizational objectives. For the marketing faction, their goal might be to increase customer satisfaction, to the engineering faction it might be building of a more reliable product. These local goals are not bad. However, local goals should not cloud allegiance to overall organizational objectives. An offshoot of the problem of in-fighting is the reluctance to engage in knowledge and information sharing. Local factions want to claim glory, at the organization's expense. In most organizations, salespersons are rewarded a commission on sales, so, the more sales they make, the more money they take home. Each salesperson is focused on making the most number of sales (local goal). It seems logical to deduce that if all sales personnel focus on achieving their local goal – making the most sales – the organization will be more successful, but this is false. The superstar sales personnel will eat up most of the sales and, in doing so, will restrict access to potential purchasing contacts. This will result in conflicts among the sales personnel, lower productivity, and decreased performance. Moreover, there will be a lack of information and knowledge sharing. The successful sales personnel will have developed tactics, skills, and the expertise to lure the customer and close the deal. Unless the sales superstars' expertise is shared with the other team members, overall sales performance will not be satisfactory. Unfortunately, organizational incentives will encourage the selfish behavior of no knowledge sharing and will comprise the goal of the organization. The organizational mission might dictate that it would like all employees to work in harmony and collectively, yet the reward structure will promote each person working as a lone wolf and protecting their own particular turf.

Finally, owing to poor knowledge and information sharing among the constituents of the organization, there will be a lack of organizational learning. Individuals in the organization may learn, but the collective entity, the organization, will not advance. When members are not focused on the core mission of the organization, trust between groups erodes. As a result of this lack of trust and the problems that arise from the lack of a clear organizational mission, obtaining honest feedback is difficult. Without trust, feedback seems like a way to pass the buck. This behavior costs the organization, since no one is willing to change their behavior to improve the organization and the organization experiences a gradual but inevitable decay.

Constantly reiterating the organizational mission is important for the knowledge chiefs for several reasons. First, it is easier to convince members of an organization about the need to manage knowledge effectively if it is framed in the context of the organization's mission rather than as a necessary chore or operational activity. Knowledge management efforts should be linked directly to the organization's core values and then to the mission statement. Effective and optimal knowledge management practices by individual employees should be considered part of the core value statement and such behavior must be rewarded. Second, by framing knowledge management efforts in the context of the organization at large, the chiefs can integrate the various, sometimes disparate, sectors of the organization. This is essential if knowledge management is to be engrained into the organization and be made part of the organizational culture. Moreover, it is also important to ensure that efforts are unified across the organization. Third, working through the organizational mission provides the chief with a way to receive cooperation from their peers, the other C-level executives, and their boss, the CEO. It is the job of the CEO to work through the core values of the organization while fostering its mission. Hence, any support that the CEO will receive towards this end will be viewed as positive. Chiefs must work diligently to reiterate the organizational mission effectively.

Every chief has an opportunity to bind the various constituents into the organization. Here are three prescriptions. First, use your imagination to make the organizational mission lively. Too often, mission statements are glorified explanations of what the purpose of the organization should be. These are most often articulated by the founders of the organization, and as a result are historic. They are distinct from the everyday realities in which the organization is involved. Not surprisingly, allegiance to the mission statement is often an afterthought. Mission statements need to be made real again – operationalized. Operationalizing the mission statement helps the front-line employees relate to them. We asked the owner of a local café what was the mission of her organization; she answered:

> To be the host of a large party…the goal is to bring in as many people into the shop, have them enjoy themselves at the party, and make sure they keep coming back for more…Like with any party, we want to build a sense of communal gathering and enjoyment.

This café owner's mission is operationalized. It is simple, yet imaginative, and is sticky. Employees of this café knew the mission and aspired to achieve it. Moreover, what is even more interesting about this mission is the use of vocabulary. The word *party* connotes fun, enjoyment, laughter, and thrill – these are the values that the owner wanted the employees to promote. She wanted to ensure that the customers were relaxed, enjoyed the café's atmosphere, and would come back for more. Not surprising, much of the café's business was through repeat customers.

The second aspect of reiterating your mission is to back your words with actions. An organization must systematically remove incentives that compromise the mission for local goals. In the sales example, this may be achieved by changing the remuneration structure from one based on individual sales to one based on departmental or team output. Actions speak louder than words. We need to measure and evaluate employees against how well they contribute to the organization's mission. Though achieving local goals is important, local goals should not compromise the global mission of the organization. In addition, employees must be judged not just on job performance, but also on how well they emulated the organization's core values. For example, if an employee puts their own task on hold and voluntarily helps other personnel with a critical project that is about to fail, such behavior needs to be acknowledged and rewarded. In most organizations today, such behavior will never make its way into the performance appraisal; moreover, it may cause an employee to fare poorly in a review because it created a delay in completing the local task.

The third aspect is to live the mission. Living the mission is difficult, but not impossible. Employees must be appropriately engaged to discuss the mission of the organization. They must feel that their views have meaning and a bearing on the core values of the organization. They must be willing to contribute to the organization's overall goal. In most democratic societies, citizens have a right to elect their government. By exercising their right to vote, they have a say in the business of the government. Yet constantly, we see low voter turnout; why? This right and privilege is taken for granted and people feel that, regardless of who they vote for, their voices will not be heard. A similar apathy occurs in organizations. When input is solicited on important matters, many employees do not share their opinion. This can be attributed to the fact that the mission of the organization is not being lived and engaged. Employees should feel part of the core mission of the organization, and in order to do so they must be able to visualize how their work contributes to the overall survival and growth of the organization. Only by focusing on the core mission and by subscribing to the core values can we take the organization a head, involving all the constituents.

The mission and core values of the organization are latent assets. If mobilized appropriately, they can contribute towards a more cogent, focused, and agile organization. If ignored, they can lead to the sub-optimal performance and demise of the organization.

Metrics

Metrics play a vital role in assigning credibility to the work conducted by a person, unit, or organization. Metrics provide a way to measure. Successful CIOs have learnt the benefits of metrics. CIOs developed metrics to show the performance, benefits, and viability of the IS function in organizations. This helped the CIOs' cause by moving the perception of IS from a luxury to a real necessity. Moreover, metrics helped CIOs argue for changing the view of IS from one of a cost center to one of a function that helps generate revenue.

The knowledge chiefs should learn from the struggles of CIOs and focus their efforts on carving up metrics. Currently, organizations face immense pressures to show profitability and cut costs; spending on all but absolutely necessary and efficient business functions is entirely absent. Only departments or practices that perform tasks or reach organizational goals, while consuming minimal resources, survive. Often, executives mistakenly view knowledge management efforts as inefficient. Executives think knowledge management does not generate revenue and therefore is an auxiliary and expendable practice that adds only marginal value to the organization. Hence, executives have cut knowledge management efforts by arguing that they are not essential to the firms' survival or core business goals.[9]

In reality, knowledge management efforts contain a second – degree efficiency component. The efforts themselves are not efficient, but enable other departments in an organization to enhance their efficiency. KM efforts enhance worker efficiency by providing employees with existing knowledge so that they will not reinvent the wheel. Moreover, knowledge management aids organizations in developing synergies between disparate knowledge objects, resulting in increased innovation. Thus, KM efforts are central to a firm's success and are capable of providing firms with significant overall efficiency gains.

Investments in personnel and infrastructure to support knowledge management are costly and by their very nature do not often yield immediate results. A firm gets a return on their investment in knowledge management when employee demand for knowledge is met with a supply of the appropriate knowledge object. Coincidentally, firms which still invest in knowledge management practices often have workers with a high demand for organizational knowledge; consulting firms are an example here. However, before this demand can be satisfied, the necessary knowledge infrastructure must be built and knowledge protocols created. Supply solutions involve the provision of knowledge repositories such as data warehouses and digital libraries, and building communities of practice. Moreover, a crucial part of knowledge management supply is to transform organizational culture so that employees embrace the concepts of knowledge sharing and re – use and can facilitate the deployment of knowledge to areas where it is in highest demand. The length of time required to build this inherently complex knowledge supply infrastructure is industry-specific. However, creating an effective knowledge supply requires considerable time and effort. Moreover, executives rarely see returns from knowledge management investments while their firm is creating and refining its knowledge supply. Thus executives, perceiving that knowledge management investments don't yield demonstrable results, often prematurely axe their knowledge management practices. In so doing, they inhibit knowledge management efforts from reaching the maturity level necessary to facilitate knowledge reuse and provide tangible benefits to the firm.

Knowledge management has moved from being a sheltered endeavor to one where results need to be visible. The knowledge chiefs must tie knowledge management initiatives to an organization's strategy in gaining competitive advantages. Chiefs must strive to identify, measure, and disseminate results that demonstrate how management of knowledge will make or save the organization money, and thus contribute to shareholder value. Metrics are a key to getting attention in the organization, since they are a clear way to demonstrate achievement. The point of knowledge management is to make a business more valuable, and the chiefs must find ways to ensure this happens and use metrics to demonstrate it. All knowledge chiefs, like the CFO and COO, are evaluated by the metrics and deliverables. Failure to create core metrics that prove the viability of knowledge management efforts puts judgments of those efforts at the mercy of the evaluator's biases.

Conclusion

In this chapter we have examined the roles played by four salient strategic players who affect knowledge management agendas in the organization. Success of knowledge management efforts in an organization can be linked to how well each chief performs their functions and the integration of efforts across the chiefs. While these chiefs are currently in distinct roles, the future has other plans.

We envision that the CKO and CLO positions will be combined, emerging as either a CKLO or a CLKO. Knowledge and learning are intermittently linked and this position will eventually come to reflect that reality. Knowledge informs learning and vice versa. One person should oversee the knowledge management and learning aspects of an organization. Management of knowledge will help inform the training and learning needs of an organization and, once training is achieved, successful knowledge management will help move expertise from one corner of the organization to another. When training needs are identified in an organization today, the CLO is normally inclined to look outside it for knowledge, perhaps by hiring an external training vendor. However, in many cases the necessary knowledge resides in-house and can be mobilized to attain the training goals. In order to do this, the CLO will need to be acquainted with the resources and the expertise possessed by the CKO, who may have an inventory detailing the types of expertise that reside in-house and the best way to leverage them. In this instance, it would be ideal to have the CKO and CLO positions combined.

The CKLO/CLKO position will be more encompassing in the future. The HR functions of the organization will be subsumed under this position. Currently, it is common to see human resource divisions operate independently from the knowledge management aspects, the only exception being the role played by the HR department in employee training. However, this is already changing. Knowledge and learning officers are better suited to handle traditional HR tasks. The current HR functions are part of knowledge intake, growth, and losses. Simply put, HR functions are responsible for bringing knowledge workers into the organization, helping the knowledge stock of the organization grow by managing employee training programs and other knowledge programs, and also by replenishing the organization's knowledge when necessary. These are knowledge and learning matters and are best managed by chiefs who are trained and proficient in these matters and have a broader view of the strategic aspects of the organization. Most of the operational niceties of the HR position have already begun to disappear from the organization, often because of the increased rate of automation. For example, today we have direct deposits of paychecks and employees can manage their benefits package via automated tools on the corporate intranet. In addition to automation, outsourcing the HR function has also become popular. Today, there are firms that specialize in every operational aspect of the HR domain. HR management is not what it used to be just a few years ago, and will not remain the same in the future. Expect the CKOs and CLOs to take more active roles in HR functions and, ultimately, to take responsibility for the strategic direction of the HR function.

The CPO and CSO positions are going to grow in popularity, prominence, and significance. With the current rise in outsourcing, strategic alliances, and other forms of contractual agreement that require sharing of information and knowledge, an organization must have adequate security and privacy measures. Most sovereign governments are creating legislation that forces organizations to comply with privacy and security requirements. In the USA, the 1996 HIPAA Act has called for mandatory changes in how medical information is managed. Legislature like this will require medical organizations to appoint a senior person to oversee such efforts.

The CSO's position is the one we expect to grow the most significantly. However, since almost every organization must have security personnel, how can we expect significant growth in the CSO position? The answer begins with the fact that while organizations may have security personnel, only a handful of organizations have a senior-level individual overseeing security issues; currently security matters are merely an operational chore. However, security matters really do need to be discussed at the strategic level, just as do matters of finance or marketing. The CSO must work with the other senior executives to ensure that organizational assets (human and non-human), processes, routines, and expertise are protected. An illustration is the case where a pharmaceutical company had a contingent of five senior researchers visiting a foreign country in South America and failed to heed the advice of senior security personnel. These warned the head of research and development (R&D) to enforce strict guidelines on the carrying of any work material outside the organization without clearance from the security department. The head of R&D felt the issue was a headache and an unnecessary step, however, and the contingent embarked on their trip carrying work-related material. During the first two days of their arrival they were victims of robbery and kidnapping and the expertise of the organization was severely compromised. Needless to say, the organization now has a CSO who has the respect and attention of all executives at the table.

In summary, if an organization takes the concept of knowledge management seriously, it is an imperative to have senior personnel leading the various components of knowledge management. Chiefs play an important role in making knowledge management visible, effective, and prominent at the strategic levels of the organization, and, without them, knowledge management will remain on the periphery. Engaging the chiefs essential in building a knowledge program that is credible, respectable, and institutionalized in the organization.

5
Engaging with Distributed Knowledge Management

'We live in a global world' has become a cliché. More recently, we have also seen considerable interest in the term '*distributed*', in the context of *distributed work, distributed teams*, and so on. A recent tragedy may help illustrate the critical issues of globalization. On September 11, 2001, the USA was attacked by the terrorist organization of Al Qaeda. The terrorists who hijacked the aircrafts resided in various geographical locations in the USA. The command-and-control centers for the coordinated attacks were based in the USA, Germany, Afghanistan, and Malaysia. The resources and skills required to carry out the attacks were garnered from multiple global locations. The success of the effort can be linked to the ability of the terrorists to blend into local cultures and go undetected by law enforcement officials. A wide assortment of communication tools were used to exchange the information and knowledge required to coordinate the attacks. Every aspect of the assault was global and distributed in nature.

As has been documented by a number of sources, the various US intelligence agencies had information that, if assembled appropriately, might have foiled the terrorist plot. The intelligence agencies failed to create knowledge in their local arenas of operations. For instance, the CIA had difficultly in eliciting knowledge on activities in Afghanistan, as their agents could not blend into the local cultures and penetrate the groups. Moreover, the various agencies did not manage incoming knowledge from their international partners. On several occasions, the US intelligence community was warned about possible attacks by their peers in Egypt, the Philippines, and other countries. Where knowledge nuggets were available within a given organization, say the CIA or the FBI, the storage of these knowledge items was haphazard. Knowledge resided mainly in the minds of individual agents and not in any systematic, organizational-wide repository. In short, the US intelligence agencies could not integrate the distributed knowledge in and around them.

Further, the various agencies failed to exchange knowledge for the global good of thwarting terrorist activities. Each agency was focused on its local goals and lost sight of the big picture. Finally, they were unable to deploy knowledge. For instance, when the FBI office in Minneapolis had information on the possible use of airplanes as weapons, they faced significant barriers in trying to relay this knowledge to their headquarters in Washington. Such delays led to delayed action in trying to round up the terrorists.

Being global and distributed is more than a catchphrase; it is a reality and must be attended to as such. An organization must be able to manage knowledge in a distributed context so that it is able to carry out optimal actions to meet the challenges of a global world. Today, there are several challenges that are of critical importance in a global community. Competition is not restricted to geographical boundaries. National economies are more tightly coupled than ever before. Economic downturns in one country can affect corporations operating in other corners of the world. The pervasiveness of the internet and the sophistication of other technologies make it easier than ever to move products and services across the globe, hence no more is one competing on issues such as local pricing, service quality, and so on. A threat to an organization's survival can come from location anywhere in the world.

An organization must also be aware that its customers reside in multiple global locations. Hence, they must sensitize their product and service offerings along with the associated delivery platforms to meet the peculiarities of local cultures and norms. Amazon.com, a global e-commerce business, has developed distinct websites for its major customer bases such as the United Kingdom, United States, Japan, Germany, France, and Spain, among others. Organizations also employ a virtual, globally distributed and dynamic workforce. Hence the knowledge required to carry out operations and implement innovations is also spread out across the globe. Unless an organization can integrate such knowledge appropriately, innovations may be lost and best practices will not be transferred from one location to another. Cultural differences are also plentiful among the various geographical locations. These ethnic differences affect the way business is conducted, and work executed, and also how people issues are managed. Moreover, in some cases cultural issues manifest themselves in how an organization deals with external parties such as governments, suppliers, business partners, and customers. For instance, in the USA it is common, in our experience, for organizations to equate business relationships to dollars and cents. This is not the case in Eastern cultures, where precursors to a viable business relationship are trust and relationship-building. How much cultural knowledge an organization has, and how aptly it can deploy such knowledge, are critical determinants of success in a global marketplace.

With all the current interest in global management, we must be clear on one thing: global operations and global enterprises are not novel concept. Historically, we had merchants that would move from one location to another. The old empires such as the Dutch, the British, and the Roman were involved in global conquest and dominance, and there are instances of global corporations dating back centuries, such as the East India Company. These global organizations, while vast and extensive, were simplistic operations owing to the absence of any excessive competitive pressures and an integrated world. It is best if we think of globalization as one dimension of a distributed environment. Organizations have distributed operations in a number of dimensions; globalization is the most prominent, but there are others. Examples include the notion of distributed projects, virtual teams – where team members are distributed and communicate using technologies – and even the prominence of contingent workers, who are distributed in terms of their organizational affiliations. Organizations must master the act of integrating disparate global sources of knowledge found within their bounds in order to create and sustain competitive advantage.[1] As Hayek notes, knowledge management can be framed as a distributed problem: "It is a problem of the utilization of knowledge not given to anyone in its totality."[2]

The focus of this chapter is to articulate issues involved in distributed knowledge management. We will spend much of it on the concept of global knowledge management and the explication of the accompanying issues of concern. In our research, we have found three common strategies employed by organizations when it comes to global knowledge management architectures. We will discuss them here. We will then examine the case of spin-offs, and what is required to manage knowledge in such settings. We conclude the chapter by looking at several distributed work arrangements – distributed projects, virtual teams, and contingent workers. In order to ground our discussion on global knowledge management, we must first visit the seminal work on global management performed by Barlett and Ghoshal.[3]

Global management strategies

The work of Barlett and Ghoshal has formed the foundation of the recent research on the strategic management of global enterprises. These authors[4] highlight four strategies for competing across borders – *global, international, multinational,* and *transnational.* We now briefly describe these.

The *global* strategy is one in which the actions of the subsidiaries are heavily regulated and controlled by the parent company. This approach ensures achieving global efficiency through economies of scale that arise from the standardization of production processes, the nature of goods produced, and the large volumes of goods manufactured. Goods are produced by the parent, or under tightly controlled processes that it supervises, and then shipped to overseas markets. The central concern of the global strategy is to minimize costs by standardizing operations. The parent retains the strategic assets and also develops strategic capabilities. Subsidiaries are tightly controlled and are considered implementers of the parent's strategy. Knowledge is created and retained by the parent. When necessary, knowledge flows from the parent to the subsidiaries in a one-directional manner.

An *international* strategy calls for the creation of a coordinated federation. The parent company transfers knowledge on processes, ideas, products, procedures, and strategies to the subsidiaries, who are free to use the incoming knowledge to better achieve their objectives and goals. Subsidiaries are accountable for their assets and goals, and depend on the parent for an influx of knowledge. As in the global strategy, knowledge flows from the parent to the subsidiaries; the difference is that knowledge implementation lies with the subsidiary and is not controlled by the parent. The role of subsidiaries is to adapt and leverage the parent's competency.

A *multinational* strategy is where a multinational company (MNC) has foreign subsidiaries that function in near autonomy, or as a loose federation. The MNC employs a strategy that focuses on national differences. The central tenet of this strategy is that the subsidiary takes responsibility of the strategy and implementation. The strategic assets and capabilities are decentralized and distributed among an organization's subsidiaries with minimal parental control. The role of the subsidiary is to sense and exploit local opportunities in the market, by demonstrating the ability to leverage local knowledge and assimilate it with the know-how from the parent, in order to devise appropriate products and services. Running autonomously enables subsidiaries to respond quickly to changes in local markets. The strategy of the organization is to produce products that meet local needs, and hence the focus is on being nationally responsive and conducting product differentiations and customizations to meet local taste, standards, and laws.

Consider automobile manufacturing. Each country has local standards and laws that govern items such as percentages of chemicals, emission standards, safety controls, and so on. The organization must, therefore, be able to customize and differentiate the product (an automobile or a quart of oil) to meet such idiosyncrasies. The multinational strategy calls for creating and managing a decentralized organization. Each subsidiary is financially accountable to the parent, and is managed very loosely. No formal systems of controls exist. Rather than attempt to manage subsidiaries uniformly as belonging to one entity, the organization takes a portfolio approach, where each subsidiary is viewed as an asset in a large investment portfolio. Here knowledge flows from the subsidiaries to the parent, because each subsidiary has core competencies and is responsible for knowledge gathering, assimilation, and application.

A *transnational* strategy is where an organization coordinates its global operations while being flexible in responding to local needs by following the maxim: 'Think locally but act globally.' Subsidiaries are viewed as providers of ideas, skills, capabilities, and knowledge that benefit the whole organization. Organizations following a transnational strategy coordinate efforts, ensuring local flexibility while exploiting the benefits of global integration and efficiencies, as well as ensuring the worldwide diffusion of new products and innovations. Each subsidiary operates independently from the parent, while appreciating its interdependence with other subsidiaries and the parent.

The transnational company incorporates features of the global, international, and multinational strategies. Having effective knowledge flows between the parent and subsidiaries and among subsidiaries is a critical determinant of a viable transnational strategy. Knowledge flows are bidirectional, from the parents to the subsidiaries and vice versa, and also between subsidiaries.

Global knowledge flows

Our discussion here will use the framework of Anil Gupta and Vijay Govindarajan, who conducted seminal work in explicating how knowledge flows between subsidiaries and the rest of the organization.[5] These authors studied the movement of knowledge about products, processes, and practices. They intentionally omitted the movement of administrative knowledge, which is mainly information such as financial statements, payroll information, and so on. Gupta and Govindarajan identified four types of subsidiaries, based on the volume of knowledge flow and the direction of the knowledge flow. Volume was noted as being either high or low, and the directions were signified as either in (inflow into the subsidiary) or out (outflow from the subsidiary to the other entities). The four types were:

Global innovator   The outflow of knowledge from the subsidiary to other entities is high, but the inflow of knowledge into the subsidiary is low. The level of global responsibility and authority given to the general manager is high. These subsidiaries work in a largely autonomous fashion and have a high tolerance for ambiguity and risks. They are leaders in their areas of operations.

Integrated player   The outflow of knowledge from the subsidiary to other entities is high, and the inflow of knowledge into the subsidiary is also high. As with the global innovator, the level of global responsibility and authority given to the general manager will be comparatively high. Integrated players are less autonomous in operations than global innovators. Since they seek to maximize synergies in knowledge residing in multiple entities of the organization, they must work with various entities interdependently to be able to tap into the various knowledge assets.

Local innovator   The outflow of knowledge from the subsidiary to other entities is low, and inflow of knowledge into the subsidiary is also low. The level of global responsibility and authority given to the general manager will be low. The manager's tolerance for ambiguity will be lower than that of global innovators and integrated players. Local innovators will focus on small areas where they can operate in a confined space without interference from other entities of the organization.

Implementer   The outflow of knowledge from the subsidiary to other entities is low, but the inflow of knowledge into the subsidiary is high. The level of global responsibility and authority given to the general manager will be low. The manager's tolerance for ambiguity will be lower than that of managers of global innovators, integrated players, and local innovators. The need for autonomy will be lowest for implementers, as they will be dependent on the rest of the organization for knowledge that they can draw on and transform into implementations.

Building global knowledge management systems[6]

How do organizations go about building knowledge management systems? In our discussions with several organizations, we uncovered the presence of three popular strategies that we now describe briefly (see Figure 5.1):

Headquarters commissioned and executed   Here, headquarters (that is the parent company) sets the tone for knowledge management initiatives, and provides technology solutions and support, training, and policies and procedures. We found this approach in companies with standardized global products and services that take advantage of economies of scale. Standardization of interfaces, procedures, and policies remains the over-riding principle.

Headquarters commissioned and regionally executed   This resembles the transnational strategy. Organizations recognized that a sweeping global order from headquarters was not the best way to carry out knowledge management. To prevent each local office from taking a unique approach, a coordinated, federation-style operation was essential. In this strategy, the parent specifies broad guidelines and policies and initiates the knowledge management dialogue. Subsequently, regional centers – hubs on each continent where the organization operates – take command of actual execution. This ensures a common theme and mission, while allowing solutions to be tailored to meet distinct regional requirements.

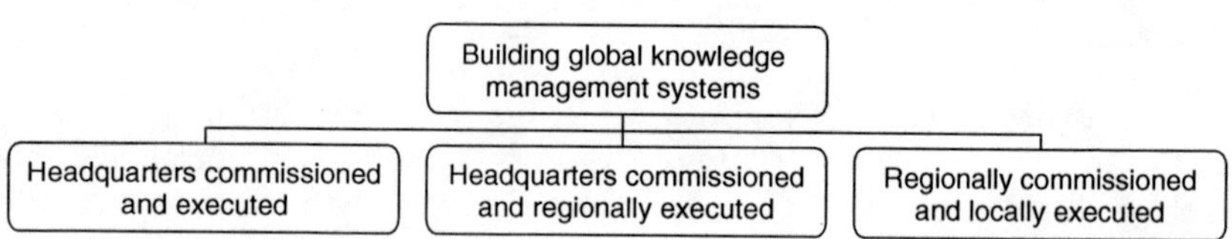

Figure 5.1   Global knowledge management strategies.

This approach is common among organizations involved in global consulting efforts and even manufacturing firms. In such organizations the parent sets out the knowledge management initiatives, such as the high-level mission, objectives, and aims of the program, and chooses the tools to ensure connectivity between offices. However, the regional centers are free to set their own specific objectives and goals in line with the specified broad directives. They also customize the technology to meet the distinct requirements of their local offices. Common customizations include modifications in language, interface, and types of knowledge bases. Since the parent dictates the technology, connectivity between offices is ensured, with each regional and local office connected to the rest of the organization, but having its own internal schema for interaction with their peer local offices. This approach enables meeting local needs while staying connected to distant global counterparts. The organization gains from local best practices by fostering knowledge exchanges between the regions and the parent. For example, suppose the Asian KMS team designs a successful user-friendly interface; given global appreciation, it could become the standard for the entire organization.

Regionally commissioned and locally executed   This strategy is the least popular. Here initiatives for knowledge management efforts come from the regional offices themselves in recognition that they need to exchange expertise on a frequent basis in order to function smoothly. Consequently, rather than go for an organization-wide effort, the regional headquarters commission a locale-specific knowledge management effort. Each field office in the region is free to execute this so as to achieve goals and policies set at the regional office – that is to 'think regionally but act locally.'

In discussion with senior managers at the regional offices, we learnt that the regional approach rather than an organization-wide endeavor gives the benefit of shorter lead-time between thought and action. Organization-wide endeavors take years to be executed owing to the sheer mass of personnel, networks, and inter-relationships that require management. Regional efforts are substantially less time-consuming owing to the close-knit ties and commonality found between local offices.

One adverse effect of this strategy was the difficulty in sharing knowledge beyond the individual regions. Since each region deployed its own tools and initiatives to capture and store knowledge, exchanges between regions became cumbersome, with email as the only viable exchange mechanism. It was difficult, although not impossible, for one region to access the knowledge database of another. However, each database was organized differently, so enabled access was problematic and involved significant learning of the schemas.

In this section, we have examined the broad organizational strategies employed in building knowledge management systems. We will next discuss an interesting organizational approach: spin-offs. These are instances of global operations, not in the rudimentary sense of having operations in a different country, but in having independently managed operations that are outside the core organization.

Spin-offs

Situations emerge where an organization has (1) more knowledge than it knows what to do with or (2) less than an ideal approach in realizing valuable knowledge residing within it. Either of these two situations normally results in knowledge leaving the organization, resulting in spin-offs. Spin-offs are new organizations that emerge around knowledge in the parent organization. When the knowledge leaving the organization is authorized and official we have a sanctioned organizational spin-off. When it is unauthorized, we have an unsanctioned spin-off.

Both sanctioned and unsanctioned spin-offs are common in the technology sector, where organizations are rich in knowledge and do not have the resources necessary to focus on every valuable insight. As a result, the organization may need to decide on its core competency, and focus on this knowledge development, while spinning off other firms that can focus on interesting but auxiliary knowledge. In some cases, an organization may spin off an entity to focus on high-risk projects. Such projects call for knowledge usage and development in areas where the organization is less sure of the intended results, and may want to insulate the parent company from risks owing to any failures and unintended consequences. Unsanctioned spin-offs can arise from frustrations on the part of employees in their efforts to leverage their knowledge and build on ideas. Charles Zeigler calls this 'fissioning' – where people who find their ideas blocked in one organization create a new entity that is more receptive and sympathetic towards them.[7]

Sometimes we can see a variant spin-off, where a new organization is not created, but where knowledge from one organization is given better reception and leveraged more successfully by another organization. For example, PARC (see Chapter 1) has routinely failed to commercialize any of its ideas. Thus while PARC developed the graphical user interface for computer systems, it was Apple which successfully commercialized it and earns royalties from the invention. This kind of spin-off is normally owing to a poor knowledge management plan, or none at all. We have discussed these chaos-and-order dimensions of knowledge management in Chapter 2.

Managing a sanctioned spin-off calls for due diligence in knowledge management. The first critical issue is balancing between exploiting the parent's knowledge and exploring to create new knowledge. Spin-offs emerge from knowledge constructed in the parent in the forms of ideas, processes, practices, and market insights. It is therefore important that this knowledge, the very reason for the creation of the spin-off, is appropriately managed in the new entity. This is no easy accomplishment. Knowledge needs to be taken out of its original context (the parent company) and moved to a new context (the spin-off). Moving knowledge and not caring appropriately for the contextual issues could make the knowledge less valuable and in some cases even a liability. As an analogy, consider the difficultly in translating a joke from its native language to a foreign one. Many a punchline is lost owing to lack of appreciation for the cultural, social, and other contextual nuances of the native region. The balancing act is further complicated by the cost issue. While a spin-off may be creative and innovative, resources will not be readily available to invest in creation of all types of knowledge. Consequently, for the spin-off to be economical the organization needs to decide how resources will be used to create new knowledge and what knowledge should be brought in or adapted from the parent. It is not wise to adapt all of the knowledge from the parent, since in many cases the spin-off arose because the original organization failed to appreciate the knowledge. Blatantly duplicating the cultural, governance, and other attributes of the parent will not lead to the creation of a new and impressive environment for new innovations.

In order to be successful, we recommend that the spin-off have the capabilities to leverage the parent's knowledge in terms of market opportunities and general administrative issues. The parent will normally have deep pockets of market knowledge that can be of vital importance to the spin-off in terms of positioning their new products and services. Spin-offs normally operate in the same industry spaces as the parent and hence do not need to reinvent knowledge about the market. Moreover, the parent will have knowledge on general administrative details, such as how to handle payroll and taxation issues. Rather than trying to reinvent the wheel here, the spin-off should tap into such knowledge and leverage on the parent's know-how. It should, however, think very carefully before importing the parent's governance mechanisms. It is better to invent mechanisms to meet the needs of the new entity than to attempt to superimpose previous structures, since the spin-off is different from the parent and may need different management protocols in order to be successful. For example, suppose a traditional manufacturing organization decides to spin off an entity to focus on cutting-edge research and development. In the traditional parent company, the key to success is efficiency through order-based protocols, where goods need to be manufactured most cost-effectively and rigid processes are essential. The new entity will not be able to function under the parent's rigid, order-based protocols, because knowledge creation requires room to innovate, to be chaotic, and to collaborate.

The second issue we have to consider is cultural cogency and trust. As mentioned above, a spin-off is better off building a culture that embraces its innovative potential. Very often, this culture is not in sync with that of the parent. Moreover, a spin-off may be viewed as the parent's 'preferred child'. During the dot-com boom, a lot of traditional organizations (brick companies) decided to spin off organizations that focused on leveraging the internet as a business avenue and marketplace (click companies). These click companies were understandably in the spotlight and received a lot of attention both in terms of reputation and resources. Esteemed employees of the parent organization were asked to move to the click company, which most often got resources such as fancy office spaces, recreation rooms, bonuses, flexible work schedules, and a lot of other goodies. Those employees who were not asked to move to the dot-com side of the business were understandably disappointed and envious. This led to rivalries and stifled knowledge transfer between the parent and the spin-off. When the spin-off needed access to critical knowledge, members in the parent organization inhibited the flow of knowledge. Additionally, when the latter wanted access to new innovations at the spin-off they were treated as second-class citizens. Neither organization gained from this attitude. Not surprisingly, most organizations eventually decided to pull back spin-offs and reintegrate them into the parent organization.

Organizations need to be mindful about maintaining trust between personnel in the parent and the spin-off. Treating either organization favorably at the expense of the other is a sure way to erode trust. Organizations should have clear communication programs that articulate the unique value proposition of creating the spin-off and how the spin-off will contribute to the core competency of the corporation. To foster and manage open communication between the two organizations, we recommend that an organization have personnel who serve as liaisons and work to bridge connections between the two entities.

The final issue deals with helping the spin-off manage knowledge. The spin-off will be busy trying to focus on its core knowledge and leveraging it to build products and services and successfully commercialize such innovations. Knowledge management may well take a back seat to this goal. Spin-offs will use knowledge, exchange it, and apply it, yet they will do so informally. The parent should help the spin-off in formalizing its knowledge management practices. This may call for the sharing of expertise, technologies, and communication architectures. The parent should not try to impose its thinking on the spin-off, but should act as a consultant by offering its experience and expertise to help the spin-off reach its objectives.

Issues in global knowledge management

In this section, we will briefly describe some of the critical issues one must consider when embarking on global knowledge management endeavors. We do not propose to have all the answers; our goal here is to raise awareness of three salient issues.

Global rather than local focus

The most dominant issue is fostering a cultural shift. Members of the organization are used to working within their local confines. After all, they go to a specific work location, meet the same sets of co-workers, and have built relationships with these individuals. This is why, when knowledge needs to be exchanged locally, this occurs mostly via informal mechanisms – a person may call up his neighbor for help, an employee talk to his peer in an adjacent cubicle, and so on. Knowledge transfer is also enhanced locally, as individuals share cultural similarities and an established context for practices and interpretations. Ironically, the very practices that promote local movement of knowledge make global knowledge management difficult.

First, if knowledge is captured and shared through informal mechanisms, how is someone outside the immediate network supposed to know of the existence of the knowledge and get access to it? The external person will visit the knowledge repository and not find any knowledge nuggets, and hence may decide to reinvent the wheel.

Second, contextual issues are important if we are to appreciate the notion of cultures. Practices common in one part of the globe may be unacceptable in others. Moreover, language issues play significant roles in how knowledge is codified and exchanged. Consider the following example. In the USA most knowledge artifacts are created in American English, in Japan artifacts are compiled in Japanese. If knowledge needs to be shared between a Japanese division and one in Detroit, the original artifact written in Japanese needs to be translated into English. Here knowledge loss can occur owing to the semantic and contextual issues of language. Misinterpretations can also arise owing to the translation procedure. Hence, knowledge created in Japan may never be appreciated fully in the USA. This often leads to the not-invented-here (NIH) syndrome-where knowledge created by the external entity is rejected because it is more prestigious to create new knowledge instead of reusing knowledge invented elsewhere.[8] Globally speaking, this would lead to an underutilization of corporate resources as knowledge existing within the organization gets recreated at the cost of resources that could be better used for productive tasks.

Third, it is important to expand search horizons. Too often, individuals in organizations confine their search for knowledge within local boundaries. This is hardly surprising as it is easy to search locally, or so it is believed. However, with advances in technology searching globally is also easy, though it is practiced less. The reason, we think, is one of cognitive biases about the effort involved in conducting a global search. Individuals may feel that it is easy just to search on their local office systems, when it may take the same effort to search the entire corporate network. Changing this mindset is an important issue, as individuals need to realize and appreciate the fact that taking a global view is a baseline requirement and not an exception or add-on to a local search for knowledge.

We argue that to be successful, organizations need to make the shift from local to global. Individuals should also be trained in the need to follow formal procedures for knowledge sharing and storage, such as the use of KMSs.

Without this, knowledge will stay in local groups and never be made available to the other sectors. It is important to frame ideas, missions, and projects in a global context and make it clear that this is the operating norm. This will, one hopes entice individuals to give up their local allegiances in favor of global success. Strong leadership is critical to focusing the organization on global efforts. Consider the case of the World Bank. When its president, James Wolfensohn, announced his vision at an annual meeting of finance ministers in October 1996, several knowledge management pilot efforts were already underway in areas such as education and private sector infra-structure. Although successful, these initial forays into knowledge management lacked the top-down support necessary to ensure their success. There was little agreement on a knowledge strategy, no dedicated budget, inadequate systems infrastructure, and no monitoring mechanisms in place to track their progress. Within months of Wolfensohn's proclamation, however, an institutional task force translated his vision into a comprehensive action plan, which provided a detailed roadmap to organizational transformation. Among the resistance points identified early on in implementation were shifting the culture toward sharing, setting and implementing quality standards, avoiding knowledge junkyards, resolving confidentiality issues, and achieving an integrated approach across the organization.

Bridging multiple knowledge spaces

Divisions of the organization may operate very different technological solutions for fostering knowledge exchanges. One company that we consulted for had 40 different enterprise resource planning (ERP) systems. ERP systems are meant to act as a singular architecture for information management across the enterprise; hence ideally there would be only one per enterprise. Different technological solutions, across the global enterprise, require knowledge integration and connectivity management. Failure to integrate appropriately the different technological architectures will lead to poor global knowledge searches and failed efforts in building a truly global knowledge management program. In order to conduct an efficient integration exercise, organizations need to standardize on their terminology (such as what a particular knowledge nugget will be called), to manage the issues of multiple languages (such as building systems that can be accessed in Japanese or English or German), and to appreciate the wide assortment of contexts that individuals will bring when accessing and contributing knowledge to the system. We will elaborate on the issues of building knowledge management systems in Chapter 9.

For now, we would like to focus on the more strategic aspect of crafting global knowledge management systems. A critical decision that the organization must make is how best to meet the needs of its diverse global user community. One option commonly employed by organizations is what we define as the averaging phenomenon. This is where the organization tries to satisfy its diverse population by making compromises on different specifications and requirements, and coming up with a system that is average, that is it meets some of the needs of each user group and ignores some other needs, and no one is terribly upset. This, in our experience, is an erroneous approach, because averaging requirements makes no one happy in totality and leads to a system that is anyway not accepted by all. Moreover, averaging the user requirements will in many cases call for compromises to the overall system design and the integrity of the system. An alternative is to build individual systems tailored for the various user communities and then integrate and connect them. This is a better approach and one that we have seen work. However, let us emphasize that this solution is workable only if the organization has foresight and has thought about the integration issues upfront, rather than trying to integrate disparate systems as an afterthought. For effective integration, there must be organizational standards in place for the management and maintenance of knowledge management systems, or things could get chaotic. We consulted for an organization where the Indian office decided to update their KMS architecture and access protocols without consulting with their European counterparts, who also were conducting a minor integration and system update project without informing the Indian team. A saying comes to mind: 'The right hand does not know what the left is doing,' or more correctly: 'The right hand washes what the left hand did.' Both KMS maintenance projects failed owing to lack of global standards of governance to assure synchronization.

Appreciating variances in knowledge management practices

Cultural differences impact how knowledge is managed in diverse countries. For instance, consider the knowledge management practices in Russian companies.[9] Subordinates intentionally hoard their knowledge because they feel that their superiors would not take kindly to their publicly revealing their superior knowledge. Knowledge is almost always shared vertically, from superior to subordinate and vice versa, and seldom moves horizontally across functions and across teams. There is a fear among many employees that if they share their knowledge it may be misinterpreted and used inappropriately, resulting in unintended consequences. These are expected and common norms in Russian enterprises. Should we try to change them to make them reflect practices in Japan or the USA? No! We must appreciate the differences in cultural knowledge management practices and figure out ways to work around them. This will call for specifying cultural assumptions and helping individuals bridge these differences through adequate training. Instead of any one culture supplanting all the others, different cultures should be respected and appreciated for their diversity.

Distributed projects

Most organizations necessarily have to conduct distributed projects, and hence must be effective in managing these assignments. Projects have moved from being simple to manage – single projects in a single location – to more complex entities spanning geographical locations, multiple occurrences, and different organizational affiliations. Information technology is the key enabler for the transformation.[10] In the realm of project management, much of the effort to incorporate technology has been in fostering ubiquitous communication between project members while also enabling easy knowledge exchange.

Projects can be distributed in multiple dimensions.[11] We can have projects that are conducted simultaneously, but involve workers at multiple physical sites. Projects can also be distributed by involving members who have different organizational affiliations (for example contingent workers) or distinct functional affiliations – that is, who are part of cross-functional assignments or teams. Here we will not list the other dimensions of distributedness, but will instead begin to focus on the salient knowledge management issues in the context of conducting distributed projects.

Project management knowledge can be segmented into knowledge *in* projects, knowledge *about* projects, and knowledge *from* projects.[12] Knowledge in projects calls for a microscopic look at the intimate insights generated within each individual project. Items of interest in this category include project schedules, milestones, minutes of meetings, training manuals, and so on. Individual project members need to know when, what, how, where, and why something is being done and by whom, the goal being to promote the efficient and effective coordination of activities. The increased exchange of relevant knowledge directly boosts team performance, as each member can learn from the others' experiences and complement the others members' endeavors. Group support systems and email are commonly used to enable sharing of knowledge in projects.

From the macro perspective, an organization must have an inventory of all projects underway at any given time. This aids in planning and control of resources to maximize utilities. Knowledge of interest includes employee assignment to projects, return on investments, cost-and-benefit analysis, deadlines, customer commitments and expectations, and so on. It is common for such knowledge to be generated at regular intervals such as through weekly, monthly, or bi-monthly reports. Executive information systems and other reporting mechanisms are commonly used to generate knowledge about projects, perform aggregation and summarization, and finally present it in a cohesive manner.

Knowledge from projects is a *post hoc* analysis and audit of key insights generated from carrying out projects. This knowledge is a key determinant of future project successes, as one can learn how to function optimally while avoiding past mistakes. Moreover, a company must preserve knowledge and experiences about past projects in order to deploy future initiatives successfully. In today's economy, employee turnover is high along with a tendency to opt for early retirement, so an organization must make every effort to capture personal knowledge to prevent loss of valuable know-how.

To efficiently manage such knowledge one must enable its availability and transferability, both across other projects being conducted at the same time and to future projects. Knowledge sharing and intellectual capital transfer that takes place in a group setting and via formation of project teams is fostered through a knowledge management system. A vast majority of such systems employ the codification approach. Here a central repository holds knowledge under categories such as project reports, programming bugs, quality control reports, new developments, and so on. An important consideration while contributing *post hoc* knowledge from a project is to capture the context in which the knowledge was generated because failure to do so will lower the real value of knowledge.

Managing each type of knowledge is essential for successfully managing distributed projects. Leveraging knowledge in projects calls for paying close attention to knowledge gatekeepers, that is the individual or group who manages what information and knowledge make their way into the project, and consequently what knowledge is sent out from the group. Most projects have gatekeepers, with the project manager as the *de facto* gatekeeper in many cases. As discussed in Chapter 4 on knowledge chiefs, gatekeepers need to be monitored so that they do not impede the flow of knowledge from projects to the rest of the organization. One reason why project gatekeepers may do this deliberately is to avoid disclosing bad news. This happens particularly when the project is failing or not on schedule.[13] Gatekeepers should be advised that rather than trying to hide such knowledge, they should seek help from the rest of the organization on how best to get the project back on track and thus improve their chances for success.

While gatekeepers are the checkpoints for knowledge entering and leaving the project, knowledge brokers seek to connect or broker knowledge between multiple entities.[14] Knowledge brokers are agents who span multiple markets and technology domains and innovate by brokering knowledge from where it is known to where it is unknown. They combine existing technology in inventive ways. Knowledge brokers are essential to the success of distributed projects as they traverse distributed spaces. They are able to collate knowledge from dispersed spaces, thereby helping to eradicate or lower occurrences of knowledge glitches – costly mistakes that could have been avoided if some of the parties involved had understood things known to other participants.[15] Most often individuals working on the project search for knowledge in their preferred domains or spaces, usually limiting their search space to their functional areas of specialties and close ties. Knowledge needed may be outside these domains, and hence may go undetected and be reinvented, thus consuming valuable organizational resources. However, worse yet, some of the existing knowledge may be in conflict with the 'new' knowledge that is being generated, posing issues more serious than those of simple costs. In one organization we consulted for, the marketing department was attempting to make a bid to a client for a significant consulting engagement. A glitch of serious magnitude occurred when the marketing department approached the client as though they were a fresh prospect. However, the client had existing relationships and projects with one of the organization's subsidiaries! This knowledge, which was not detected and used in a timely manner, could have made for a better marketing pitch by tapping into the existing relationship rather than taking a cold-call approach. Consider what McKinsey has decided to do to avoid similar and related issues such as knowledge identification and transfer issues. McKinsey has rapid response teams who find answers to questions within 12 to 24 hours by scanning multiple knowledge environments. For an endeavor like this to succeed, the knowledge space of the organization must be mapped.[16]

In addition to having access to different knowledge spaces, it is important that project managers seek to have *requisite variety* to understand and appreciate knowledge from different sources. One might equate requisite variety to having enough knowledge to engage in and appreciate thoughts and ideas from a wide array of locations. Project managers who do not have adequate requisite variety are limited to thinking within their silos and niches, thus increasing the chances of knowledge from the outside being ignored and hence of propagating knowledge glitches.

Organizations must remember that projects are distributed across time as well. It is important that organizations seek ways to leverage knowledge from past projects and use them to inform current and future behaviors. We posit that the dismal findings in project success rates, especially in cases of new product development and information systems development efforts, can be traced to poor organizational learning mechanisms in software organizations. A manager at the Motorola Labs in Illinois, USA, put it best: "We make mistakes, and we know these mistakes were done in the past, yet we constantly reuse mistakes."[17] Learning in and around projects is not an option; it is a must for organizational survival. We cannot afford to constantly reuse our past mistakes. In order to prevent repeating mistakes, we must pay attention to the process of projects. We must learn from past processes and seek ways to improve them. The process is tacit, and in order to foster organizational learning, these tacit insights need to be captured in an explicit format so that they can be reused easily in future projects. Tacit insights, in this context, can be likened to project management lessons.

George Santayana put it succinctly: "Those who cannot remember the past are condemned to fulfil it" (*Life of Reason*, vol. 1, ch. 12). Postmortems are mechanisms for remembering and recalling what transpired during a project so that we may use these lessons to inform future behavior and actions. Postmortems can be conducted at either the completion of a milestone or the termination of the project.[18] For small projects and non-complex endeavors it may suffice to have a postmortem when the project ends. For large-scale projects it is advisable to conduct postmortems on completion of milestones, so that lessons learnt can be incorporated to improve the processes for the remainder of the project and also improve efforts in future projects. The motivation is to reflect on what happened in the project in order to improve future practice – for the individuals that have participated in the project and for the organization as a whole. The objective of a postmortem should be learning, and not project evaluation. Evaluation can lead to people not sharing experiences that they think may embarrass them. Learning through postmortems must occur at three levels – the individual, the team, and the organization.

There are several ways to perform postmortem reviews. Some companies use a simple checklist in a meeting, while others use half-day workshops, or three-day meetings away from the normal work area, and some use a combination of methods. Some do not organize a postmortem meeting, but gather data through interviews. Apple Computers has used a method that includes designing a project survey, collecting objective project information, conducting a debriefing meeting, holding a project history day, and finally publishing the results. The project survey is used to gather subjective data on how the project was conducted, followed by the gathering of objective data – costs, time to completion, defects, and so on. The debriefing meeting and project history day help in eliciting tacit insights, engaging in dialogues, and extracting lessons learnt. The postmortem culminates with publishing the postmortem report. At Microsoft much effort is put into writing post-mortem reports containing discussions on what worked well in the last project, what did not work well, and what the group should do to improve its work in the next project.

It is important for an organization to have a well-defined process in place when conducting postmortems.[19] While postmortems can differ in the range, scope, and depth, based on the characteristics of the organization and the project, most postmortems follow the basic process used by Apple Computers that we have described above.

Participation is tied to the intended goals of the project postmortem. If the goal is to foster individual learning, the postmortem may be restricted to the members of the project team, probably with an external facilitator whose role is to structure discussions and lead different exercises to stimulate reflection. For team learning, it is important to have an external facilitator to moderate the discussions among team members and also to keep the project manager in check. In our experience, it is common to have postmortem analyses turn into disasters without a facilitator, since leadership of the postmortem discussion is then assumed by the project manager, who is biased, will not take kindly to criticisms, and may show favoritism to individual project members. The success of a project postmortem is heavily reliant on how open participants are to taking accurate stock of the situation. The use of an external facilitator can greatly contribute to open discussions, as the members perceive the facilitator to be unbiased, neutral, and with no hidden agenda. To foster organizational learning, it is possible to invite either people from similar projects that are starting up, or people who have an organization-wide role, for instance as a CKO or quality department member, roles which are more common in software companies.

Outcomes of postmortems can vary in their length, scope, and depth. We have seen postmortem reports that range from 3 pages to over 100. Depending on the nature of the project, postmortem reports are written by individual team members, jointly by teams, or by the project manager or the external facilitator.

There are two main kinds of postmortem reports. The first is a traditional report. As the name implies, this is like any other report – a structured presentation of lessons learnt during a project. Reports are built using predefined organizational templates, that is every project report has the same layout with only the content being different. A typical template for a report includes an introduction with information about the project and how the postmortem was conducted, lists of issues that went well or did not go well with corresponding analyses of the most important issues, and finally appendixes with full listings of the postmortem agenda, and possibly transcripts of discussions.

The second is a narrative report, or a story used to develop learning histories. Learning histories are a means to use narratives to transfer experience, taking into account the importance of storytelling and myths in organizations. A learning history is created by interviewing participants in an individual project, and then working on the material to create a story starting with a curtain-raiser, a kernel paragraph, and an exposition containing the main points of the story. The main story is presented as a jointly told tale, with the narrator's voice in one column and the direct voice in another. Usually, the main story is organized into thematic chapters with their own kernel paragraphs and expositions. The conclusion of the story connects to the curtain-raiser.

Postmortems are knowledge objects in their rudimentary sense, and they need to be mined to detect patterns in behavior. It is therefore important for an organization to have a structured collection of postmortems to enable easy analysis. The organization should conduct semi-annual or annual evaluations of postmortem reports to extract macro lessons that can help make strategic changes to how an organization conducts its project management effort. For example, an organization might be able to gauge an ideal team size to avoid communication problems, or be able to learn how much colocation is needed for successful project completion. It is important to build a history of lessons learnt, as lessons that need to be learnt several times over are not being learnt effectively. For example, if all projects suggest that more slack time needs to be accounted for during the testing phase of product development, and this has never been implemented in subsequent projects, there is a fundamental management problem here that needs to be addressed. Patterns help in rethinking existing behaviors and changing the governing principles on which the organization operates.

Virtual teams

Distributed projects are engagements with a finite deadline or termination point, after which the team or organization is normally dissolved and members move on to other organizational tasks. In contrast, virtual team engagements are normally longer, though in some cases they could be disguised as distributed projects. There is no clear-cut definition of a virtual team. Some use the terms 'distributed teams,' 'teleworking,' and 'virtual workplaces' to mean virtual teams. For our purposes, we will use the term to represent long-term and ongoing work structures that involve members collaborating, most often using electronic communication technologies rather than traditional, face-to-face approaches. The difference, as we see it, between virtual teams and distributed projects is that the latter are more long-term and permanent in nature. While the team members might change, the team remains a going concern and continues to accomplish its goals. Virtual teams also rely heavily on the use of communication technologies to coordinate work assignments and collaborate on work. Much like other distributed engagements, the success or failures of virtual teams is heavily dependent on how knowledge is managed between the various team members. Knowledge transfer and integration issues become salient here.

It is absolutely essential that managers work diligently and effectively to help virtual team members generate and maintain sufficient levels of trust among themselves. Virtual teams do not have the same latitude on trust as would be possible with a face-to-face team. Much of the communication being handled via technologies results in the sacrifice of non-verbal cues, which play an important role in the development of trust. For instance, one of the authors of this book (K.C.D.) resists virtual meetings because there is no clear sense of how someone is reacting to information being transmitted. One cannot "look into the other's eyes" to ensure that the message is received properly, nor can one adequately read body language cues. Even with sophisticated videoconferencing technologies, the richness of non-verbal cues is not the same as in a face-to-face meeting.

Another reason why trust issues are a serious concern is the fact that most virtual team engagements, especially during the initial stages, are between people who do not have a rich history working together. Hence, they may not have a good read on the others' behaviors or nuances, which may possibly lead to misinterpretations. Trust development in virtual teams affects the ability to share knowledge, as trust helps relationships between members and helps construct adequate social relationships, which in turn can act as channels for knowledge transfer. If two or more individuals do not necessarily trust one another, they may view any knowledge transferred with suspicion and contempt. This is where the message being transferred will lose significance, since the overriding focus will be on the sender.

In order to manage trust effectively, managers have a lot of upfront work ahead. During the initial stages of the team's engagement, it is important that adequate training is provided for the various members on trust issues. Additionally, there should be an initial socialization or initiation period during which team members engage in activities, which could be virtual, to get to know one another. Once the foundation is laid, managers must pay particular attention to the initial stage of the team's life and look out for early signs of conflict and struggle. These early indicators should be taken seriously and appropriate interventions should be introduced to resolve them. Failure to attend to these signals from the onset will definitely jeopardize the team's future. One of the critical characteristics of the younger generation is their apparent ability to work easily in virtual contexts. For instance, it is not uncommon to see high school or university students comfortably use technologies such as instant messaging to communicate with their peers in different geographical locations. A whole set of new communication codes have emerged from such interactions that use shorthand to get messages across easily. For all we know, people may not have many issues on the dimension of trust in virtual contexts in future. Only time will tell.

The second issue in trust management is balancing between diversity and commonalities in member composition. One of the advantages of having virtual teams is that it allows us to bring people with diverse backgrounds, varied geographical locations, and in different time zones together for collective work. While this is true in spirit and on paper, there is a hidden cost of diversity that needs attention. The greater the diversity of team member composition, the higher is the probability of difficulty in transferring knowledge. This is because each team member will not share sufficient common contexts with other members, making it difficult to appreciate the others' knowledge. It is very like having engineers talk to accountants and accountants to physicists. The lack of common context will mean there are differences in use of terminologies, languages and semantics, work styles, and other norms. For instance, were one to visit a construction site and compare this with an accounting department, sharp contrasts would be visible in just how people work, how they refer to one another, and how instructions are given and knowledge transferred. Virtual teams must tread a fine line between having too much versus too little diversity in team composition. Too little diversity, for example in a virtual team involving only members from the accounting department, might raise the question: Why have a virtual team at all? The virtual team would be justified only if the accountants are from different geographical locations.

To our knowledge, there are three best practices to manage diversity. First, it is important to be cognizant of the differences in contexts, and set up clearly specified communication protocols from the start. For instance, if the team involves people from the USA, India, and the UK, certain protocols must be specified from the start: the time zone of reference, the metric or non-metric system used, the expected norms of email replies, and so on. Being clear about these practices up front will avert a lot of confusion. Second, and just as important as training on trust, is clarifying contextual issues that the team will face, from the onset. Raising awareness of these issues will make the team members conscious of them and will, one may hope, provide them ways to manage issues as they arise. Lastly, it is also important that a virtual team have access to knowledge brokers, as addressed previously, so that they can help move knowledge across the various distributed spaces.

Contingent workers

Most organizations employ contingent workers in their workforce, that is, temporary staff, consultants, advisers, and independent contractors. These individuals work on specific projects, normally for a fixed duration. In the USA, for example, during the months of December through April, most tax accounting firms hire temporary staff to help them manage their workload, since it is unusually high during this period. Hence, instead of keeping additional staff on their payroll for the entire year, they hire as needed to complete projects during their peak period. The advantage is cost savings. Keeping a salaried worker on full-time would require the additional expenditure of fringe benefits; it is far more economical and expedient to hire someone on a temporary basis.

Organizations also hire contingent workers with specialized knowledge, usually as consultants. Consultants normally possess specialized knowledge in their domains, which is aligned to the area of interest to the organization. For instance, hiring consultants from Andersen Consulting on supply chain management or hiring strategists from Bain & Company will provide the organization with several benefits. First, the organization will have access to knowledge not available internally. This external knowledge can be realized to better improve the organization's operations. The quality of such knowledge is normally higher, as consulting organizations have the benefit of experiences with a large number of clients. Hence, the organization is getting knowledge that, in many cases, has been applied in multiple environments and by subject-matter experts. Second, the organization does not have to invest in the fixed costs for resources needed to create the knowledge they are going to access; they only pay a fee to access and use such knowledge, which is most often cheaper than creating the know-how from scratch.

Hiring contingent workers also provides the organization with knowledge without the cost of replenishment or updates, that is organizations seldom pay the training costs of their contingent workers. Contingent workers are expected to be knowledgeable in their domains, and they bear the cost and responsibility of keeping their knowledge up to date. Monies saved on training costs can be devoted to other organizational endeavors. In addition, contingent workers help the organization move from a fixed-cost model to a variable-cost one.

There are several issues to be addressed when it comes to hiring and managing contingent workers. The first question is: What kind of contingent worker are we hiring? It is best if the organization thinks in terms of the type of task and the knowledge they are seeking. On the one hand, it can hire workers that do not necessarily bring knowledge of interest to the organization, but are being sought to implement knowledge possessed by the organization a priori. These contingent workers are normally required to help in the execution of tasks, and are best managed by tightly controlled approaches. As discussed in Chapter 2, when managing workers who are expected to perform routine tasks by utilizing knowledge, we can measure their performance by how well they followed the articulated process. Conversely, our decision to hire contingent workers is motivated by the fact that we are seeking new knowledge for the organization. This occurs mainly when we hire specialists in areas like management consultancy. Here we do not necessarily want them to exclusively utilize knowledge owned by the organization. Rather, we want them to help move the organization forward by sharing their insights and know-how, and by improving organizational performance.

An example of how best to manage contingent workers can be found in government parties trying to win elections. The core of the party and the main candidate seeking election victory represent less than 5 percent of all the people involved. The success or failure of an election campaign lies in how well the remaining 95 percent or so are mobilized. Most of these are volunteers, are distributed, and have no direct or economic ties to the party. They do, however, have strong allegiances towards their party and their candidate. So how are these workers mobilized? Normally, the candidate has a close group of advisers and confidants – the high-end knowledge workers that bring in new knowledge and insights. These insights shape the direction of campaigns and propaganda. Much of the campaign's success is related to how well the other 95 percent of the distributed volunteers work to execute the knowledge from the top. They will be asked to follow rather structured processes of rallying support by making phone calls, holding fundraisers, and so on. All these are examples of executing knowledge passed on from the headquarters. If one or more of the volunteers decides to drift off and conduct events independently, there will be lack of efforts coordination and this will reflect poorly on the caliber of the candidate. In the final analysis, the high-end knowledge workers are brought in to inform the candidate's agenda and campaign, while the rest of the knowledge workers, who are also a contingent workforce, are there to apply knowledge, and do so rapidly, to build support for the candidate.

One of the critical issues is how to manage the weak affiliations that contingent workers have with organizations. Contingent workers, in many cases, especially when it comes to high-end knowledge work, serve multiple clients at a given time. The organization must be certain that adequate knowledge protection capabilities are in place to prevent knowledge from leaving the organization and being used elsewhere. Often, preventive measures call for excellent legal contracts and work assignment documents being prepared that demand adherence to tight security policies. As a rule, it may be best that contingent workers are not used in highly sensitive areas, as it may be just too risky in terms of knowledge protection, especially since knowledge will be mobile, both into and out of the organization and also across organizational boundaries between the organization and the contingent workers. In cases where an organization sees a need for contingent workers in these areas, it may want to think instead about hiring employees of the required caliber into the mainstream of the organization.

Knowledge hostility issues between contingent workers and the traditional workforce of the organization need to be addressed. The traditional workers may demonstrate hostility towards the contingent workers owing to the fear of job loss and the envy of higher pay for the same work. These issues need to be managed, especially when the contingent workers are actually working for less. It is interesting to note that, in our experience, regular staff are less likely to get agitated when contingent workers are paid more than they are, than when they are paid less. The reason is economic threat: paying external workers less indicates to the workforce that their salary could be proportionately lowered or they could be out of a job, while paying more indicates that the organization is paying a premium for the external knowledge. Regular staff feel that this works to their advantage – they have an opportunity to pick up such knowledge and improve their position in the organization. Managing hostility issues can be very easily handled by clear communication and articulation by management. Management needs to clearly state their intention in hiring the contingent workers, how such hires will benefit (or hurt) the current employees, and how organizational goals will be furthered. Without clear instructions, grapevines open and rumor mills start to run – seldom a positive thing.

Conclusion

In this chapter we have discussed the concept of distributed knowledge management. An organization must be engaged with the global context of knowledge management. Most organizations operate in the global space, or at least face competition from global adversaries. As a result, they must be thoroughly and systematically engaged with what it takes to manage knowledge across the globe and how best to position their various subsidiaries to leverage local market knowledge for the global good of the organization.

6

Engaging Knowledge Management in Strategic Alliances

The prominence of strategic alliances continues to grow as we move through the knowledge era of competition. Having accepted that they must intensify focus on their core competencies, organizations find that they must strategically outsource their non-core tasks to organizations that are better at those activities.

No organization is an island, nor can it operate effectively in isolation. To cite a recent case, consider the effects of the mostly unilateral US foreign policy. A misguided belief in its own solitary and unchallenged supremacy left the US government unprepared to deal with the impending threat of terrorism before 9/11 and leaves it unprepared to counter it today. On numerous occasions before 9/11, foreign intelligence agencies in Egypt, the Philippines, the UAE, and Germany provided the US Intelligence Services with information about terrorist plans. Granted, these nuggets of knowledge were not complete, but they did represent valid clues. For the most part, the US intelligence agencies failed to grasp the need to *listen* to these foreign knowledge sources and use them towards their goal – protecting the US homeland from attacks. One reason that can be attributed to ignoring foreign knowledge sources is a sense of arrogance and invincibility. Organizations that fail to appreciate external sources of knowledge are most likely obsessed with generating knowledge internally and independent from external parties. Most times this is regrettable.

While the above illustration is dramatic and will become one for the history books, it is not the only instance of failure to appreciate foreign knowledge sources. The music recording industry in the USA, represented by the Recording Industry Association of America (RIAA), failed to grasp the severity of customer preferences and how peer-to-peer (P2P) technologies would impact the recording industry.[1] In the beginning, the RIAA considered P2P technologies and file-sharing platforms, such as Napster, to be a passing fad, a mere outcome of the dot-com boom. Then, when they realized that P2P sharing of music was a serious competitive contender, they responded unimaginatively by filing lawsuits. All this did was slow down the pace of the illegal music sharing platforms, and encourage rapid growth of various offshoots of Napster. Even today, the RIAA is playing catch-up to the several Napster clones that are now selling music directly to customers. In this case, the RIAA failed to *leverage* customer knowledge. They missed the simple fact that customers wanted the ability to customize their music collection rather than being forced to buy pre-packaged products. In addition to the failure of leveraging external knowledge, they also failed to *link* up to the external sources of knowledge; they did not connect with their customers. As a result, they are still struggling to reconnect with their customers and sell music profitably.

Organizations that fail to *listen*, *link*, and *leverage* their external sources of knowledge make themselves vulnerable to crises such as competitive surprises, loss of customers, innovation failures, bad press, and many other negativities. In this chapter we will discuss how organizations can better tap into the external sources of knowledge, and demonstrate why the future of competition will call for organizations to have not just good but excellent competencies in listening, linking, and leveraging knowledge from external sources. We will begin by explicating the needs for forging strategic alliances. Next, we will discuss the various types of external knowledge sources, why an organization should *listen* to these sources, and what they should be listening for. Following this, we will discuss how an organization can *link* up to these external sources of knowledge. We survey a range of alliances an organization can forge with external knowledge sources. Finally, we explain *leveraging* knowledge from external sources.

Why have strategic alliances?

Organizations must forge alliances with external entities for several reasons, the most prominent drivers being cost reductions, sharing risks, gaining access to foreign sources of knowledge, and strategic advantages to enhance competitiveness.[2] The cost reduction factor can be explained through the theory of transaction cost economics.[3] If a firm wants to process its payroll, for instance, it has two basic options: make or buy. If it has competency in the specified processing and the necessary resources, it chooses the make option. However, if it lacks the necessary resources, or does not want to invest in the required resources, it will be better off choosing to buy, that is purchase finished goods from the market.

Now, in purchasing goods, one may choose to purchase items on an ad-hoc basis or via a structured relationship. The former has the benefits of being flexible and customizable to changing needs over time. For example, we can change the place from where we purchase resources based on changes in the prices offered. However, the benefits do come at a cost. Conducting business on an ad-hoc basis is not stable – there is no telling that the price today will not go up instead of down tomorrow, nor is there any guarantee that the purchaser's needs will be prioritized. These weaknesses can be addressed by entering into structured relationships, also known as alliances. Alliances help firms collaborate on the exchange of resources in a structured manner for mutual benefit.

Entering into alliances can be conducive to helping firms lower their risks in new endeavors. Let us consider the example of a firm looking to expand into a new geographical region, say, an American company wanting to launch operations in Qatar, an emerging economy in the Middle East. Qatar continues to expand and grow at an astounding pace, with foreign investments largely driving its economic growth. Now, the American company can decide to enter the market either on its own or through an alliance with a local firm. The first option would be unwise, as the American company would lack sufficient appreciation of local cultural and management practices. Accepted practices in a Detroit mall may not be acceptable in a Qatari store. Moreover, there are crucial distinctions between the two disparate regions in the very way business is conducted, in how business deals are framed, how advertising is devised, and how local laws affect the conduct of commerce. Hence, it may be wise for the American company to enter into an alliance with a local company and penetrate the Qatari market through this alliance. This strategy will help the organization lower the risk of doing business, as it will be able to lower its investment and use some of the existing infrastructure of the local ally. In addition, it will be able to use some of the local knowledge to better inform its planning and strategic decision-making, hopefully making these more effective.

Alliances can also help improve a firm's strategic posture in the market-place. For example, firms may enter into mergers and/or acquisitions to increase their market share, merge assets and resources, and also improve the delivery of products and services to customers. Complementarity is a salient concept here.[4] Some of the external entities' resources may complement the firm's own resources. Since resources that have complementarities are strengthened when used in conjunction with the complements, the organization may enter into alliances to build coalitions where resources are exchanged between trading partners. For example, suppose a company has a well-designed and appreciated product but lacks a good distribution and logistical network. Rather than go the long route of creating its own distribution network, it may choose to engage in a distribution alliance with a company that already has inroads with retailers that are willing to stock the product. Companies can also collaborate when they try to surmount barriers to markets or enter new niche areas. For example, two or more smaller firms may collaborate in an effort to share administrative overheads associated with shipping their products to an overseas market. None of the firms could enter the market individually, but sharing the cost opens up a new market opportunity. By entering into alliances, a firm can also curtail its competitor responses. For example, should a firm learn about an emerging new competitor who is a threat in its marketplace, it might choose to enter into a series of alliances with the other players in the market. The objective would be to make the market more integrated and increase its dominance, thereby increasing the cost for the new competitor to penetrate the market.

There are many more subtle reasons for forging alliances that are beyond the scope of this chapter. In this chapter, we focus on the knowledge component of strategic alliances. We begin by exploring the relevant external sources of knowledge representing those entities with which alliances need to be forged to gain external knowledge.

External sources of knowledge

Most organizations need to concern themselves with the following external sources of knowledge: (1) business partners, (2) customers, (3) government and regulatory bodies, (4) academia, and (5) competitors (see Figure 6.1). Depending on the organization's industry sector, some sources of external knowledge may carry greater weight than others.

Business partners

Business partners may be seen as a collection of entities representing suppliers of raw materials for production and also suppliers of administrative and support needs such as legal services, financial affairs management, and logistic and distribution knowledge. Suppliers are an important factor in an organization's operations, being the providers of raw materials, work-in-progress, or finished goods that an organization consumes to attain its goals.

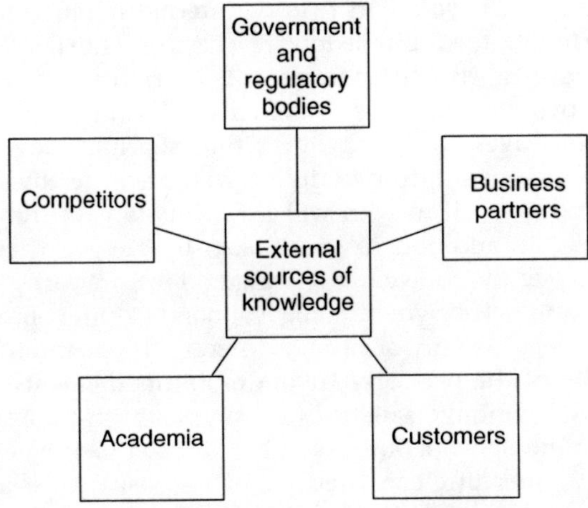

Figure 6.1   External sources of knowledge.

Suppliers need not provide exclusively physical products such as nuts and bolts. In the consulting and service sectors, they provide intangible products such as ideas, insights, and advice. Suppliers normally have focused and narrow niches and can be said to possess deep knowledge in their domains. Consequently, the organization must turn to the knowledge sources aligned to their areas of specialization. For a car manufacturer, say, this will involve listening to suppliers about inventions and innovations in automobile parts. Suppliers of products and services are seldom exclusive to one organization; in most cases they serve multiple organizations. In the automobile industry, it is not uncommon to find a supplier of one product to serve two or more organizations who may be competitors. In this case, the organization has an opportunity to gain knowledge about its competitors through the supplier.

A case in point: the Toyota knowledge sharing network

Toyota, the automobile manufacturing giant and supply chain innovator, has created an interesting knowledge sharing network to connect its suppliers and achieve superior results.[5] The network promotes the exchange and transfer of explicit and tacit knowledge. Explicit knowledge, mainly documents, is exchanged electronically, while tacit know-how is exchanged via social mechanisms such as networking events and conferences. Toyota hosts plant tours and quality management conferences, where members can learn from observations of work and discussions with senior leaders.

The supplier network is also a good avenue for Toyota to impart some of its administrative knowledge, such as procedures and policies, to its suppliers by sending consultants to supplier worksites. In this service, which is free for participants in the suppliers network, experienced consultants are dispatched to suppliers and provide 'on-site' assistance. The consultant is the expert who has knowledge about Toyota – its history, internal systems, administration, and so on. The involvement can be for a few days or for extended time periods up to several months. Also, inter-firm employee transfers enable knowledge transfer from Toyota to suppliers. Experienced Toyota engineers are sent to suppliers as executives. Toyota believes that sharing knowledge with its suppliers will help them improve their operations, thereby lowering their cost of operations, which in turn will help Toyota gain from the lowered cost of materials. In addition to steps taken by Toyota, the suppliers can organize themselves for knowledge sharing and integration.

An example might be where some suppliers form voluntary learning teams to work on problems of mutual interest. To maintain the integrity and the viability of the network, Toyota monitors incidents of free-riding, and may impose economic sanctions on suppliers who do not share their knowledge with the network but seek only to exploit it. The network mission of *"kyozon kyoei"*, meaning coexistence and co-prosperity, is also given due respect and eliminates any notion of proprietary knowledge, while retaining focus on collective and social knowledge.

In addition to suppliers, an organization must interact with other business partners. These include office equipment manufacturers, technology providers, legal firms, logistics and distribution centers, advertising houses, and so on. Each of these entities provides the organization with goods or services of value that enable it to be more efficient in meeting its objectives. Like suppliers, business partners have deep knowledge in their areas of focus, as this represents their bread and butter. The organization must look to these partners for knowledge on improving internal operations. No organization can be self-sufficient in the various activities needed to deliver customer value. Any organization that thinks it is autonomous is not optimizing the use of its resources, at the cost of lost opportunities. An organization must forge the right type of agreement with the business partner, depending on the type of knowledge it seeks.

Sometimes knowledge management may be the reason to engage in an alliance. Tokio Marine & Fire Insurance Co. (now Tokio Marine & Nichido Fire Insurance), an able provider of insurance services, forged an alliance with NTT Communications Corp., which has experience in the management of data and information protection. The two companies chose to integrate their strengths to calibrate a joint product – insurance against information and data leaks.

Customers

All businesses exist to serve their customers, who provide the organization with revenues to keep them going and improve their status. Failure to listen adequately to customers has been shown, time and again, to be detrimental to the health of an organization. In historic times, an organization could design, build, and price a product without engaging the customer. Those days are long gone. Today, unless an organization can understand its customers' needs, transform those needs into products and services, and manage the relationship with customers, it is unlikely to survive the marketplace. We will elaborate on the concept of customer knowledge management in Chapter 7.

Government and regulatory bodies

Most organizations resist and despise interacting with the government and its various regulatory bodies such as the Food and Drug Administration or the Internal Revenue Services. We do not blame them. Working with the government, in our experiences, can be painful, though the pain is subdued with experience and frequent interaction. By the very nature of their work, government and regulatory agencies have knowledge that is, in many cases, rare and protected. For example, if an organization is facing issues with instances of electronic fraud or online theft, working with the Electronic Crimes Taskforce of the FBI or other agencies will provide the organization with access to knowledge they lack. We believe most organizations make the mistake of working with the government and regulatory agencies only after the fact, for example following a theft or a fire. Often it takes an unwelcome incident for the organization to willingly embrace inspections by the police and fire departments, such inspections having been viewed before the incident as a burden and an unnecessary chore.

Rather than being reactive, we suggest being proactive. An organization must have the ability to tap into these external sources for knowledge on the environment, changes in laws, effects of political conditions on businesses, and many other categories of knowledge. Government organizations routinely conduct research projects on topics of interest. In the USA, the Government Accounting Office regularly publishes reports on topical issues. These represent viable knowledge resources that an organization can use to benchmark their practices with those of the industry. It is also common for government organizations to host forums, usually panel discussions and debates, where private sector enterprises are invited to participate. An organization must embrace such opportunities and actively participate in them to tap into a rich source of knowledge.

Academia

Academia, especially business schools and engineering science teaching establishments, represents a viable external source of knowledge for business organizations. A computer manufacturer has vested interest in keeping abreast with developments in premier computer engineering departments, in order to get access to new knowledge, inventions, discoveries, or lessons learnt. Researchers at universities, colleges, and research institutions steadily generate new knowledge. Much of it is made available via working papers, research reports, discussions and panel presentations, conferences, meetings, symposiums, and industry–academic collaborations.

Researchers and scholars, who work on cutting-edge problems and have greater slack for experimentation, are sometime better at knowledge generation than the private sector. Many of these studies take a global perspective of the problem, and hence knowledge generated is widely applicable to any business in a given industry or facing a similar problem. Academics have the advantage of being neutral in their analyses and can access wider data points than can a private organization. A salient competency of academicians is that, by promising non-disclosure of sensitive material, they are privy to confidential data. Gaining access to a wide range of data points allows the knowledge generated to be more rigorously calibrated to attain a higher value.

Academic knowledge must be tapped by seeking explicit and tacit sources. Explicit sources of knowledge are databases that house academic journals and other outlets for dissemination of research. Tacit knowledge is gained by interacting with academicians through attending presentations, inviting academicians to act as consultants, and working out industry–academia collaborative efforts.

Competitors

Organizations must also get knowledge from their competitors. Today, we can find many instances of competing organizations cooperating for mutual benefits. Take the example of the strategic engagement between two classic rivals: Amazon and Borders. Amazon, the pioneer online retailer, started out as an online bookseller. Their competitors were the traditional bookstores like Borders and Barnes & Noble. After failing to compete adequately with Amazon, Borders decided to forge an alliance, a marketing and distribution agreement, with the internet giant. Amazon shared its technical expertise with Borders and helped them manage their book inventory system to establish a dominating presence on the internet. Amazon gained access to Borders' customer base, which Borders had acquired through endless effort over decades.

Besides the one-to-one competitor agreements, there are situations where it may be viable for a whole slew of competitors to engage in a collaborative space. One example of this is Eli Lilly's InnoCentive solution.[6] This is a web-based collaborative platform that allows pharmaceutical companies to post problems and find solutions for difficult problems, with cash rewards for scientists who provide solutions.

Competitors normally have different areas of strengths and weaknesses; one's strength may be another's weakness. This knowledge can be used to improve the positioning of one's products and services, or to forge successful alliances. Building coalitions is one way to get competitors to collaborate, wherein each organization provides a piece of their strength to counter another member organization's weakness, and make the coalition stronger. Today, we can find many instances where traditional competitors are engaged in cooperative relationships. Consider three competitors in the electronics space – Hitachi, Toshiba, and Matsushita – forming an alliance to manufacture and sell LCD panels for flat-panel TVs. Such joint ventures will become more prominent in the future, as competitive pressures increase and firms realize that their core competencies need to be integrated with external competencies that may reside with their competitors. The notion of external competency complementarities is salient here. This is where the strength of a firm's competency, such as marketing, is made more powerful and valuable when it is integrated with an externally residing competency, such as packaging. The organization must seek the means to gain better access to its competitors' knowledge and also engage with its competitors in a cooperative spirit in order to use existing knowledge more effectively and create new products and services.

Engaging with competitors does not have to be limited to issues of products and services, but can also be for non-value-added services or administrative functions. In Japan, 300 drugstores that are traditional competitors have decided to create a private school to train employees on management functions such as store management, merchandising, and human resource management. The school is intended to help improve the education level of knowledge and service provided by the associates at the member companies, thus helping them retain the drug sales market and prevent new entrants. Recently, supermarkets and convenience stores – competitors with the traditional drugstores – were given permission to sell drugs. Hence, by forging an alliance even with their regular competitors, the traditional drugstores are better able to prepare themselves to deal with new entrants in the marketplace. An organization that is not agile in tapping into competition knowledge is risking disaster.

Listening to the external sources of knowledge

Having an inventory of external sources of knowledge is important but not sufficient. An organization must *listen* to these external sources in order to receive knowledge. They must recognize, identify, and capture the knowledge from those external sources. As mentioned earlier, ignorance of such knowledge, intentionally or inadvertently, invites disasters.

Knowledge from external sources can range from highly explicit to highly tacit. Knowledge that is explicit can be transmitted easily from source to destination, because it can be easily articulated and understood. Knowledge that is highly tacit, on the other hand, cannot be easily transmitted or assimilated. Gathering knowledge from new ideas or emerging innovations normally calls for discussions, many of which need to be face-to-face. Such knowledge is high in ambiguity and requires detailed explanation, much of which cannot be sufficiently addressed in a report.

An organization can deploy human or mechanical means to listen to knowledge. Obviously, technical mechanisms such as scanning newsletters, subscribing to discussion groups, monitoring competitor websites, and searching databases are apt for accessing external sources of knowledge in an explicit format. Alternatively, human mechanisms are better suited to listen to and interact with knowledge that is highly tacit. Regardless of whether an organization embarks on technical or human mechanisms to capture knowledge from external sources, it needs to forge the appropriate *link* with the external source. We will now discuss the wide assortment of alliances the organization can forge with external sources in order to obtain knowledge from them.

Linking up to external sources of knowledge

There are several ways an organization can connect to external sources of knowledge: (1) licensing agreements, (2) marketing and distribution agreements, (3) production and development agreements, (4) minority equity investments, (5) joint ventures, and (6) mergers and acquisitions. Linking up to external sources is important to access knowledge that is external to the organization. Alliances help an organization achieve goals by tapping into resources held by other parties; in many cases a goal will remain unachievable without an alliance. Alliances can range in scope and depth. We will begin by discussing the simpler forms of alliance and move on to more complex arrangements (see Figure 6.2).

Licensing agreements

A licensing agreement allows an organization or individual to use a product or service for a specified purpose and duration. The most common licensing agreements deal with the purchase and usage of software. When someone purchases a piece of software, they are purchasing a license to use the technology within prescribed boundaries. The licensing agreement gives them access to external knowledge that is already in a codified state. Entering into a licensing agreement seldom provides access to the knowledge source, the programmer of the software, but does provide access to the knowledge artifact, the software. A licensing agreements is therefore best suited for knowledge needs where the organization wants to apply knowledge in a packaged solution without much care for insights into domain knowledge.

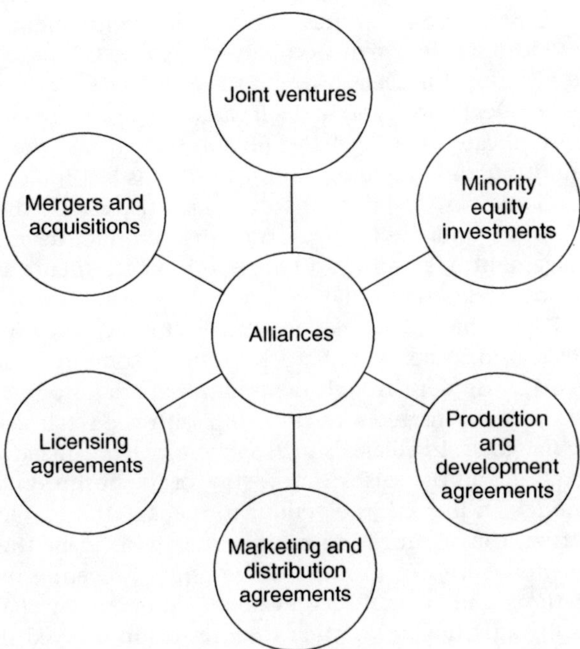

Figure 6.2   Linking with external sources of knowledge.

Most organizations enter into licensing agreements to tap into external sources of knowledge from business partners. Besides the popular technology licensing agreements, licensing agreements are found in legal and consulting services. Hiring a consultant on a specialized project can be considered akin to a licensing agreement. While we do not have a physical product here, the organization is still restricted to accessing knowledge in a prepared format. It is best to enter into a licensing agreement when the organization does not want to control the source of knowledge or the knowledge asset, but just to have access to use it for operational purposes. Using a licensing agreement enables a firm to employ specific outputs of an external entity's knowledge process without internalizing the core knowledge of the entity. This is very suitable for simple needs, especially when they represent an organization's non-core activities.

Marketing and distribution agreements

As the name implies, these agreements deal with an organization's outbound goods and services. Once an organization calibrates its products and services, they need to be moved to the customer. This calls for informing, enticing, and educating the customer about the products, packaging them, and then transporting them to the customer. In today's era of specialization, where we have organizations specializing in marketing and logistics, it is in an organization's best interest to enter into alliances with them, rather than attempting to do it on its own. Companies such as UPS and FedEx have sophisticated offerings for their customers that include product packaging, distribution, after-sales returns, and so on. It would be unwise for an organization to attempt to duplicate the knowledge possessed by firms who specialize in product distribution and marketing. Simply put, it is just too costly.

An organization's best response is to tap into the knowledge housed in the external parties, and use it to inform better product development and revenue management. Marketing and distribution agreements do not necessarily need to be exclusively structured with marketing or logistic houses. Compaq and Radio Shack, the retail electronic store, entered into an agreement whereby Radio Shack would stock Compaq computers and help sell them to the end consumer through the traditional brick store. The Gateway computer firm recently forged a relationship with the retail giant Best Buy to achieve similar goals. In alliances such as these, the organization is tapping into the marketing and/or logistics know-how of the business partner.

It is not enough to just ask the vendor to manage the marketing and/or logistics function; the organization must be able to leverage the knowledge in these domains to inform product development, revenue management, customer relations, and overall achievement of organizational goals. For example, if using a particular logistic carrier results in delayed shipments to customers causing them to switch to competitors, this knowledge must be acted upon immediately. Everything does not have to be negative: in one case that we know of, the logistic carrier informed a retail organization that they should enter into an alliance whereby customers could return their products directly at the carrier's drop-off centers. Doing so would ease customer tension about product returns in electronic transactions, which would boost sales. The logistic carrier was right! The client started to see positive responses from their easy-return initiative, and was able to reach customers who were not known to make high-value online purchases.

For several reasons, entering into marketing and distribution agreements is a more involved task than signing a licensing agreement. First, for the alliance to be successful, an organization has to go beyond getting access to an outsider's knowledge to also sharing some of its own. An organization wanting to hire an advertising agency to handle sales promotions and media ads must be willing to engage in a dialogue with the agency, so that the ad designers have a good grasp of the organization's values, policies, features, product details, and persona to calibrate an appropriate ad. Second, a marketing and distribution agreement calls for reliance on the vendor's knowledge application capability. An organization does not have direct access to a product; the agreement just means that a knowledge service will be delivered. The organization is not using the knowledge directly, but is entering into an agreement for the vendor to use specialized knowledge to meet the goals of the organization.

Marketing and distribution agreements are excellent in situations where an organization wants to have access to the knowledge source and is interested in exerting some control over how the knowledge service is executed. For example, an organization can state particular delivery times, transit times, product packaging issues, and so on with a logistics company. For our purposes we would like to stress that, along with the physical control items such as the ones above, the organization can exert control over the knowledge. For instance, an organization should ask for specifics in terms of information reports, knowledge sharing mechanisms, training, knowledge transfer agreements, and so on. Wal-Mart, the retail giant, has been very successful in streamlining the flow of knowledge between its suppliers and itself. Anyone who wants to supply products to Wal-Mart will have to play strictly by their rules in knowledge sharing. This excellent management of information and knowledge has helped Wal-Mart improve its business operations significantly.

Marketing agreements help an organization gain access to knowledge from the market. A marketing research firm will have access to market information that will not easily be available to the organization, because the marketing research firm is in the business of studying the market. Moreover, marketing firms can provide an organization with access to customer knowledge by outsourcing aspects of product research on customer preferences, pricing preferences, tastes, and so on. In addition, marketing firms have access to large data sets of demographic customer information. Via marketing and distribution agreements, an organization may be able to tap into its vendor's knowledge about government and regulatory matters. This is a common practice when an organization decides to start operations in a foreign country, where teaming up with a local marketer and distributor with deep knowledge about local operation enables market penetration.

Production and development agreements

Production and development agreements are more complex than marketing and distribution agreements. First, in addition to engaging in a dialogue with an external party, knowledge work is jointly conducted by two or more organizations. This involves far greater cooperation than the previous types of alliances. Here, not only is knowledge shared between parties, but the fusion of knowledge from diverse sources also leads to the development of new products and services.

Second, in our experience, production and development agreements are more long-term than marketing or distribution engagements. Most organizations are very careful before committing to joint work, because entering into a production and development agreement calls for greater effort in terms of integration and coordination. Common manufacturing practices: such as the use of just-in-time (JIT) systems, require highly streamlined integration and coordination mechanisms. The need for effective integration demands a high investment in the alliance, in the form of upfront cost, so organizations are less likely to terminate these agreements at short notice.

When entering into production and development agreements an organization must clearly examine its rationale, the key question being: Are we entering into an agreement for dependence on capacity or knowledge?[7] Dependence on capacity is important when a firm has the requisite knowledge to design a product but lacks the appropriate infrastructure and resources to transfer logical designs into physical products and services. This type of agreement calls for the firm to transfer specific design requirements to an external entity, which will then take the knowledge and implement it to create products and services. Dependence on knowledge is a more complex endeavor. Here, the organization is seeking to engage in the exchange of knowledge so that products can be calibrated. It knows that it does not have all the knowledge it needs to build the product and hence must engage external parties.

Organizations can enter into joint production and development agreements in order to gain access to knowledge from suppliers, business partners, academia, and even customers. Alliances will be forged when an organization needs to work closely with its suppliers to build a product. This is common in the case of automobile manufacturing, where small suppliers may collaborate to produce parts by jointly sharing resources and knowledge. Most computer manufacturers, such as Gateway and Dell, also engage in production agreements.

We must address an important point here: the issue of responsibility. Unlike the prior two forms of alliances, production and development agreements place a greater burden of accountability on the organization. By this we mean answering stakeholders. We were made aware of a case where one of the suppliers of a PC manufacturer was having difficulty getting a component to the manufacturer, forcing it to delay shipments to the end consumer. Can you guess who end consumers held responsible? The PC manufacturer, since it did not matter to them that an external party was the cause of the delay. The PC manufacturer got a bad reputation with consumers and was forced to sell computers at highly discounted rates to prevent order cancellations.

To return to our earlier point, effective integration, both in terms of physical and knowledge resources, is essential for a production and development agreement to be successful. Though rare, production and development agreements can be entered into with business partners. Here, the organization may be looking to enhance its core product or service by collaborating on certain components with its business partners. The service industry shows us popular instances of such agreements. For example, a restaurant chain may collaborate with an interior architecture firm to help design and build the décor and furnishings of the restaurant. The added ambience is a component of the overall service proposition that the restaurant offers its customers.

Increasingly, we are beginning to see industry–academia alliances that follow the paradigm of production and development agreements. In fact, this book can be thought of as an outcome of a number of such alliances. Academics work with organizations, either onsite or offsite, to help the organization better construct its products and services. The academic gains by having access to business data that can be used for research studies. Organizations can also farm out research and development assignments to academic labs, a practice very common in the engineering sciences. Organizations will fund research undertakings on topics of interest to them. This is an excellent, low-cost method for an organization to show commitment towards scientific projects and get involved with academia. The organization can gain from external sources of expertise and knowledge without much risk, since it makes only minor financial commitments to the endeavor. Production and development agreements are being used to transfer knowledge from customers into companies (we will discuss this point in detail in the chapter 7).

A point worth noting is that production and development agreements are not static. Changes in organizational environment, competition, and business dynamics will call for changes to existing production and development agreements. If, over time, the organization realizes that a particular business partner is not delivering products of quality, it will find it necessary to replace the partner. If, however, the supplier is performing extraordinarily well, it would be wise to look at shipping other production needs to that supplier. More important, however, is the notion of changing dependency on supplier knowledge. If, over time, the organization realizes that the supplier's knowledge is continuing to increase in value and may be the root cause of successful product differentiation efforts, it may consider internalizing this knowledge by acquiring the supplier. Careful considerations about integrative compatibility are required at this stage, an issue we will discuss later in this chapter.

Minority equity investments (MEIs)

The alliances we have discussed till now do not involve putting up equity or seeking ownership of the knowledge source. Starting with MEIs, we begin by considering ownership of the external knowledge source. MEIs are considered the simplest form of equity-based alliances, and involve one organization purchasing a *minority* interest in another organization.

MEIs are usually employed extensively to gain access to new and emerging knowledge sources. Pharmaceutical companies routinely use them to gain access to new biotechnology startups and other academically spun-off research incubators. Technology giants like Microsoft have also been known to invest in upcoming startups that they see as promising, and aim to acquire in the future.

MEIs are normally viewed as a stepping-stone toward a more complex equity-based collaborative relationship, such as a joint venture or a merger or acquisition. As such, they provide the organization with a testing ground to analyze the potential of the investment before entering into the more complex agreements. In an MEI, an organization will have limited access and control of the knowledge source. However, owing to minority ownership, it will retain a connection to the source and be able to monitor its growth and development.

Intel is one company that has been successful in using MEIs to gain access to emerging knowledge. One of the largest R&D spenders, Intel has invested over $13 billion in R&D since 2001. A significant amount of this spending goes into funding emerging companies. For example, in 2004 Intel's investments included companies involved in developing technologies to create networked homes that let people access digital content. In 2003, the investments were made in companies such as DRAM makers Micron Technology Inc. and Elpida Memory Inc. Intel has also invested in Elpida Memory Inc., a Swiss designer of low-cost chips for linking home devices, Entropic Communications Inc., which designs chips for home networking systems over standard coaxial cable, and Musicmatch Inc., which sells software for recording, organizing, and playing music on digital devices. Intel's most-far-reaching investments will let people videoconference, play games, and even watch movies via their cellphones. Intel recognizes that, since only a small fraction of its knowledge needs reside in-house, and since successful innovations may stem from outside entities, they had better have a procedure to seek these out and invest in them systematically. Twice a year, Intel hosts developers' forums to brief suppliers and innovators on its needs and to encourage innovative work.

Joint ventures

Joint ventures are agreements whereby two or more organizations decide to pool resources and create a new entity that has its own corporate identity, resources, and structure. Entering into joint ventures helps an organization share risks and costs, and also forces engagement with the external source in an effective manner. The success of a joint venture is closely tied to how well the parent organizations share their resources – not the least of which is know-how – and integrate the resources into a holistic entity.

Joint ventures are popular when firms seek to enter new markets or are undertaking high-risk R&D projects. In the first case, a joint venture can help an organization to introduce products and/or services into a foreign country by collaborating with a local firm. In the second case, it can help an organization share risks with a business partner who has similar interests in the research. Moreover, by creating a joint venture, both parents isolate their traditional businesses from associated risk.

Joint ventures are also common between firms who may be competitors, but see a reason to engage for mutual benefit. In the automobile industry, for instance, there have been numerous instances of joint ventures between American and Japanese car manufacturers. CAMI Automotive Inc., a joint venture between GM and Suzuki, proved to be very successful. Suzuki gained access to the North American market by accessing the GM dealer network, while GM was able to leverage Suzuki's knowledge to produce efficient low-priced automobiles.[8] A similar case is that of Philips and Whirlpool. Philips's appliance division was a valuable segment, but did not represent the company's core strength, since Philips lacked adequate knowledge of how to market and distribute their appliances. Whirlpool had adequate knowledge of marketing and distributing appliance products, but lacked the comprehensiveness of the Philips products. A joint venture enabled both organizations to leverage each other's strengths. Similarly, the competitors Toshiba and Motorola collaborated to share their knowledge of DRAM and microprocessors to develop better products.[9]

Since knowledge generated by the joint venture must benefit the parent companies, there must be effective mechanisms for knowledge transfer. We found some of the best practices in companies that have been successful in tapping into the knowledge of the joint venture include: (1) regular meetings between staff of the parent company and the joint venture, (2) meetings between all parent companies and the joint ventures, (3) joint work on projects, and (4) development of common collaborative platforms, such as extranets, that can be used to post knowledge nuggets from the parents and joint venture, resulting in knowledge sharing and connections between the organizations. Unless a joint venture is able to successfully integrate and synthesize knowledge from the parents, the chances of failure are high. Moreover, if knowledge does not flow from the joint venture to the parent organization, the principal organizations have little to show for their investment.

Mergers and acquisitions

Mergers and acquisitions are the most complex form of equity-based engagements. Here one organization combines with another in a merger, or subsumes another – an acquisition. Mergers and acquisitions are common between erstwhile competitors, to increase the new entity's chance of competing in the marketplace. Consider the case of JP Morgan, the bank ranked second in the USA, acquiring Bank One of Chicago, ranked sixth in the industry. The motivation behind consolidations is simple – united we stand, divided we fall. In this case, while neither JP Morgan nor Bank One had the individual assets to compete with the industry leader, Citigroup, consolidating their assets has positioned them to compete successfully.

Not all consolidations occur between companies of equal equity and size. It is more common for a large organization to acquire a smaller firm. This is especially viable when the smaller firm has distinct competencies that can be better leveraged using the infrastructure of the larger organization. The most common scenario is where the larger organization would like to acquire the R&D capabilities of the smaller company. First Data Corporation, a leader in the domain of electronic commerce payment services, acquired Concord EFS, a leader of process-automated teller machine transactions. First Data Corporation can now extend market share by tapping into the Concord EFS's customers and can offer these customers a deeper and broader range of products and services. Acquisition of small organizations by larger ones is common in the high-technology industries. Microsoft is infamous for acquiring smaller IT and software organizations possessing innovative ideas, products, and services that either complement or compete with Microsoft's product offerings. Many large pharmaceutical companies also routinely acquire smaller biotechnology firms that are on the verge of innovative breakthroughs in medical drug discovery and treatments.

It is critical to address knowledge management issues when engaging in a merger or acquisition. The acquirer must have the capability to integrate knowledge from the organization it is acquiring. Many organizations fail to do this, as they focus heavily on the issues of financial gains, market reactions, and other short-term metrics. We postulate that the long-term success of a merger or acquisition is linked to success in knowledge integration. Organizations need to address issues such as knowledge loss that will occur after a merger or acquisition owing to staff reductions, duplicate processes, and so on., and how these will affect the end-consumer.

Organizational culture issues also need to be addressed upfront; that two organizations look good on paper does not mean that they will be able to work symbiotically. Since entering into a merger or acquisition is a long-term contract, an organization must have the patience and resolve to work through the preliminary hurdles, setbacks, and issues in knowledge integration.

Leveraging external sources of knowledge

In order to better address how external sources of knowledge can be leveraged, let us contrast internal and external sources in two dimensions – control and coordination.

Control

The organization can exert control over internal sources and dictate, to a large degree, their tasks, roles, responsibilities, and behavior. This control makes it comparatively easy to manage the knowledge they contain and also the behavior that results from the knowledge. For example, an organization can create teams to blend together individuals who have varying expertise and know-how. It can also mandate and provide incentives for the usage of knowledge management systems and the contribution of knowledge to these systems. Failure on the part of an internal source to comply with organizational mandates could result in termination of employment. For efficient knowledge management, control over knowledge sources is an important advantage.

External sources of knowledge are, by definition, located outside the organization. As such, the organization has limited control over their behavior, actions, or motivations. Hence, the organization must learn how to manage knowledge without the complete control that can be exerted when controlling internal sources. Consider a simple example: if an organization such as a retail store like Best Buy, Sears, or Gap wants to elicit knowledge from its customers, it must have a knowledge management program that is strongly geared to its customers. This will call for providing incentives such as purchase discounts, coupons, and so on for knowledge and information shared with the company. There is a cost to exerting control over external sources of knowledge and this cost must be justified in terms of coordination.

Coordination

In exerting control over the internal sources of knowledge, the act of ensuring coordination among these sources is also controlled to a large extent. For example, an organization can devise protocols such as cross-functional team and/or department meetings to ensure that the various units are coordinating their efforts in pursuit of the overall objectives. Work schedules and work arrangements can also be coordinated. Consider the traditional work shifts, where, when one batch of employees leaves there is a new group ready to manage the service, so that coordination remains efficient and effective. Internal information systems can also be coordinated to effectively interact with one another.

Now, consider the problem of coordination when it comes to external sources of knowledge. Can you tell your customers and suppliers how to coordinate their activities? Well, at first thought you may dismiss this question as ridiculous. Give it a second, though. Most of the time, you cannot coordinate the activities of your customers, but you definitely can control the behavior of your suppliers. Think Wal-Mart! Suppliers to Wal-Mart are controlled by Wal-Mart, who dictates the products to be stocked, the quantities of such products, the order and replenishment times, and the flow of knowledge and information. How is Wal-Mart able to do this? Simple – they can exert control over their suppliers owing to their sheer size, market position, and market dominance.

Control and coordination

The various alliance options discussed in this chapter can be weighed on this two-dimensional scale of control and coordination. Licensing agreements represent the lowest degrees in both dimensions. They are followed by marketing and distribution agreements, which call for increased coordination efforts, but retain minimal control of the external knowledge source. Production and development agreements call for increased coordination efforts, and here an organization can exert control of the external knowledge source. MEIs are interesting, in that the amount of coordination and control depends on the context. In some MEIs the investing firm can exert serious control of the knowledge source; in others this may not be possible. One factor that governs the amount of control is that the number of MEI investors is an inverse relationship, that is the greater the number of MEIs, the less control any single one can exert and vice versa. Joint ventures result in the creation of new external knowledge sources that are heavily controlled by the parent firms. And finally, mergers and acquisitions result in the most control of the external sources of knowledge, and call for the greatest efforts in terms of coordination. For example, Amazon.com acquired Joyo.com, a Chinese online company, to gain essential knowledge about the Chinese market, and succeeded in gaining complete control and assimilation of the Chinese company's knowledge. However, control and coordination of knowledge was far from easy, given the difference in organizational and national cultures.

Alliances as relationships: a life-cycle perspective

In our opinion, organizations should look at the various types of alliances as a phase or process model. An organization might consider beginning with a licensing agreement with the external knowledge source. Depending on how things progress, the alliance can increase in sophistication to a marketing and distribution or a production and development agreement. If the organization realizes that its dependence on the source is increasing, it may consider an MEI or even a joint venture. Over time, depending on how valuable the external source is and the extent of organizational dependence on it, a merger or acquisition may be an option. Starting with simple alliances and moving towards more complex ones provides the organization with a way to test the elasticity of the relationship and build up integration and coordination capabilities.

Knowledge issues in strategic alliances can be studied from a life-cycle perspective, by comparing alliance formation, management, and termination in individual relationships. Forging organizational alliances is in many ways similar to how individuals manage relationships. Without an adequate sense of their own needs it will be very difficult for an individual to enter and sustain a successful relationship. As a first step, we must ask: Am I ready for a relationship? This is hardly a trivial question. The answer will depend on the individual's current situation, goals, and aspirations, life style, time, resources, and so on. Unless an individual seriously contemplates this question, there is a risk of entering into the wrong the type of relationship or entering into a relationship with the wrong kind of individual. In certain situations we may also have an individual who poorly estimates the need for a relationship and hence could remain in seclusion erroneously. All these outcomes are undesirable.

Once we decide there is a justified need for a relationship, the next step is to seek out the right type of relationship and partner. It is important to differentiate between the right relationship and the right partner. Relationship types can vary from finding a pen pal and making acquaintances or friends to seeking a soulmate. Each relationship has its associated sets of benefits and costs – conceivably, the effort needed for sustaining a friendship will be less than for courting a soulmate.

After we identify the type of relationship, we are ready to begin the search for the right partner, ideally one who meets our individual needs and is willing to engage in the relationship of our choice. This ideal, as anyone experienced in forging relationships knows, is not always realistic. The partner we might want may not want to engage in the relationship of our choice, or we may not find the right partner to meet the peculiarities of the relationships we want. To ensure a good match, we must engage in a process of getting to know the partner and begin dialogue. Negotiations normally occur during the initial courtship phase. Failure to reach appropriate compromises could lead to early termination of the relationship. If an agreement is reached, the relationship begins "officially." This could be signified by the signing of a contract, as in the case of a marriage, or a handshake or similar formal gestures.

With the relationship underway, the parties will need to evaluate each other's performance in terms of living up to the compromises and promises made. Both parties know that the early road may be rough. While good communication will help clear up confusions during this period and reaffirm expectations, poor communication can kill the relationship in its formative stage. During the course of the relationship, both parties must ensure that they are receiving as much as they are giving. Failure to ensure this results in discrepancies and will be a cause for conflict.

As the relationship continues, we expect each partner to grow individually. They may run into new scenarios in their lives, changes may occur in their environment, and needs and desires may be reprioritized. Clear communication about these changes between partners would be ideal. A successful relationship is reaffirmed through continuation. In the case of irresolvable differences, good communication would go a long way toward a peaceful end to the relationship. During termination, it would be best if both parties had appropriate backup plans and appropriate exit strategies. While having these in place never guarantees an amicable end to the relationship, it increases the likelihood. However, if one party discovers the other has violated the terms of the agreement, such as by one spouse cheating on the other, the termination of the relationship could be volatile and disastrous.

On termination, the individual may decide to stay in seclusion for a period or to sign up with a new partner. This signals the start of the cycle again. Hopefully, the individual will use the lessons learnt from its prior relationships to make better choices in the future. As we get older and – hopefully – wiser, we are better able to determine who would meet our needs, and we can easily detect signs of an impending relationship failure.

We are all familiar with this cycle. We engage in building and managing social relationships on a daily basis. Organizations work in a similar fashion. We will now use this analogy to highlight key issues in knowledge management during alliance construction, management, and renewal or termination (see Figure 6.3).

Constructing the right alliance with the right partner

In order to construct the right alliance, an organization must be able to manage and effectively leverage several types of knowledge. The first is knowledge about the organization's current state, both internally and as the external world views it. Internally, the organization must have a sense of its core strengths and weaknesses, its areas of competencies and deficiencies, and its current goals and objectives. It must also know how it fares in comparison with the external world. Is the organization viewed as a low-cost provider of goods and services, or as a high-end product differentiator? Is it an industry leader or a follower? What are its relative strengths and weaknesses compared with other competitors? Knowing these details will

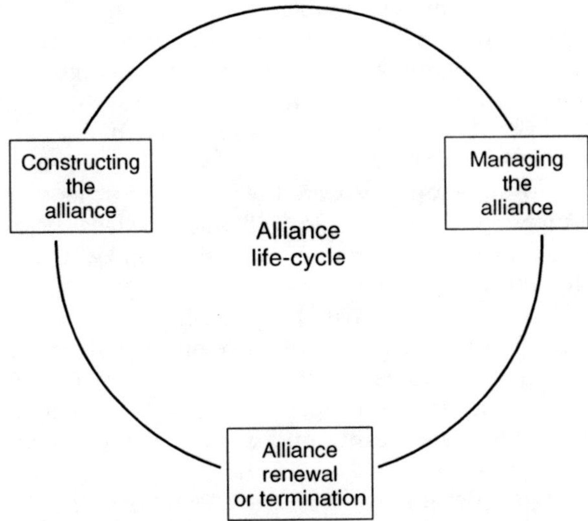

Figure 6.3   Alliance life-cycle.

provide the organization with a good starting point from which to plan for alliances.

The second type of knowledge that is needed is about the future state. This calls for forecasting the organization's end-state vision after the alliance is commissioned. What does one seek to gain from the alliance and how will this impact the future of the organization? Since entering an alliance of any sort calls for some changes to the organization's strategic posture, strategic implications must be considered.

After the strategic details are sorted out, the next item is knowledge about the alliance. Here, the first question is: 'What is the object of interest; what is being exchanged in the alliance and what will the alliance involve?' An organization must consider the knowledge implications of the object of the alliance and outline the pros and cons of entering into an alliance versus conducting the activity in-house. The next question is: 'What type of alliance do we engage in?' This will require the evaluation of the control and coordination issues outlined in the previous sections.

Once the alliance type is identified, the organization must then solicit the right business partner. This is probably the most difficult phase of the life-cycle. While there might be a number of partners willing to provide the goods and services of interest, the critical question becomes: Can synergies be developed for knowledge and resource integration? If an organization is just seeking to get access to resources, knowledge exchange moves to the background. However, in most cases today organizations want to engage in alliances for resources as well as knowledge exchange.

Learning from one's business partner is a critical part of the engagement, as the organization can use new learning to improve its activities and be more competitive. Gaining knowledge on how synergies will manifest themselves during the engagement is imperative. This will call for analyzing integration issues in the people, process, strategic, and cultural issues of the organization. The organization must also evaluate a partner's knowledge creation and innovative capacity. Can it rely on the partner to innovate and generate new knowledge in the domain? Will this knowledge help organization to improve the nature of its own business operations, and will such innovations be shared with the organization? These are important issues to consider before engaging in a knowledge-based relationship.

Once the right partner is chosen, we move on to crafting the agreement. Here, legal knowledge and knowledge of the operating environment are of paramount interest. Contracts, properly drawn up, can help all parties in the alliance by clearly stating assumptions, goals, and expectations. During this phase, it is important that tacit assumptions be spelt out. Often, this will call for lengthy debate and discussion, activities that should not be bypassed in the interest of hurrying up the alliance. A stitch in time saves nine – dialogue must be encouraged, so that all possible ramifications are clarified before the engagement is commissioned and formalized. It is also important for an organization to craft out an exit strategy on how to proceed if the engagement turns sour. Thinking about this upfront will lead an organization to be better prepared for the future, and also impact how the contract will be structured to account for contingencies. Organizations that do not spend time thinking things through leave many of the termination issues to chance, and can be taken hostage by the external entity owing to poor preparedness.

Managing the alliance

Once the alliance gets underway, our experience indicates that the initial phase can be characterized as bumpy and chaotic. Just how much will depend on the care executed in the preceding steps. Regardless of all possible diligence, a plan on paper is one thing, while getting operations going quite another. Consequently, organizations need to be tolerant, and work to resolve matters through an open-dialogue attitude. Knowledge must be shared effectively between the business partners during the initial phase to enable quick resolution of issues. Trust must be built between the partners. Effective knowledge sharing and openness are sure ways to build that trust and avoid a disastrous partnership.

After the initial period, knowledge sharing and management need to become routine and automatic, with procedures in place to dictate knowledge flows, contact personnel for knowledge, discussion or meeting times, personnel rotation mechanisms, and knowledge documentation practices. These procedures should be used to help knowledge move between partners and to govern the relationship. It is equally important that, over time, there is knowledge input to better help the knowledge management process and improve its efficiency. It is not sufficient to have processes that merely generate knowledge; knowledge must be used effectively to optimize the knowledge process. For instance, if the organization realizes that emails between its personnel and the alliance partner's are not being answered promptly enough, this knowledge must be used to devise a more effective communication protocol.

Alliance renewal or termination

Once a fixed milestone is reached, either at the end of a specified time period such as a year or six months or else at the end of the engagement in the case of short contracts, it is time to review the agreement and take the next steps.

If the alliance has been successful then the contract may be worth renewing, specially if there is high compatibility in terms of knowledge and resource sharing. A common mistake organizations make is being penny wise and pound foolish during contract renewal. Being extremely focused on minor cost savings as a quick way to renew a good business relationship is hardly sound practice. While the organization may be able to save a few dollars, it will immediately lose the trust and esteem of a good business partner.

Another common mistake is to compare an existing alliance to a hypothetical relationship. If an organization has a good relationship with company X, comparing the cost and benefits of a potential alliance with company Y is unwise. While anything can look good on paper, going through a relationship is where the rubber meets the road, so to speak. It is important to be conscious about the comparative factor so that knowledge generated is of value. A measurable comparison is the knowledge exchange range. Is the organization getting the same amount of knowledge as it is imparting? Is the knowledge of the same superior level? And is the knowledge useful? Obviously, if the organization is getting more than it is giving, things may be looking good, at least in the short term. However, in the long run, the external vendor may catch on to this discrepancy and resist sharing knowledge. On the other hand, if the organization is getting little for what it is giving, there must be a discussion to fix this and attain equality in knowledge exchange.

Knowledge that should be generated at the end of a milestone is comparing the performance of the business partners with the contractual agreements. Contracts always specify service level agreements (SLAs) that need to be evaluated to see if they were met. Serious violations of the SLA demand a termination of the agreement. However, if most SLA standards were met and there are only stray issues, a revision of the contract for improved knowledge exchange can resolve such issues.

In considering abrupt termination, the organization must seriously contemplate issues of knowledge loss and knowledge continuity. Instead of instantaneous terminations, it is better to phase down alliances, by reducing dependency on the alliance and then move towards termination in graded phases. Lowering the intensity of alliances gives the organization an opportunity to re-evaluate its needs, find a new business partner if warranted, and then commission a new agreement. Having backups in place and taking the time to document existing knowledge can also minimize knowledge loss. Regardless of the decision to terminate or continue the alliance, the organization must reconduct the need analysis process to examine how its current state and future definitions have changed, and such changes should be reflected in the new alliance engagement.

A dedicated alliance manager function

As indicated by Jeffrey Dyer, Prashant Kale, and Harbir Singh, organizations that had a dedicated alliance management function were able to claim greater returns on alliances than those that did not.[10] Dyer *et al.* remark: "The dedicated function coordinates all alliance-related activity within the organization and is charged with institutionalizing processes and systems to teach, share and leverage prior alliance-management experience and know-how throughout the company." We recommend that organizations follow this model.

Managing alliances is a knowledge-intensive activity. It is important that organizations have a methodology to (1) systematize the process of alliance construction, management, and termination, (2) manage their portfolio of alliances, and (3) learn from successful and failed alliance management efforts, so as to improve future efforts.

Managing knowledge effectively is central to achieving these outcomes. Lotus Corporation created what it calls its '35 rules of thumb' to manage each phase of an alliance, from formation to termination. Hewlett Packard developed 60 different tools and templates, included in a 300-page manual to guide decision-making in specific alliance situations. The manual included such tools as a template for making the business case for an alliance, a partner evaluation form, a negotiations template outlining the roles and responsibilities of different departments, a list of ways to measure alliance performance and an alliance termination checklist. The alliance function should help in both internal integration and external coordination activities. One approach is increasing the visibility of the alliance function. Rather than have the alliance function spread all over the organization, one group is responsible and accountable for such activities. Consequently, it must also have the authority to take charge of the alliances. Tacit knowledge must be passed through training and education programs.

As organizations become increasingly involved with multiple partners in simultaneous multiple alliances, understanding the synergies and constraints of multiple alliances becomes more important than ever. The success of an alliance no longer comes from managing an individual alliance, but depends on how organizations design and manage multiple alliances. In order to be successful here, an organization must have the capacity to import lessons learnt from prior and current alliances and apply such insights for current and future needs. Eli Lilly created an Office of Alliance Management (OAM) that facilitates the development and implementation of best practices throughout the company. Alliance management in the OAM is responsible for capturing and codifying knowledge about the management of their alliances for future references. Learning is critical to improve the management of alliances. The alliance management process can gain from feedback, both positive and negative. Lack of prioritization in such matters will result in repeated mistakes and continued failures.

Conclusion

External knowledge is becoming more important than ever if organizations are to be competitive enough in the current and future market. *Listening, linking,* and *leveraging* knowledge from external sources is an organizational imperative. In order to be successful at leveraging external knowledge, an organization must forge the right alliance with an external source. Managing the alliance will call for appreciation of the knowledge component. Unless an organization is concerned with how knowledge is created, transferred, moved, and applicable to its alliances, its benefits from such arrangements will be meager.

7
Engaging with Customer Knowledge Management

Businesses exist to serve their customers' needs. Customers can make or break or a business. Historically, an organization could design, build, and price a product without engaging the customer. Those days are long gone. Today, unless an organization can understand its customers' needs, transform those needs into products and services, and manage their relationship with customers, they will not survive in the marketplace. Why? In his most recent book, the strategy guru C.K. Prahalad and his colleague Venkat Ramaswamy identify several trends changing the way organizations manage customer interaction.[1]

Customers have greater access to information on products and services than ever before. As a result, organizations can no longer gain from information asymmetry – that is, from having more information on products and services than their customers. The internet and other technologies, like intelligent agents, allow customers to compare products and services on multiple criteria. Such product comparisons will hopefully lead to a more informed purchase. Customers are also no longer restricted to their geographical area when making a purchase, since the internet makes information available from all corners of the globe.

The internet has led to the creation of customer communities. A potential customer can turn to these communities to gain first hand-insights on product issues like bugs, warranty services, usage issues, and many more topics. The emergence of such communities has changed how customers are informed on products and services. In the past, the organization controlled the flow of information on their products and the most common method of information dissemination was through advertisements. Today, in addition to advertisements, customers have a forum in which they can seek information from peer users. The organization cannot control such information. Research has shown that customers value information from user communities more than information coming directly from the organization. Customers are more likely to share their opinions openly with peers since they are not being influenced by the product manufacturer and do not have ulterior motives in such a situation. Communities provide customers with a medium in which they can voice issues and promote activism. Product activist communities can be good or bad for an organization, depending on the issues of concern. America Online's AOL Watch has been bad for AOL since it has served primarily to illustrate problems, negative opinions, and complaints from former AOL customers. The Harley Davidson User Community has been good for the company in securing sales. Sales generated by referrals from current Harley riders are estimated to be as significant as those from the organization's paid advertisement programs. The Harley Community helps riders share routes and driving tips, plan and organize riding excursions, exchange knowledge, and interact with fellow riders. Potential Harley customers can ask seasoned riders questions and learn about their biking experiences. This positive activism has helped Harley retain its brand image and lure new customers. Potential motorcycle buyers are attracted by the fact that when riding a Harley, they are not just riding a bike but are members of a community of bikers with whom they can connect.

The internet has also made experimenting with products and services a popular concept. Customers today can often try a product or service before committing to a purchase; online vendors provide trial software versions, music samples, no-risk trial periods for services, and so on. In light of this culture of sampling, it has become more difficult to lock customers into a purchase before providing them a taste of what to expect from the product or service. Customers must have more knowledge now about the product or service before they are willing to make a purchase decision. This requires the organization to make such knowledge available in easily digestible formats, devise mechanisms that allow the customer a sense of the expected product benefits without releasing the entire product for free, and ensure that knowledge is openly shared with and received from the customer. When purchasing a book, a reader needs a synopsis, the author's credentials, the reviews, price and other pieces of knowledge to inform their purchase decision. One reason why companies like Amazon continue to be successful is the tremendous sophistication by which such information is presented to a potential buyer. Most electronic products today can be sampled over the internet. Book publishers allow readers to read a few pages of the text, usually the introductory material, to help the customer get a better sense of the product. Similarly, online music vendors provide song samples for their listeners. These mechanisms allow the user to get a sense of the product, but do not give the complete product away. Experimentation is the requirement of this constant knowledge exchange; knowledge must flow freely from the customer to the organization and vice versa.

Organizations must be more engaged with their customers than ever. They must more actively involve their customers in all phases of product development, marketing, testing, and selling. As noted by Prahalad and Ramaswamy, organizations must work with their customers to co-create product value.

In order to be successful, an organization must be able to manage customer knowledge. Managing customer knowledge is critical to ensure an organization's future. Anyone who fails to manage such knowledge could be out of business. But if they leverage customer knowledge they could begin luring their competitors' customers. Most organizations find it difficult to grasp the concept of customer knowledge management. One key reason is that it is hard to define. Just as the construct of knowledge management has many definitions and interpretations, customer knowledge management conjures a variety of reactions. To some, managing customer knowledge means leveraging customer data and information into actionable knowledge, to others it means using knowledge management to support customers, and to others still it is the process of eliciting and managing customer feedback. Which of the above is the true definition of customer knowledge management? All of them are!

Customer knowledge management must leverage three types of customer knowledge – *about* the customer, *to support* the customer, and *from* the customer. Most organizations incorrectly focus on only one type of customer knowledge. Moreover, even organizations that recognize the three distinct types of customer knowledge fail to appropriately integrate knowledge management activities across the three types. This inevitably leads to an incomplete customer knowledge management program.

This chapter highlights the three types of customer knowledge that must be managed to construct a comprehensive customer knowledge management agenda. We must stress that success in leveraging customer knowledge demands that an organization find ways to integrate all three types of customer knowledge. The chapter also discusses key challenges faced by organizations in attempting to leverage the various types of customer knowledge.

The customer

Before trying to engage in customer knowledge management, an organization must understand who their customer is. Identifying customers will depend on the defining question's context. Customers can be categorized according to a number of dimensions. Customers can be internal or external to the organization. To an IT help-desk team of the organization, the employees of the organization represent their customers. To the marketing department, the customers may be end consumers of the products and services. Customers can be individuals, businesses, or a combination of the two. IBM serves individual computer users, businesses, governments, and educational institutions. A corner delicatessen serves the individuals and local businesses that rent space for office parties. Customers can also be segmented on a temporal dimension. Many an organization has a group of customers that are permanent – those with whom long-term relationships have been established – and this is in contrast to its dynamic customers – those with whom the organization's relationship is more temporary. Customers also differ on the amount of knowledge or expertise they possess on the product or service. Those purchasing computers can be experts or novices, and managing the customer interaction with an expert will be different from serving a novice.

The above classifications are neither an exhaustive listing nor the only ones possible. However, the important issue is that an organization will have multiple definitions of a customer, depending on the context. Every organization (and units within the organization) exists to fulfill the needs of more than one type of customer. Actively engaging the customer will define how successful the entity is in achieving their objectives and missions. Each entity takes input from a *supplier*, processes this input, and then releases the finished product to a customer. The entity's value is normally tied to the internal and external value generated. The internal value is the income an entity can earn, the external value is determined by customer satisfaction. The internal value is generated by process efficiency, since efficiency can lower costs. External value, on the other hand, is tied to effectiveness – specifically, how effective the organization is in meeting the requirements of the external world, especially in serving its customers. The ideal entity will recognize and appreciate the customer dimension in every interaction. For example, the ideal human resource department will treat the organization's employees as customers and will aim to serve their needs holistically, just as a winery aims to serve the needs of both the connoisseurs and the novices who are interested in sampling their wines.

The three dimensions of customer knowledge management

Regardless of the customer in question, the three types of knowledge – *from, about*, and *to support* the customer – must be managed. We will explore each dimension in detail.

Knowledge about the customer

We can define knowledge *about* the customer as processed demographic, psychographic, and behavioral information. Knowledge about the customer is generated primarily through information processing activities. In the past, information available about customers was limited for two reasons. First, organizations thought they did not need to care about their customer's needs. This line of thinking can be best summarized by the original thinking present at giant automobile companies. Ford were willing to paint any of their cars "any colour – so long as it's black." This thinking was acceptable when there was little market competition and customers had limited choices. As time passed and competition grew fierce between organizations, gathering information about the customer became of paramount interest. In the automobile sector, American companies lost ground to their Japanese counterparts because the latter took great pride in gathering information about the customer, transforming the information into actionable knowledge, and devising suitable products that met those needs. For example, compact and affordable Japanese automobiles caught US customers, which surprised US automobile companies who had believed that Americans preferred a bigger car.

The second reason for the scant availability of information about customers was the unsophisticated nature of technology. A few decades ago, when you ran to the grocery store for a quart of milk and some bread, the cashier probably calculated your bill using pen and paper and then wrote you a receipt. The diffusion of calculators and basic cash registers helped improve the efficiency of this process, eliminated many of the errors in arithmetic, and provided the customer with a receipt for record keeping. Yet calculators and cash registers were still not able to capture the intricacies of your purchase. The grocery store owner had still to rely on observing the customer purchase to gain only approximate knowledge about the customer and the goods they chose to purchase or ignore. Barcode scanners and electronic cash registers came next. These tools helped not only streamline the process of capturing customer purchase data by lowering the number of errors in data capture, but also enabled the grocery store to track what goods were being purchased and in what combination. For example, the store could see if milk and diapers were typically purchased on one register ticket. Each item in the store had a unique bar code that could be used to track the product. Product identification helped the groceries compare the various brands of a product. For example, grocers could tell if Energizer batteries were selling better than Duracell. The only missing piece of the puzzle was a way to uniquely identify the customers who frequented the store.

More recently, the advent of grocery store cards and credit cards have helped refine the process of capturing customer data to include this final piece of the puzzle. Each customer was assigned a unique identification number on their store card and these cards enabled stores to capture the identity of individual customers and track their purchases. An individual store and the larger parent company could develop histories and profiles for each customer.

Grocery stores are not alone. Today, organizations have an abundance of information on customers. Customer information is collected from multiple sources like financial institutions, credit reporting agencies, and local stores. Information is collected about customers on a near-constant basis, whether they know it or not. We are able to gather information in finer detail. Online companies like Yahoo! record every click made by a visitor to their website; to this effect, they collect an estimated over 500 billion bytes of data daily. Information collection and identification devices like store cards and radio-frequency identification (RFID) devices enable organizations to collect accurate information on the purchasing behavior of customers. RFID devices can be attached to products in a grocery store to track their movement within the store. In addition to the sophistication of data and information capturing tools, we are able to record and store such information with ease because data storage media are so inexpensive now. Communication networks – like the internet – have also advanced in sophistication, and this advancement has made sharing information between entities more feasible and economical. Almost all organizations have begun to exploit the internet and its variants to facilitate information sharing. The end result of all these advancements is that customer information is available in a larger volume and in finer detail than at any other time in history.

Managing information overload

The abundance of data available on customers is certainly owing to technological advancements, yet nothing is free. The abundance of information has posed a new challenge to organizations: they must now avoid information overload. An organization must be able to extract relevant knowledge from the information stores in an effective and efficient manner. Unless knowledge is extracted from these information stores, they serve no purpose for the organization and it is impossible to inspect manually all the customer data an organization possesses to discover knowledge. Today, organizations must rely on technological solutions to sift through and process the vast quantities of information. Extracting relevant knowledge is conducted by processing the information through mathematical, statistical, and logical analysis techniques. Statistical analyses and, more recently, data mining are the most common. Statistical approaches include trend, regression, and cluster analyses. Statistical analyses test our pre-existing hypotheses. For example, if we think recently that milk purchases have increased, we can plot the number of quarts of milk sold and see if there is an increasing positive trend. Data mining seeks to uncover the hidden relevant patterns (that is knowledge) from vast amounts of information. It is not used to test hypotheses, but discovers latent patterns residing in the information store. Once patterns, trends, and insights are extracted, the use of automated report generation tools helps present the knowledge in a usable format.

TGI Friday's, a restaurant chain, used knowledge about its customers to redefine its food offerings.[2] The restaurant managers began to observe that customers were seeking more healthy options in their food orders; for example, they gave customers the option of replacing French fries with baked potatoes or green vegetables. The restaurant used data mining analysis on their point-of-sale data to uncover the patterns and combinations in how their patrons customized the standard offerings. The results of this study led to the creation of diet menu items. TGI Friday's signed an agreement with the creators of the Atkins Diet to offer low-calorie meals for the health-conscious customer. What TGI Friday's were able to achieve would have been impossible had their diners' customizations chosen food not been captured and analyzed.

Gathering knowledge about customers is a fairly straightforward task. Customer involvement is minimal since most of the information needed to generate knowledge is readily available and able to be captured without direct customer involvement. Credit card companies do not need to involve the customer to analyze purchasing behavior. The organization gets data and information on its customers regularly and can process the information easily. Knowledge about customers helps an organization gain a sense of its current customers and about its target population of customers. In the case of TGI Friday's, understanding current customers' eating patterns led the organization to modify its product offerings.

Customer churn

Analyzing customer information helps lower the *customer churn*, the movement of customers from one organization to another in search of better and cheaper alternatives. Customer churn is popular in saturated industries, where competition is fierce and customers have a wide selection of competitive choices. In the USA, recent regulation on wireless phone services has had many companies worried about customer churns. Prior to the legislation, a customer switching telecommunications carriers had to switch their mobile phone number too, a hassle that prevented many from changing their service providers and acted as a mechanism to lock customers. Today, a customer can switch telephone carriers without changing their number and this has given customers increased mobility among providers. Since the legislation was passed, customer churns have become a problem for the wireless industry. Customer churns can result in significant cost for the organizations, primarily in the activation and deactivation charges the telecommunications carrier pays. It is cheaper to keep existing customers than lose them to competitors.

Organizations have begun to thoroughly analyze their existing information on customer behavior to see how they can provide better alternatives that may prevent them from switching to a new provider. Most mobile phone companies in the USA have begun to offer users the option to personalize their telephone plans, on the basis of their peculiar usage behavior. In addition, most organizations now try to offer packaged solutions. A customer can, in many cases, get their cable, internet service, home telephone, and mobile phone bill from a single service provider. Getting customers to commit to a bundled service is beneficial to the organization since it increases the switching cost of a customer. For the customer, signing up for a packaged service will save costs compared with purchasing each item individually. Selling bundled products or cross-selling is one way to increasing the revenue per customer. Coffee shops sell coffee and pastries; movie theaters sell tickets, snacks, and drinks. Analyzing information on customer purchases can help an organization detect associations among products. Once an organization detects associations between two products, they can devise promotions designed to entice customers to purchase the two products together. Most coffee shops or restaurants offer products in sets. The cost of purchasing a value meal is lower than the cost of purchasing a burger, fry, and soda individually.

Unless an organization constantly monitors information and data on its current customers, it will be unable to detect emerging patterns of purchasing behavior and predict future purchasing trends. This will lead the organization to lose customers since it will unable to embrace future needs quickly. There are many classic failure stories of successful companies who lost a sizable market share to new companies because of their inadequate appreciation of customer knowledge. IBM suffered this fate in the personal computer market and Apple Computers gave Microsoft an open door that eventually shrank Apple's market share dramatically. Analyzing the information about current customers can open up avenues for targeting new products and services to existing customers and can increase the revenue stream per customer.

Attracting new customers

Knowing the customer is one thing; attracting new customers is more difficult. One reason why new products and services fail is the lack of adequate demand. Sony's expensive MiniDisc failed in the USA and WebTV failed to become popular as an internet access mechanism for households. An organization must expend appropriate efforts to create and carefully examine knowledge about *potential* customers before deciding how to market existing products and devise new products to meet their needs. Acquiring new customers is not easy, nor will it become easier in the foreseeable future. Customers will increasingly have more power to choose the offering that best meets their needs. The wise organization will study the vast amount of information available on potential customers to be effective in targeting customers. For example, Kevin had four different types of bank account in one large global banking organization; two of these accounts were traditional checking and saving accounts, while the remaining two were investment accounts. Kevin had an adequate number of accounts for his needs and was pleased with the bank's offerings; he even had a personal banker with whom he conducted most of his financial business. One afternoon, a telemarketer called trying to sell him a credit card account with a different financial institution. The marketer's efforts were futile, wasteful, and annoying. Why? The competing financial organization did not know there was a very low probability, based on his current bank's offerings, his service agreement, and his level of satisfaction, that Kevin would switch his four accounts to a new bank. The telemarketer could not offer anything of value beyond his existing services (in fact, Kevin would have lost services by switching); no economically rational individual would have taken the proposed offer. Lastly, the organization for whom the telemarketer worked had not studied and uncovered that Kevin had never made a purchase from a telemarketer. What is interesting is the following: a basic analysis of the credit history or rating on Kevin would have flagged Kevin as a low-probability potential customer and would have saved the company the cost of the cold call and its brand name (Kevin has a very negative opinion on this bank and warns all his friends about it).

Analyzing information on potential customers can help an organization better target its marketing messages and also lure potential customers. Customers, existing and potential, do not want to be sold products or services for which they have no use.

Currently we have a larger number of mediums through which customers can be solicited; however, the effectiveness of these media is still contested. We can send messages to customers through email, instant messenger ads, pop-up ads, and messages on their mobile phones. Despite the popularity of such ads, the chance of a customer committing to a purchase after seeing them is low. It is important to remember that sharing information with customers who do not solicit the information is never a good idea. Unsolicited emails, for example, are more of a nuisance than a valuable marketing strategy. While they may be successful in enticing the most noble and innocent customers into a sale, they will do significant harm to the organizational name and image. Most customers are irritated when they receive unsolicited email, since it clutters inboxes and distracts their energy and time from more important matters, and legislation is being considered in several countries, like those belonging to the European Union, that will make it a crime to send unsolicited email. While the cost of soliciting customers may continue to decrease – compare the cost of a TV advertisement with the cost of an email – remember that unless the customer's time and attention is respected and marketing campaigns are targeted carefully, such misgives are worthless and may hurt the organization. Countries belonging to the European Union, for instance, have taken serious stances against sending of unsolicited emails and have setup procedures whereby individuals can sue senders of nuisance emails. Permission marketing is the right approach. An organization must target customers who are willing to receive their information and will appropriately utilize it, rather than trying a blanket unsolicited marketing campaign.

Knowledge about customers helps an organization to improve product and service offerings to its existing customers and also to improve the effectiveness of attracting potential customers. Knowing customers helps us entice customers to purchase product and service offerings, but, once the sale is complete, an organization's success is based on how well it can *support* the customer in using the purchased products and services.

Knowledge to support the customer

Knowledge *to support* the customer is knowledge that improves the user experience with products and services. Managing knowledge that provides support for the customer requires an organization to leverage transaction data and information to personalize the pre-purchase, purchase, and post-purchase experiences. Ensuring a pleasant user-experience is critical for retaining customers. Organizations estimate that it is nearly five times more expensive to draw a new customer than to retain an existing one. As noted earlier, the growth of electronic markets and the ease of conducting commerce on the internet means it is even more important to ensure pleasurable user experiences.

Today it is difficult to completely differentiate a product based on its features alone. This results in a low degree of error tolerance for poor customer support functions. Organizations commonly imitate the industry leader. Hence, most competitive advantages based on differentiation are only temporary. The computing industry is a testament to this. All computer manufacturers produce almost similar products in terms of computing performance, features, styles, and so on. So how does a customer choose a Gateway, Dell, or other personal computer? The answers to this questions often lies in the quality of customer support – how quickly an organization can resolve customer queries and complaints. For example, not all organizations provide customer service personnel 24 hours a day, and for some purchasers, this will be an important feature of customer support; in the highly competitive marketplaces of today, a small difference makes the difference. A positive shopping experience can be a key differentiating factor for positioning products and services.

A historic tour of customer support

A quick look at the commercial history of customer support will provide some useful insights for today's organizations. In the early 1980s, if you had wanted to purchase a good audio system, how would you have gone about it? First you would have gone to the electronics store in your neighborhood. You would have surveyed your choices and their associated prices; the salesperson would have been knowledgeable in the area of electronics and would likely have shared this knowledge with you. Once ready to purchase the system, you would have paid for it, then used it. Had it broken, you would have taken it to the service and repair center and they would have fixed it. Simple! Yes, but at what cost? You would not have known if the audio system you had purchased was indeed the best model available since the local store may not have carried a particular make or model, and also it would not have been clear whether you had received the best deal, since comparing costs would have been difficult and you would often have been restricted to the local store for purchases. However, not all was bad; you would have had a good relationship with the store and trusted the sales personnel when making the purchase. In the past, it was rare to find an individual who lacked competency in a product or service trying to sell it. The same rules applied for purchasing a service, such as finding a house painter. You relied on word-of-mouth recommendations from your friends to find the most suitable person for your job. Seldom did you do an all-out price comparison to find the best deal or the most competent person. You relied on recommendations to vouch for a person's credibility and reliability. You relied on local knowledge and information to make purchases and receive post-sale support. In this local environment, you – the customer – were pleased with most purchases.

Shopping began to change a bit in the mid 1980s when it became popular to move products and services to the customer. You could order a product from a catalog and have it delivered to your home. Companies such as Sears and Lands' End led this commercial effort in the USA, while stores such as Mothercare led in the UK and abroad for catalog-based sales. You could call a number, or order by mail, and the goods would be delivered within 4 to 6 weeks, or longer for international shipments. You could pay for your order with a variety of payment options such as payment on delivery, money order, and so on. The variety of product choices available to a customer had increased, but it was still difficult to compare prices or information. Moreover, purchasing outside the locality requires you to spend time waiting for your product. Returning defective merchandise to the seller was time-consuming and a hassle. The catalog business did not affect the service business much at the time. For services, most people still went to the location of the service provider.

The first wave of the internet boom hit near the late 1990s. Consumers could purchase products and services over the internet. Geographical barriers and time constraints (such as store hours) were eliminated. Goods could be purchased from around the globe and at any time of the day or night. As information processing tools – like search engines and intelligent agents – increased, you became able to compare products using a number of dimensions: price, manufacturer, features and so on. One of the first intelligent product comparison agents was developed at Andersen Consulting (now Accenture) and was called Bargain Finder. Bargain Finder searched the posted prices of products on a number of manufacturers' websites and then summarized the information for a would-be purchaser. The consumer could then choose the best option and make a purchase. The first waves of the internet hype helped customers gain power and prominence in product sales and post-sales activities. No more could a company compete on information asymmetries. Customers could go to the lowest-price seller for certain goods and also seek out the highest-quality merchants. However, one thing was lacking: the sophistication of back-end services. Customers frequently ran into problems getting their orders – just ask anyone who got snipped by Toys"Я"Us making a holiday purchase in 2000. Many organizations failed to properly integrate their e-commerce systems with their traditional order processing systems, and consequently there were routine hiccups and issues owing to lack of synchronization. Moreover, many online vendors failed to work out all of the kinks in their logistic and distribution services. So while the first wave of the internet hype definitely gave consumers the chance to get an appreciation of the power of information, knowledge, and choices in products and services, internet shopping was not yet without its problems.

The internet business landscape of today is mature. Most people now order products online to save themselves the hassle of visiting a mall. It is unusual for a customer to experience logistical or distribution issues. The process of selling services has also been transformed owing to a mature internet. Take the healthcare industry for example. An individual can search medical information, research symptoms, find doctors, and even schedule appointments using the internet. Some mature healthcare providers also allow their patients to chat electronically with doctors and exchange emails with them about healthcare issues.

Organizations that survived the first internet wave realized that they must ramp up their pre-sales, sales, and post-sale efforts. Those organizations have realized that they must provide an all-inclusive, integrated customer service agenda. Today, companies like Barnes & Noble allow you to purchase a product online and return it at a local store if you are not satisfied. Companies like the electronics store Circuit City allow you to order your products online and pick them up from your local store. Best Buy, another electronic store, allows customers to use in-store kiosks to customize products, and thus provide the same flexibility as that available if purchasing on the internet. These flexibility enhancements have been possible because of large-scale efforts to integrate customer management systems, most notably customer relationship management systems.

Customer relationship management systems

Customer relationship management (CRM) systems are used to track interactions with customers and improve the delivery of products and services. Organizations have also embraced the internet as an avenue through which to deploy customer support knowledge. The internet is used to transmit product documentation, troubleshooting guides, repair manuals, and other forms of support knowledge. Some organizations have gone a step further and are now using the internet as an interactive medium to handle customer support queries. Through the use of chat rooms, emails, and structured reasoning systems, customers can find their queries answered and problems resolved online. For instance, most computer manufacturers have interactive web-based programs that allow their customers to find answers and debug problems with their products. For example, if you choose to purchase a Gateway computer, you can chat electronically with a sales associate who will walk you through the ordering process and answer any of your questions about customizing the computer.

While the use of automated and technology-enabled mechanisms for customer support knowledge delivery has increased in recent times, we cannot completely overlook the human element. Automated techniques work well for supporting well-structured and easy-to-solve problems, when there is little need for a detailed explanation of solutions and processes. For ill-structured problems and problems related to complex products, we still need to employ human agents to transfer and apply customer support knowledge. Take the case of the banking industry. Many had envisioned that the rise in internet banking would do away with bank tellers and reduce the staff of branches. This has not happened. While most individuals use the internet to conduct routine transactions such as paying bills, transferring funds, and so on, bank tellers are needed to help support customers who want to engage in complex transactions like choosing a retirement account. Moreover, highly valued customers and those with large portfolios are more accustomed to managing their finances through interaction with their personal bankers. These customers have established a history with their personal bankers; hence, the use of technology alternatives is very costly since it is difficult to encode the history into technology artifacts.

Personalization

One aspect of managing knowledge to support the customer requires an organization to personalize the shopping experience. Organizations can use transaction data and customer information to personalize the shopping experience, especially for those purchases conducted on the internet or through other electronic media like PDAs or mobile phones. For a frequent traveler making travel arrangements, entering their preferences into a ticketing system for every voyage is time-consuming and annoying. In the past, we would have gone to a travel agent who knew our preferences and would have made our arrangements accordingly. These travel agents were knowledgeable, not only about the various destinations, but also about our preferences: window seat, non-smoking, two double beds, make and model of rental car we prefer, and so on. Today, an electronic customer reservation system can handle many of these details. For example, the two of us made several writing excursions while preparing this text. Many of these trips required us to research various knowledge management issues and to simply write the text. During this time, we relied exclusively on the Hilton chain of hotels. The Hilton Honors customer system allows its frequent travelers to store histories of past stays, accumulate points for each stay, find suitable locations, provide descriptions of each hotel and its surrounding attractions, and interact with customer service representatives – a one-stop shop. Just as with any other sophisticated reservation system, you do not have to repeatedly enter your particulars and this makes scheduling the trip a bit more pleasant. Using your particulars, the electronic system can personalize the booking and travel experience. Moreover, in addition to using the system, we were very pleased with another fact. Of the nearly fifteen trips taken while writing the book, we frequented one particular hotel four times. We were thrilled by the fact that not only did the system remember our preferences, but so did the receptionist staff at the hotel. These individuals helped capture and apply knowledge not available in the system. They remembered that one of us liked the working desk to face the window and not the wall...yes we are picky writers! We share this example, as it shows the nicety that can occur when human customer support is integrated with the technology support. In the Hilton instance, the technology personalization helped ensure that we would stay at the Hotel and the human personalization of services ensured we would have a pleasant stay. Personalization is a viable method to lock customers into an organization's products and services.

Outsourcing customer support knowledge

The discipline of customer support is undergoing some dramatic changes because of the recent interest in outsourcing. Advances in technology and the low cost of communication mean we do not need to locate customer call centers with the customers. Today, most of the call centers are located in developing rather than developed countries. Simple economic dictates that, all else being equal, we must choose an alterative that offers the lowest cost to increase profitability. While outsourcing endeavors, especially those concerned with offshore outsourcing, will continue to rise in the foreseeable future, we must ensure that customers are happy with the service they receive. Some organizations have recently decided to withdraw some of their offshore call centers owing to low customer satisfaction. One of the main reasons cited for low customer satisfaction is the difficulty in communication with service personnel. It is our belief that these withdrawals are only temporary and that as we get more accustomed to competing and operating in a global and distributed landscape, there is no economic justification for keeping call centers in high-cost locations. We must remember that, to the customer, it does not matter where a call center is located if they are apt at solving and resolving queries.

Organizations must strive to be global in their approach to customer support, especially when it comes to call centers. Customers are global in their orientation; some may speak good English, while some others may have a good grasp of American English but have a hard time appreciating a conversation in a British accent. Again, for example, in the USA, anyone calling an 800 customer support number is restricted to speaking to service personnel in English or Spanish, so a Japanese- or Hindi-speaking tourist has no shot at all. If an organization seeks to expand its market globally, it must consider such issues. It must be able to support customers who have varied global orientations. The first steps are being taken on the internet today: most large organizations deploy their websites in multiple languages. One word of caution must be added here. It is important to appreciate the context in addition to the languages that connect with global customers. For instance, there are certain colors that are have distinct connation in a given culture; an organization must be trained enough to appreciate these subtleties so they can avoid offending a customer segment.

The future of customer support knowledge

We envision a future where there will be no physical call centers. Products will have in-built help and service functionalities and the internet will be way to resolve customer issues. For many products today, help functions are built into the product. For example, each new IBM notebook computer comes with "Access IBM." Access IBM is a software program that can resolve most computer issues without the need for human intervention. To reload software, just click the Access IBM button. You can also learn about computer maintenance issues such as backup and password issues, and so on. A similar mechanism, though less sophisticated, has been deployed in mobile phones and other electronic devices. The internet is emerging and establishing itself as *the* customer support platform. Owing to advancements in telecommunications, especially the increase in bandwidth, the deployment of video and voice technologies over the internet has become economical. In the past, it would take days to download a movie from the internet, today; an average cable modem can download a full-length movie in hours or minutes. Moreover, through technologies such as chat-rooms, messaging devices, and email systems, customer queries can be answered electronically by virtually contacting support personnel.

In summary, successful customer support demands that an organization manage knowledge and use customer information to enhance the quality of pre-sale, sale, and post-sale support. Organizations must ensure the user has a pleasant experience while consuming the product or service. Knowledge *about* and *to support* the customer have focused on leveraging data and information to generate customer knowledge. The final key component is eliciting knowledge *from* the customer.

Knowledge from the customer

Knowledge *from* the customer can be defined as the insights, ideas, thoughts, and information the organization receives from its customers. These insights can be about current products and services, customer trends and future needs, and ideas for product innovations. Knowledge from the customer is not the same as complaints or product queries. Queries and complaints fall into the *support knowledge* category; knowledge from the customer as discussed in this section elicits ideas and feedback from customers. Ideas for successful product innovations most likely stem from end-users and customers of the products and not from the within organizational quarters. As such, an organization must actively seek such knowledge to be better prepared to conduct product enhancements and innovations. It is important to design, manufacture, and sell a product that customers want, rather than trying to convince customers that they want a product. Listening to customers is important for successful innovations. For example, Hewlett Packard modified its Laser Jet V printer design by adding handles, after observing that more than 30 percent of its customers moved printers routinely.[3] Furthermore, HP noticed that women most often moved the printers and designed the handles to be large enough to prevent them from breaking fingernails.

User-toolkits

Customers know the products better than the organizations that produce them; as such, they represent a viable source of knowledge. Organizations have always struggled to find ways to tap into this source of knowledge; this knowledge's inherently "sticky" nature is the reason customers can never properly articulate their knowledge;[4] The language customers use to express their issues may not match the technical jargon used by the engineer who created the product. Designers and customers of information systems, for example, constantly engage in battles over design specifications because neither party can communicate optimally with one another. To address this issue, many organizations have deployed user toolkits that enable customers to innovate with products and services.[5] By using these toolkits, customers can directly innovate, modify, and customize products to meet their peculiar needs and preferences. PDAs, for example, are specifically designed to ensure that each customer has the ability to customize, modify, and personalize the tool to meet their peculiarities. Customers can format the design of the screens, change greeting messages and alerts, and download additional software as needed. Bush Boake Allen allows its clients – like Nestlé – to develop their own specialty flavors using an internet-based tool.[6] The customer can create a special flavor by using a database of flavors, and then send the new flavor design to an automated machine that will manufacture a sample within minutes. After tasting the flavor, the customer can make modifications and request a new sample. When the design formula is final, the customer can place a special order and receive their flavor.

Using toolkits reduces the burden on the manufacturer to conduct iterations to find the right flavor, reduces the time of the design cycle, and is a more effective way to elicit customer knowledge. The organization can focus its energy on deploying one artifact that can be customized by a wide-ranging user community, rather than by deploying individual solutions to meet the idiosyncratic needs of every customer. A toolkit must have four essential capabilities: (1) It must allow a customer to modify a product by conducting design iterations. (2) It must be user-friendly. (3) It must contain a library of existing components that a customer can use while designing and customizing the product. (4) It must have a help function that informs the customer how to conduct the customizations.

Tapping lead users

In addition to empowering customers, many organizations are now beginning to consciously tap into their "lead user" segments for knowledge. Research has shown that the present pressing needs of lead users will become requirements for other users in the marketplace within months or years.[7] Lead users have foresight (knowledge) that can help an organization better plan for product improvements and both incremental and radical innovations. Organizations have begun to host user conferences for the specific purpose of better understanding how customers utilize their products and how they customize or modify the products to meet their peculiar usage contexts. As products become more sophisticated, it is rare that we will find all customers using the products in a unified way. Most products have options for customization. For example, we can customize our computers to meet our needs. We can customize the settings on our cappuccino makers and the features that come with our automobiles. Understanding how users engage in these customizations opens an organization to possible product enhancements and innovations. Most software organizations consciously tap into their lead users to discover new routines, methods, and enhancements that have been conducted on the technology. These modifications, if they have a broad appeal, can be made part of upgrades or newer versions of the software. We will discuss user innovation to KMSs in Chapter 9.

Simple economics dictate that an organization cannot seek knowledge from all its customers; this is possible only in a boutique store or a small enterprise. To best choose the customer segment to be polled for knowledge, organizations must have mechanisms in place to adequately segment its customer base. Companies such as US West and FedEx can determine how profitable a given customer will be for them by examining historic cost information related to serving the various customer segments.[8] It would be wise for a company to expend proportionally greater resources to listen to customers that historically conduct a large volume of transactions and are repeat customers, than spending time polling temporary or non-routine ones. Customers who have repeated interactions with a product will be more cognizant of the product features, their current value propositions, and areas for future improvements. For example, if one interviews a pipe-smoking enthusiast, it will be clear that a pipe is not just a pipe. To a regular pipe smoker, his pipe has great value and is chosen for a number of features. The shape of the pipe, for instance, has bearings on how the smoke will flow and taste, and the texture has similar significance. Ask a novice about the design of a pipe and the chances are high you would not be able to elicit rich knowledge. For customers that purchase on an infrequent basis, it is important that an organization focus on using knowledge *about* and *to support* them to improve the chances that they will increase the volume of their purchases and become profitable.

We offer a word of caution about eliciting customer feedback. Many organizations spend an inordinate amount of resources trying to devise surveys, interviews, and so on to seek out knowledge from customers. It is important to note that such mechanisms are only as good as the questions they ask, the method by which they are administered, and their rationale. Questions framed incorrectly can bias the customer's response. We suggest an organization takes great care in devising the right questions to capture the information and that it also conducts extensive pre-testing before soliciting responses. The administering method is also a critical ingredient. If a customer is asked, for feedback while running to catch a bus their response will be useless. In fact, a large coffee shop chain once decided that it would offer customers free coffee to complete a brief survey. This was a list of 20 multiple-choice questions that would take, on average, two minutes to complete. Sounds reasonable, right? It would have been had they not chosen to conduct the survey during the morning rush. Most individuals were hurrying to work and filled out the survey without reading the questions, just to get a free coffee. In this case, the responses were worthless – a male respondent chose his sex as female, an executive chose his occupation as a student, and so on.

Finally, an organization must be clear about why they are eliciting customer knowledge. If it seeks feedback on customer preferences in products and services, the responses should not be used for making decisions about store locations. In fact, organizations routinely use customer knowledge gathered for one purpose to inform decisions in a totally different context, and this mistake can be fatal. Asking a customer questions about product preferences or features may have very little to do with customer churn management. Reichheld's research found that customers who describe themselves as satisfied are not necessarily loyal; 60–80 percent of defecting customers described themselves as "satisfied" or "very satisfied" in their last survey prior to purchase.[9] Valuable knowledge in one context may be absolutely useless in another. An organization should not be miserly about allocating resources when eliciting knowledge from customers; knowledge from customers is an asset and must be treated appropriately.

Customer engagement platforms

Organizations have also begun to create platforms where users can interact and engage in dialogue. Amazon, Barnes & Noble, and many others have set up dedicated portals and avenues on their websites for users to share reviews on products. This helps in building a sense of community for the users and provides future customers with information to make better purchase decisions. The organization can use these insights to decide which products to stock and which to abandon owing to their poor quality. While fostering dialogue between customers is important, it is also important to engage and promote discussions between organizational members who have access to customers. Siemens Information and Communications Network's ShareNet system allows sales personnel to share their experiences, tips, and insights; this has led to increased revenues in the £17 million range by increased success identifying opportunities for new or joint businesses and development.

The managing of knowledge *from* the customer has a greater human element than managing the other the two types (knowledge *about* customers is almost completely leveraged via the use of technology, and knowledge *to support* customers has a balanced mix of technology and human components). Technology plays a support role in the management of knowledge *from* customers; human interaction plays the primary role. An organization requires the human ability to comprehend the incoming knowledge about novel ideas and potential product innovation. In comparison with the other two types, knowledge *from* the customer is high in equivocality. Engaging such knowledge calls for a rich interaction between source and recipients. In pursuit of such valuable knowledge, most organizations try to promote rich human-to-human interactions.

The customer knowledge management construct

Collectively, the three types of knowledge (about, to support, and from) make up the CKM construct (see Figure 7.1). Each of the dimensions of customer knowledge needs to be managed optimally. Unless an organization can show competency in leveraging all three components, its CKM agenda will be have an inherent weakness.

Management efforts in each dimension have a bearing on the other dimensions. If an organization is unable to utilize its knowledge about customers to devise appropriate products, it will fail miserably in deploying support knowledge or in eliciting knowledge from customers. Similarly, if it does not adequately deploy customer support knowledge, this will lead to hostility from the customers and they will avoid sharing knowledge. If an organization does not listen to the knowledge provided by customers, it will lose market share and not be able to gain from their customer knowledge. Hence, an organization cannot completely ignore any of the three types of

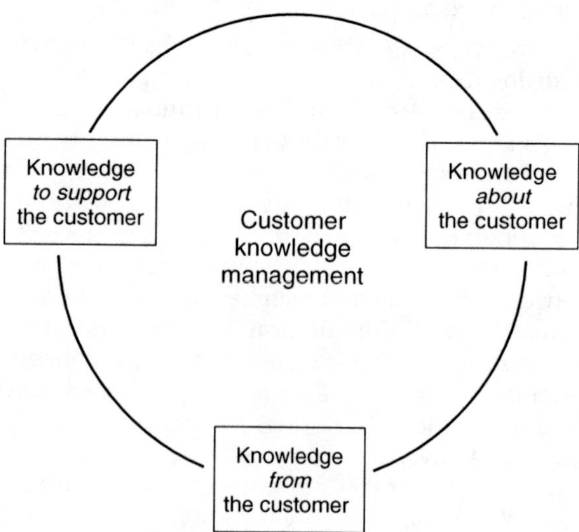

Figure 7.1   The customer knowledge management construct.

customer knowledge. However, depending on an organization's strategic orientation, competitive strategy, and industry characteristics, an organization may weigh the management of one type of customer knowledge heavier than another. An organization that focuses on being a low-cost provider of products in a mature industry will focus more effort on managing knowledge about customer and supporting the customer. Knowledge from the customer will be of lower interest, since the organization's focus is not on innovation but on sustaining its current position in the industry. However, if an organization is competing in a dynamic industry like the current technology sector, it must focus intensely on managing knowledge from its customers so that it is able to innovate successfully.

Challenges in leveraging customer knowledge

Customer knowledge management is not what it was just a decade ago. The rise of internet technologies, the resulting sophistication of products and services, globalization, and other factors have changed the face of customer knowledge management. To leverage customer knowledge adequately, several challenges need to be addressed: (1) segmentation; (2) integration; (3) distribution; (4) application.

Segmentation

The ability to segment, as discussed previously, is critical to conducting optimal knowledge management. Segmentation calls for the separation, categorization, and classification of objects. In the context of knowledge about customers, we must segment the data and information we possess on customers. We must segment information before we analyze it; failing to do so will prevent us from extrapolating rich knowledge on specific clusters of customers. For instance, segmenting customers by their income levels could lead to a richer analysis of predictive buying behavior than were we to lump all customers together and then try to predict buying behavior. Similarly, we can segment customers by geography, expertise levels, age, and many other factors. Segmentation is essential because it provides a rich understanding (knowledge) of our customers. Through segmentation, we are able to classify and categorize customers according to certain features. These features, if managed appropriately, will help us better serve the customers. For example, were we to segment our customers by disposable income, and analyze their inclination to purchase our products, we could learn how we might position the product better by improving our marketing campaigns or how we could provide lower-cost alternatives if the customers are price-sensitive. Today, we are able to collect vast amounts of customer information on a number of attributes; the challenge is to choose the right categories (attributes) into which to segment the data prior to analysis. We must recognize that attributes used to segment customer data are transient and dynamic. What is a key attribute today may not be important tomorrow. Several years ago, access to the internet was considered a significant attribute. However, the pervasiveness of internet connectivity has rendered this significance nearly obsolete.

In the context of knowledge to support customers, we must appreciate that not all customers behave and interact with products the same way. Customers differ in their degree of knowledge and expertise with products and services; this dramatically affects their interaction with the products and services. Knowledge management efforts targeted to support customers need to be cognizant of these differences. An organization must be able to clearly segment and target knowledge management efforts to meet the needs of the different customer segments. If both a novice and an expert make computer purchases, the novice will need more support since they will not have the necessary knowledge to manage the purchasing decision. The novice will need to be provided with knowledge to choose a computer based on their usage needs. They will need help framing their questions and help getting the technology operational. By comparison, the expert will have a good idea of their computer needs; they will, however, have complex questions about intricate hardware and software features. Providing the same level of knowledge to both customer groups will result in a frustrating user experience for both individuals. Organizations must find ways to better understand who is being served and to apply the right knowledge management strategy. An experienced customer feels irritated when treated like a novice. One of the managers we interviewed put a frustrating customer's experience succinctly:

> I am an IT manager [the customer], I have been using technology and managing it for over two decades; why is this kid [the customer service representative] giving me the litany on computer hardware? Just take my order and don't screw it up!

Capturing information on customer experiences, past history, place of usage, level of usage, and other details for products might be a good place to start when trying to sense the customer's background in order to provide them with the right kind of knowledge in most appropriate way. In addition to segmenting customers, the organization must be able to segment its knowledge delivery personnel. Not all customer service personnel will have the same experience handling customer queries. It is likely that those who have a longer tenure with the organization are more apt at handling complex calls than those new to it. It is essential for an organization to have an adequate process in place to route knowledge queries to the right person. It will be unwise to have an experienced customer service professional handle a simple problem that can be answered by a novice customer service representative. It will be ineffective for a novice to handle a complex query since they will not be able to provide the right answer and will eventually need to route the call to a technical expert. Efficiently segmenting knowledge delivery personnel can lead to quicker resolution of the problem and better customer service. Moreover, it will allow for experienced customer service professionals to spend their time training novice professionals, rather than answering routine customer queries.

In the context of knowledge from the customer, the organization must be able to segment its users according to how they consume the product and service. A common classification scheme used to segment technology users is: beginners, intermediates, experts, and super-users. Segmenting users in this manner gives the organization a better sense of how to manage the incoming knowledge from each group. Lead users or super-users will have extensive knowledge about the product; incentives should be made available to these users to get them to share their knowledge with the organization. By contrast, beginners will need to be provided with more support and it is best not to make them the focus of knowledge-eliciting efforts. The organization can also set up various user communities based on the different user segments, and this will help users facing similar problems interact with their peers. Building user communities is an apt way to foster dialogue between various product users. If used properly, the community can be a viable source of advertising and goodwill and can help build trust, not only among community users but also in the organization; however, if poorly set up, such a community can lead to the organization's quick demise since bad news will spread faster than good.

Integration

Integration is the act of assimilating dispersed and diverse entities. In the context of knowledge about customers, we must be able integrate the various repositories of customer information. Customer information is collected and housed by multiple organizations: banks, credit reporting agencies, work places, grocery stores, credit card companies. The organization must be able to integrate the various information objects received from these disparate sources to create a unified view of the customer. Failure to do so could lead to conflicts in the analysis of customer information, an analysis predicated around incorrect or missing data, and an inability to understand customer information. Triangulation of information is a salient task. It is rare to find synchronization in customer information coming from multiple sources; it is more common to find discrepancies. These discrepancies need to be high-lighted and addressed before conducting an analysis. The Bank of New York went through a turbulent process while trying to integrate its customer information. Through a process of over 80 acquisitions, the bank had amassed thousands of institutional customers and well over 700,000 retail customers. Integrating the massive amount of customer information proved a challenge. The bank had customer data scattered in many different applications, databases, and business groups. As a result, sales personnel found it difficult to provide services since each locality could see only a local view of customer information.

Existing customers were called and solicited for new business. Opportunities for cross-selling and for providing packaged solutions were not detected or managed. Customer support was a disaster. In March 2004, the bank introduced a centralized system to manage customer information. The new system can be better used to extract knowledge about customers and manage customer relationships.

In the context of knowledge to support the customer, the challenge is to integrate the various channels, media, and methods for delivery of support knowledge. In the past, customers were restricted in the media and channels they could use to seek information about products and services. Today, information and knowledge can be accessed using the internet, telephone, mobile phones, PDAs, mobile computers, and many other devices. An organization must ensure that it can support its customers through an assortment of media and it must be able to communicate its knowledge to customers in multiple languages and across multiple contexts. Customer support systems must be compatible with multiple environments, platforms, and systems. For example, an organization must be able to support both Windows and Macintosh environments; in addition, it must be able to use both the non-metric and metric scales. It is even more important for the organization to integrate its support functions so that customers get near-similar support experiences regardless of the access medium they choose. Some organizations have begun to appreciate the concept of integrating channels. Stores such as REI.com and CircuitCity.com allow their customers to place their orders on the internet and retrieve the items from local stores. This is attractive for customers who do not want to spend time waiting for mail delivery or to pay shipping charges, and also helps the organization attract web customers to their local stores. Customers are also allowed to return items to their local store, rather than dealing with the hassle of shipping it back to a warehouse. These organizations have noticed that integrating channels allows them to better meet customer needs and service them better. For this type of integration to succeed, it is essential for the organization to have connectivity between their information systems.

Finally, the integration of knowledge is key. In the past, a bookstore's sales personnel were knowledgeable about the books on the shelf. If you wanted to know about an author or where a particular book was shelved, they would be able to show you the right location. In most chain bookstores today, sales associates likely do not have such a rich knowledge base. Sales personnel depend on databases to help them locate books in the stores and for other information. As such, it is vital that the databases they use have accurate and timely information. As mentioned in Chapter 6, Borders, a large US bookstore chain, teamed up with Amazon.com to manage their online bookstore. We decided to do a little experiment. We chose several book titles and checked their particulars using both an in-store kiosk and the Borders internet site run by Amazon. We found 10 percent of the titles had different information on the two data stores. For instance, one title was priced at $61 if ordered in the store and $75 if purchased on the internet. The correct price of the book was $75. Some titles were annotated as "out of print" online and were listed as forthcoming books by the in-store kiosk. This is a case of poor integration of knowledge between business partners and it will cost the organization revenue. If an organization is going to ally with a business partner, it is has to make sure that information provided to the customers is in sync; a customer who receives two different answers to a simple query will not have a positive experience and will see the organization as fragmented.

In the context of knowledge from the customer, the organization faces the challenge of integrating various units of the organization that must attend knowledge from the customers. It is not sufficient for such knowledge to stay within the marketing domain. The knowledge must be shared with product engineering, research and development, and the customer service departments. Unless knowledge from the customer is integrated and shared across the various units, its use will not be optimal. In addition, building user communities requires the organization to create mechanisms whereby it can integrate and foster communication between product users. Integrating the various types of users is important to resolve inconsistencies in knowledge. If we ask three experts how they think we should redesign a product component, we will probably receive three different answers – all of which may be right. If we frame the problem to the three experts as a team or community, they will work together and resolve any discrepancies and develop one solution to our problem. When they cannot come up with one solution, the community will still have the ability to evaluate alternative solutions and try different models. The end result will provide more crisp, refined, and tested knowledge. Also knowledge from customers must be integrated with the extant literature available in external sources (see Chapter 6 for in-depth coverage on external sources of knowledge). By example, academicians and consultants publish working papers, journal articles, and conference papers; these may provide valuable insights into knowledge from customers. An organization must look outside its boundaries for knowledge from customers and try to integrate the knowledge with the insights they possess. Outsiders can also provide new insights that are not available in-house. Harley Davidson routinely asks marketing professors to help them understand and interpret customer knowledge. It is also not bad to collaborate with competitors, especially in extracting customer knowledge. Mercedes and Swatch have entered into an alliance to develop the Smart car, in addition to collaborating on innovations; they are sharing their unique perspectives of knowledge from the customer to gain rich insights.

Distribution

Distribution calls for movement of knowledge within and across the organization. The challenge of distribution in the context of knowledge about the customer is to communicate such knowledge in usable formats to the various sectors of the organization. Different organizational sectors will have different requirements and uses for the knowledge. The engineering department would need to know how much customers are willing to spend on a product and use this knowledge to constrain design considerations; the marketing department will need to know how to position the product in the marketplace. Unless we are cognizant about these different needs, we risk subjecting the staff to information overload. This will lead them to abandon such knowledge and work without it, preventing the knowledge from informing and improving the organization. One of the challenges organizations face is to appreciate the different languages of its departments. Engineering terminology is different from the terminology of marketing or finance. It is not uncommon to find different terms being used to describe a single concept. Reports on knowledge about the customers need to account for these language differences by translating the knowledge into multiple terminology sets depending on the reports' users. Reports can be distributed to the users using push or pull mechanisms. Some of the knowledge about customers will need to be pushed to organizational members by pre-defined reporting schemes. Organizational members will also need to have the flexibility to pull knowledge to meet their specific tasks and the ad-hoc problems they face. This will require organizational members to have access to knowledge repositories and the ability to extract knowledge quickly. By example, one organization we consulted for had a large mobile sales force. The sales force was accustomed to making sales during personal visits to the client offices. In 2000, sales personnel were provided with laptops to enable them to record the sales instantaneously, show clients presentations, make brochures available electronically, and even conduct product documentation. One of the most salient reasons why the organization provided the laptops was to have the sales personnel interact with the knowledge base of the organization and answer client queries on the spot. To do so, the each salesperson had to connect their laptop to the local internet connection at the client site to access the database via a secure protocol. Six months after the program was commissioned, the organization gathered the access statistics of their knowledge base and found that less than 10 percent of the sales personnel had accessed the knowledge from an off-site location. The reason was simple – the database's search and access times were too high when accessed off-site. The organization had never run a test to see how long it would take to pass through security protocols and execute a search query off-site. Providing access to the knowledge base is important; however, the cost of accessing the knowledge base should be low for employees to take the time and use the knowledge.

In the context of knowledge to support customers, the critical concern is the timeliness of knowledge delivery. It is useless for an organization to have a large knowledge repository if it cannot answer a customer's question quickly. Customers want their queries answered in real time. An organization must ensure that knowledge can be accessed instantaneously. Moreover, the organization has an additional burden in ensuring the available knowledge is current. Delivering outdated knowledge reflects poorly on the competencies and the abilities of the organization.

Continental Airlines experienced the advantage of a current knowledge database.[10] We've all had a frustrating experience while flying: the flight was delayed or overbooked, our luggage was lost or damaged, or we may have experienced all of these frustrations on one flight. Frustrating airline experiences lead customers to switch frequently between travel providers. In the current economic times, airlines cannot afford to lose their customers – especially the patrons who fly frequently and on their more profitable segments. Continental Airlines developed a knowledge management system to help leverage customer knowledge to improve service delivery. One function of the system is to arm its flight attendants with knowledge about frequent travelers on the aircraft, their likes and dislikes, their past flying histories, and these individuals' experiences with previous flights; this knowledge can help the attendants provide better customer service. For instance, if the airline loses a customer's baggage and the attendant knows that customer has had a similar experience in the past, the attendant can make accommodations to compensate for the unfortunate experience and foster goodwill. If a business or frequent traveler's flight is delayed, an airline attendant can decide whether it would be better to put the passenger on a competitor's flight to preserve their business or ask them to wait and inconvenience their personal agenda. Using the system, Continental Airlines has seen an increase of $200 in spending from its valued customers and $800 from its most profitable clientele.

In the context of knowledge from the customers, the challenge is to quickly apply insights gleaned from customers in order to save organizational resources and make timely product enhancements and innovations. For instance, consider the case of customers innovating with software. Microsoft routinely taps into knowledge from customers to provide patches, fixes, and bug cleaners. The company must act quickly on knowledge provided by the customers to prevent unscrupulous individuals from attacking the vulnerabilities of its software. Knowledge from the customers can be acted upon quickly only if the organization has a process in place to route incoming knowledge to the right decision-makers. Also, providing a timely fix or product enhancement will result in lower call loads at the customer center and will also improve customer satisfaction, while if problems are not fixed quickly, customers will lose their confidence in the organization's ability to service their needs.

Application

The most serious concern in applying knowledge about customers is privacy. How does an organization use the information and knowledge gathered from its customers? Customers will share knowledge and information with organizations they trust. Trust can be in two forms: trust in the organization and trust in the way the organization will utilize the knowledge. Customers will be willing to share information if they believe the information they provide will help the organization improve customer support, products, and services. Customers are reluctant to share information if they believe the information will be used in unscrupulous, unauthorized, and hidden ways. An organization needs to have a clear statement about their intent in collecting knowledge from customers and how they plan to use that knowledge. It must clearly state and disclose any secondary uses of collected customer information.[11] Failure to do so could make the organization vulnerable to legal problems and a loss of customer trust. We must remember that access to customer information and knowledge is a privilege and treats it as such. If we misuse this privilege, by sending SPAM or by making unsolicited calls, we risk alienating the very people we are trying to attract.

In the context of knowledge to support customers, a focus of many organizations is to make the delivery of customer knowledge more interactive. Internet channels should not be used to display static customer knowledge; rather, they should be enabled for interactivity using video and voice technologies. Moreover, advancements in artificial-intelligence-based computation will also help make these applications more intelligent and smart. We must remember that while information can be delivered in a static manner, knowledge is interactive and dynamic and must be delivered vivaciously.

As mentioned earlier, personalization is another important consideration in delivery of support knowledge.[12] Not all knowledge possessed by an organization about its products and services will be relevant for each user. Each user needs only a small part of the organization's knowledge. An organization must build mechanisms that enable users to personalize their views of an organization's knowledge repository. Most organizations have already begun to take the first steps toward this personalization. Today, users can enter the details of the product they have purchased, the way they use those products, their skill level, and other information into customer support portals. This information helps the organization push relevant knowledge to the user according to their peculiarities.

A word of caution: if the customer feels that personalizing the customer support portal requires a significant investment of time and resources, the chances are high that they will abandon the effort. A common mistake committed by organizations is in requiring customers to complete lengthy surveys while personalizing the portal. Long surveys are an excellent way to deter customers from completing personalization efforts. As a rule, organizations are better off obtaining piecemeal information from the customer. Reusing knowledge is also an important challenge. Organizations do not want to constantly need to recreate the same knowledge (we discuss this issue in a later chapter). It is vital that an organization take steps to build a knowledge repository so it can reuse knowledge. Other than the obvious benefit of saving money and time, a knowledge repository also allows the organization to provide customers with one knowledge view, so that regardless of who answers a customer query, the customer will receive the same answer. A customer should never receive two answers (for example, one provided by the internet and a different one from a customer service professional) to the same question. If a customer calls a customer specialist about a problem and the customer has already checked the corporate website, the customer service specialist should not reiterate information presented on the web. Reiterating such knowledge will frustrate the customer because calling the specialist will seem like a waste of time. Instead, the service representative must figure out what other knowledge could be used to solve the problem.

It is imperative that knowledge to support the customer increase customer value. One way to conceptualize customer value is the difference between "customer-perceived benefits" and "customer-perceived costs."[13] Perceived costs like searching for a product, getting service or queries answered, handling warranty information, and so on can be lowered by providing knowledge to the customer about how to conduct these tasks effectively and efficiently. Moreover, by providing such knowledge, an organization can also increase the perceived benefits of a product or service. If a computer manufacturer provides its customers with a rich array of knowledge on how to integrate its devices with other peripherals, training on how to use software, and a community of fellow-users, the organization contributes to increasing the perceived benefits of the computer. Quite frankly, this is what will eventually differentiate market leaders like Dell, IBM, and others from the laggards and those on the brink of extinction.

In the context of knowledge from customers, the challenge is to view customers as co-producers of knowledge. This is more important for organizations with business customers, but is also applicable for organizations that serve individual or personal customers. When engaging with a customer, an organization must see it as an opportunity to produce new knowledge in collaboration with their customers. Management consulting firms have engaged in this behavior since their inception. To be successful at co-producing knowledge with customers, the organization must be selective in how it chooses its customers. It must seek customers who have open knowledge sharing cultures, are willing to engage in learning and knowledge creating activities, and are willing to share a certain amount of risk.[14] Organizations must be ready to learn as well as to teach. Organizations should be less receptive to taking on customers who are unwilling to co-produce knowledge, since the cost of engaging these customers will be high. While every bit of revenue increases profitability, not every revenue stream is equal in expended costs and effort. All else being equal, it is better to engage a customer who is willing to share, learn, and create knowledge than one that is hostile and closed to knowledge sharing. Organizations must begin to embrace the principle that value can only be co-created with customers, not in isolation.

Conclusion

Managing customer knowledge is a strategic imperative, not an operational chore. Most organizations know the value of their customers. However, many organizations overlook the need to be systematic in how knowledge is elicited, processed, and shared with customers. Overlooking knowledge management dimensions leads to ineffective and inefficient interactions with customers. The end results lead inevitably to disgruntled and disappointed customers who are likely to switch to a competitor's offerings. Customer knowledge, if managed optimally, can help an organization differentiate its products and services. Managing and deploying customer knowledge effectively can increase the value a customer receives from a product and service and reduce the cost of deploying the product and service to the customer – it is a win–win situation. Engaging with customers is a must, and *knowledge* is the key to successful engagement.

8
Engaging to Construct Knowledge Markets

Malls and markets are part and parcel of our daily life. Imagine life without designated markets. Where would we go to purchase a quart of milk or a pint of ale? Additionally, consider life without the regulations that govern markets. How do we verify that the can of soup we purchase actually contains the stated ingredients? How do we know that the sign 'Closeout Sale' signifies a bargain? While most of us take the existence of markets and their regulators for granted, life would be very difficult without them.

A market can be defined as a collection of buyers and sellers who interact to exchange goods and services. Markets are systems of exchange.[1] Exchanges can be either altruistically or economically motivated. Altruistic motivations lead to unequal exchanges, where one entity – an individual or an organization – exchanges services with another entity at no cost, or at miniscule cost. Volunteer and non-profit organizations are examples of altruistic markets. Economic markets, on the other hand, are governed by equality, where all parties involved in an exchange must contribute some resources to the transaction.

History tells us that economic markets began as the barter system – goods for goods. Individuals exchanged the goods they produced for those that they needed but could not produce. For example, a farmer would exchange wheat for wool. Over time, markets graduated to a price system, made possible by the emergence of currencies that provided individuals with a common unit on which to govern exchanges. The governing dynamics of markets have changed very little since the early days of currency usage. Instead, the behavior of buyers and sellers has changed, given the advancements in information technology.

An 'electronic market' is one that is conducted or facilitated using technology; this kind is found most commonly on the internet. Examples are Amazon.com and eBay.com. Before electronic markets, we were restricted to making purchases locally. Today, we can purchase goods from around the world using the internet. In the past, buyers had limited information on the market. Today, we can use the internet to search for numerous products, make comparisons, negotiate with multiple sellers, and then make the purchase within minutes.

While the internet has dramatically improved the way markets operate, the fundamentals remain firmly rooted – to make a profit, sellers need to receive a price that is higher than their production cost and lower than the buyer's intended utility for the goods or services. Electronic markets are adept at bringing technological and human issues together in speedy and integrated collaboration. While sophisticated technology enables electronic markets, these markets retain the human and traditional elements of the buying experience such as searching, negotiating, exchanging payments, and receiving the product or service. A buyer can engage in the same kinds of behavior through the use of various technologies. The only difference is that in an electronic market these processes are much faster.

In this chapter, we will discuss a variant of the electronic markets: the knowledge market. Our discussion will focus on economic markets instead of altruistic ones. We assert that the knowledge market is to twenty-first century organizational knowledge management what the campfire was to prehistoric storytellers: a place for all organizational and cultural knowledge to be preserved and promulgated.[2] Just as we cannot imagine life without a neighborhood mall today, knowledge markets will become an integral part of our future. Knowledge, the critical resource of our times, will be priced and exchanged, and workers will be compensated through this knowledge currency.

Why have knowledge markets?

Current knowledge management agendas in organizations operate under the assumptions of altruism, leading to several problems. Knowledge markets can aid in alleviating these problems.

The first problem is knowledge valuation. Markets allow us a way to value goods and services. In a grocery store you know how much a carton of milk costs. However, in an organization you seldom know the real value of knowledge. How much is Jill's idea worth? Are John's skills of value to the organization? These are difficult questions to answer. In our current organizations, besides receiving a paycheck and an occasional bonus, employees are not rewarded for what they know. Since current reward systems focus on what the employee does, *doing* is valued more than *knowing*. We do not want to undermine the value of doing; after all, actions convert knowledge into operations. However, we must also reward employees for what they *know*, the skills they bring to the organization, and the knowledge they produce and share with it. Knowledge markets provide us with a means to take a stab at the problem of *knowledge valuation*. Knowledge producers can then be provided with incentives for taking the time to document their know-how. These incentives can be part of their performance reviews and annual evaluation.

The second problem is one of *knowledge contribution*. Today, knowledge in organizations is taken for granted. In most organizations we see the prevalence of the 80/20 rule: 20 percent of the employees provide 80 percent of the knowledge to run the organization. Yet they are seldom rewarded. The lack of incentives leads to a system of disincentives. The people who contribute their knowledge and share it do so under the assumption that the rest of the organization will follow suit and share knowledge. However, owing to lack of overall participation in knowledge management, the original producers do not get the return on their investment of time and energy spent codifying their insights. After all, their effort produces knowledge for consumption by their peers, not themselves. As we will discuss in the forthcoming sections, internal knowledge markets, that is markets within an organization, force one to participate in order to receive knowledge. Participation can take a variety of forms. In internal knowledge markets, to purchase a nugget of knowledge a buyer must be able to pay the price requested by the seller. The buyer can earn points by contributing knowledge to the system. Hence, anyone who wants to get some knowledge from the market must be ready to give some knowledge to it.

The third problem is one of *collaboration* and engagement between knowledge workers. Knowledge markets provide employees with a space to interact. Just as going to the mall allows buyers to engage with sellers, a knowledge market allows employees the space to exchange their knowledge. Today, knowledge is exchanged through private interaction. For example, if John needs a document from Mary, he will email her and request the document. This arrangement has several problems. First, Mary is not formally rewarded for possessing and sharing requisite knowledge. At best, she can assume that if she needs a favor in future, John will understand and help out. Second, other members who may not know Mary will not know that such knowledge exists in the organization and might spend time and effort recreating it, resulting in wastage of organizational resources. Now consider the case where an organization has a knowledge market. Mary can post her knowledge object on the market. Potential buyers can then purchase it from her for a designated price. Besides helping Mary to understand the value of her knowledge object, this interaction gives the organization a way to track and manage the flow of knowledge.

The space provided by the market can be used to facilitate dialogue. Buyers can post comments and reviews on knowledge artifacts. Sellers can engage with other knowledge producers to build better products that are a result of their combined competencies. Exchanges between buyers and sellers help develop trust among market participants. The creation of dialogue is an ideal way to build a knowledge-sharing culture for the organization. This is akin to going to your favorite store or mall for a pleasurable experience, where you have people ready to help you with your needs, you feel that you have made fair purchases, and your needs have been met. Similarly, knowledge exchanges in organizations must meet the conditions of a gratifying shopping experience.

Overall, the knowledge market makes knowledge management a formalized program that aids in legitimizing knowledge management within the organization. The above issues pertain to leveraging knowledge within the organization; the internal knowledge market will help address the issues. However, internal knowledge markets are not the only kind of knowledge markets.

Knowledge markets – types and components

We define a knowledge market as a logical space where buyers and sellers can exchange knowledge products and services. It is important to note that we are concerned here with a *logical* space, such as the internet, and not a *physical* space such as the office building. Owing to advancements in information technology, a knowledge market, like an electronic market, can be housed exclusively in a logical space with several advantages. For one thing, market participants do not need to meet physically at a location. This opens up the avenue for the global participation of buyers and sellers. Market interactions can be handled virtually. Another dual advantage is that the market can operate 24/7/365 and yet be more cost-efficient.

Types of knowledge market

A knowledge market can be classified according to the market maker, who is the entity responsible for setting up the market. Having the requisite infrastructure, inviting buyers and sellers, and determining the rules of the market are all the tasks of the market maker. We can have three types of market makers – private organizations, consortiums, and third parties.

Internal knowledge market

An organization can be a market maker by creating an internal knowledge market. Participation in the knowledge market is controlled by the organization and restricted to organizational members. An internal knowledge market is created to provide a means for employees to exchange knowledge. It is also a viable means to address some of the earlier concerns we raised about getting employee participation, providing incentives, valuing knowledge, and promoting dialogue between employees.

Fujitsu has developed an internal knowledge market for engineers across Japan, where knowledge producers set prices for their registered knowledge and users pay for them upon download.[3] When system engineers, the knowledge providers, register their knowledge in the system, they set the price of that knowledge. When a knowledge seeker chooses a knowledge document, its price appears. If the knowledge seeker decides to purchase the knowledge, the price of the knowledge document is charged to the knowledge seeker's department. If the knowledge is available in electronic format, it is sent via email. If not, a fee for paper copies is also charged. The knowledge provider's department receives revenues from the sales generated by knowledge exchanged.

Infosys has implemented a similar knowledge market called K-Shop. Employees can submit research papers, project experiences, and other types of knowledge goods through a website. Experts review the submission, and if it is found suitable, publish it. The reviewer and author are compensated via knowledge currency units (KCUs). Each reader of the document must pay a certain number of KCUs to utilize the document. KCUs can be redeemed for cash and other gifts. The practice helps entice users to participate actively in the knowledge market.

Consortium markets

A consortium is an organization whose members collaborate to achieve common goals normally beyond the resource of one member; it can play the role of market maker in order to allow knowledge exchanges between the various partner organizations. Unlike an internal knowledge market, a consortium market seeks to stimulate knowledge flows between organizations rather than within them. Trading partners own their knowledge and exchange it in the market. The consortium manages the market. A consortium market is ideal when a group of companies belonging to a given industry can jointly collaborate on an endeavor. Since the consortium acts as an independent organization, it does not show favoritism to any of the founding members, yet serves as a viable means to restrict membership to those organizations that are chosen and approved by the founding members.

In 2000, DaimlerChrysler, Ford Motor Company, and General Motors jointly created a single business-to-business supplier exchange, Covisint, located at www.covisint.com. Covisint enables raw material suppliers, original equipment manufacturers, and retailers to interact in a holistic manner by facilitating connection, communication, and collaboration between trading partners. While Covisint is not a pure knowledge market, it does allow for knowledge exchange, much of which is supplementary to the movement of physical goods and services. Shop.org, the online presence of the National Retail Federation, is another consortium knowledge market devoted exclusively to helping established retail organizations to exchange lessons learnt, case-studies, and marketing and intelligence reports on a wide range of issues in multi-channel retailing.

Third-party knowledge markets

We can also have knowledge markets that are managed by third parties, where membership will be open to participants meeting specified criteria. A third-party market maker is an independent organization which seeks to bring together buyers and sellers for exchange of specific knowledge. The third-party market maker must earn revenues to cover their expenses in setting up the market and to make a profit (see the section below, "Revenue models for knowledge markets"). A third-party market is ideal when there are a large number of individual buyers and sellers who have limited resources, yet would like to interact. The market takes advantage of the economies of scale. Each buyer and seller pays only a small fee to the market – the technique is to attract enough traffic to cover the cost of the market.

Answers.Google.com is a third-party knowledge market that helps users find answers to their questions. The knowledge provider, a researcher, searches for and locates the information and knowledge requested by the buyer, posts it to Answers.Google.com, and notifies the buyer, who is charged a fee for the answer. Keen.com, a third-party knowledge market, connects individuals seeking advice on a wide array of topics with the relevant domain experts. Individuals can search for experts ranging from psychics and astrology to professional services and technology. After an expert is identified, the buyer is connected to the expert via a telephone call for exchange of knowledge at a per-minute fee. Keen.com makes a commission based on the duration of the call. Ingenio.com is a similar knowledge market, connecting individuals seeking advice on business and professional matters.

There are two types of third-party markets – all-in-one and focused markets. An all-in-one market is akin to eBay.com, where sellers offer a diverse range of goods and services. A focused third-party market, as the name implies, focuses on a select product or service category. For example, Ingenio.com is focused on the exchange of management and business knowledge. Third-party markets are also popular in the arena of intellectual property exchange. TechEx.com, conceived at Yale University's Office of Cooperative Research, is a business-to-business knowledge market for technology licensing in the biomedical industry. The market brings together various technology and research providers – such as university, research and development labs, and private researchers – with technology purchasers and licensees such as government and business organizations. The market acts as matchmaker between the various parties to promote the commercialization of research and innovation.

Components of the knowledge market

In addition to the market maker, we have buyers and sellers, rules of the market, and market space as the components of the knowledge market.

Buyers and sellers

Buyers and sellers interact in the market to enable exchange. Buyers are the recipients of knowledge products and services offered by sellers. Membership into the market as either a buyer or seller is a function of the type of market – internal, consortium, or third-party.

In the internal knowledge market, the market maker allows its employees access to the market. Depending on the sophistication of the internal knowledge market, each member might have different access to goods being exchanged in the knowledge market. Such an arrangement is common in highly sensitive organizations, such as defense departments, where each member will need to possess a security clearance to access specified knowledge artifacts.

In a consortium market, buyers and sellers are screened by the existing members of the consortium before being allowed into the market. The organization's role as a business partner, vendor, supplier, purchaser, and so on. will determine the type of access it has to the market. For instance, the supplier view of the market will be very different from what a purchasing organization will see.

Third-party markets are the most dynamic in terms of membership. Most third parties allow members to switch roles between a knowledge provider and a knowledge purchaser, depending on the transaction. Moreover, members may join and leave the organization at will and at little cost. Third-party markets may or may not pre-screen buyers and sellers. Screening of knowledge providers is aimed to evaluate whether they have the requisite skills and know-how they claim. At Answers.Google.com, Google carefully screens the knowledge providers responsible for answering users' questions. Third-party markets may also screen buyers for their ability to pay for goods and services provided. Some third-party markets screen the knowledge products being traded in the market. At IdeaExchange.com, company representatives ensure that all knowledge products that are traded undergo a quality assurance process. Trading is permitted only if they pass this screening.

It is important to note that buyers and sellers can be human, that is employees or individuals, or artificial, that is electronic agents who conduct transactions on behalf of their human principals. Intelligent artificial agents are popular in all fields of commerce. For example, we can have intelligent agents that search for products based on a given set of purchase parameters. Similarly, we can have an agent that negotiates a price based on our price and demand elasticity. As the internet becomes more sophisticated, we can expect to see an exponential rise in the number of artificial agents participating in electronic markets. Knowledge markets are no exception.

Market rules

Market exchanges are governed by market rules on how buyers and sellers will interact. These are defined a priori and determine the exchange and pricing mechanisms. Market rules should address two questions: What goods and services will be bought and sold? How will the goods and services be paid for?

Knowledge markets can be devised to facilitate the exchange of either explicit or tacit knowledge or a combination of both. Explicit knowledge is traded in the form of products that come in a variety of forms such as working papers, research reports, business presentations, software code, business plans, and so on. Knowledge is codified into some explicit form and is exchanged with a person. The focus here is on a person-to-document exchange. Both Fujitsu and Infosys knowledge markets allow for the exchange of such explicit *knowledge objects*. Tacit knowledge exchanges, on the other hand, are *knowledge services*. The focus here is on connecting a knowledge service provider to a knowledge service recipient – a person-to-person exchange. The market acts as a connector between the two individuals; once connected the parties will decide on the medium of the knowledge services. Going back to the examples of Keen.com or Ingenio.com, here tacit knowledge is exchanged via a telephone conversation. Unlike the exchange of explicit knowledge, tacit knowledge exchange calls for access to the source (the knowledge provider), and not just the object (the knowledge document). Therefore, it is important that the knowledge market knows which sources are present in the market at any given time. If the knowledge source is not available, their knowledge will not be available to the market. At Keen.com and Ingenio.com, availability is indicated by a sign saying: 'Call Now'. If the source is not available, a buyer has the option to use another knowledge source or wait until the provider becomes available.

Knowledge markets can also facilitate the exchange of combined explicit and tacit knowledge in the context of a project. Knowledge markets such as BrainBid.com, sycaNet.com, and Techies.com allow buyers and sellers to bid on *knowledge work* or projects. An individual can post a project for sale on the market; potential knowledge workers can then bid for the work. BrainBid.com handles proposals through a sealed bid that is displayed only to the project owner. Once all bids are in, the project owner can choose the person to whom the project will be outsourced. The projects normally entail exchange of both tacit and explicit knowledge.

In addition to deciding the nature of goods sold, a market also dictates the medium of payment. In knowledge markets, products and services are exchanged for a common medium: currency. For internal knowledge markets, many corporations use proxies to represent real monetary value for knowledge products and services traded. Common examples include purchase points, coupons, and so on. Each player in the market is given a starting allowance of points to get the market in operation, that is to make initial purchases, following which players can gain more points by selling knowledge objects and services they create. In third-party and consortium knowledge markets, buyers and sellers use monetary currency such as pounds sterling or Japanese yen to trade. Monies are exchanged through the use of credit cards, debits from checking accounts, or even through phone bills. The way knowledge goods and services are priced can vary. We will discuss this aspect later (see the section below, "Pricing knowledge").

Market space

So what exactly constitutes market space? Consider the traditional department store or shopping mall. These market settings have several salient features.

First, we have some notion of *organization*. In a department store, for instance, all kitchen items are lined up in one aisle, all clothing goods in another. This provides buyers with quick access to products, to create a friendly shopping experience. Second, most malls have a map or a placard that helps in *navigation*. Someone new to the mall, or who needs to find a certain store, can consult this and traverse the marketplace. Without a navigation map, buyers will have increased search times and poor shopping experiences. Third, a mall's ambience is highly conducive to retaining buyers within its confines for long durations. Malls have benches, restrooms, soda fountains, entertainment, all of which contribute to increasing the *stickiness* factor. Finally, the market also enforces *rules* that buyers and sellers must abide by. Sellers will be punished if they sell defective material or engage in cheating practices. Customers cannot steal material from the buyers or use fraudulent currency.

The knowledge space of the organization must have features similar to those of a traditional market space. Knowledge products and services should be presented in an organized manner. The layout of the logical space, most commonly a website, should be user-friendly to promote easy navigation through an organized interface. Consider Answers.Google.com. The design of the logical space is the most simple when it comes to aesthetics, yet it is one of the easiest to navigate. Answers.Google.com allows users the functionality to search for knowledge questions based on popular categories and genres. The better designed a website, the greater are the chances that the user is going to have an enjoyable experience and return to it. A user should also be allowed to personalize and customize their views of the market. Customization helps users navigate the website efficiently and allows them easy access to items of interest.

Knowledge markets should also have avenues to foster dialogue between the various players of the market. The use of discussion forums, chat rooms, listservs, and bulletin boards can all be used to engage users to share their feedback on the market experience, engage with other users, and provide the market maker with suggestions on how to improve the market.

Probably the most important component of the market space is the help function. Users must have ready access to help whenever they need it. A help function is a knowledge provider – knowledge is provided to users when they encounter a problem in the market. Users should be allowed to search through a FAQ list to find answers to routine queries. In addition, they must have the option of interacting with a live customer service or help assistant to discuss novel or difficult problems via live chat, email, or even the telephone. The thing to remember is that just as the knowledge market is open for business 24/7/365, so must the help function be available without interruption. While having an effective and timely help function can do wonders to improve the quality of user experience, an ineffective help function can cause grave harm to user morale and result in lost customer traffic.

The market maker, buyers, sellers, rules, and space are the components of the knowledge market. Any market, including a knowledge market, must help support the basic trading process, which can be broken down into the activities of search, pricing, payment, and authentication.[4] The search process is the sum of all actions involved in the identification and comparison of trading opportunities by buyers and sellers. The pricing process is the procedure for the discovery, negotiating, and setting of prices for products. The payment process involves procedures for transfer of funds and goods between buyers and sellers. The authentication process helps verify the quality of goods sold and the credibility of buyers and sellers executing the trade. Since the trading process of a knowledge market is very similar to trading goods in a traditional market, we will not explore this topic here. The interested reader is referred to our bibliography for a listing of suggested reading. We will now discuss some of the intricacies and peculiarities of a knowledge market, beginning with the nature of knowledge products and services.

Knowledge products and services

Drawing on the economics literature, we can classify products and services as *search*, *experience*, or *credence*. Search products and services are those for which value can be determined prior to purchase. Experience products and services are those for which value can be determined only after purchase. Credence products and services are those for which value cannot be completely determined even after the purchase, because buyers lack the skills and abilities to interpret the necessary information for credence. This classification of goods and services has important bearings on how they are accounted for in knowledge markets.

Search goods are the most basic. A consumer understands the nature of these items and can make value judgments before committing to a purchase. History with the product or service is one reason why consumers can make pre-purchase judgments. If you are familiar with a brand of beer, say Heineken, every successive bottle of it you purchase is a search product. You know the value before you shell out. Similarly, if you frequent a local hairdresser, you know the value of the service and are purchasing a search service.

Experience goods are those that need to be tried before you can make a value judgment, such as going to a new restaurant or purchasing a resort vacation. Unless you actually experience the product or service you will not be able to evaluate it appropriately. Credence goods are the most difficult to evaluate, for several reasons. First, verifiability: because of the idiosyncratic nature of credence goods, it is difficult to determine their value. Second, when compared with experience and search goods, credence goods may seem riskier purchases. Here is where the seller's good reputation in satisfying buyers may be the differentiator.

In knowledge markets too, search goods are basic. They are easy to understand and limited in scope. If we purchase a basic piece of software code that computes the sum of 100 numbers, we are purchasing a search knowledge product. We know the value of the knowledge prior to using it. Search knowledge services are also basic in nature and normally involve a history between the seller and the buyer. For example, if we need to get a document edited and hire the services of an editor with whom we have a history, we are purchasing a search knowledge service. Going back to the case of Answers.Google.com, when knowledge seekers post a query to the expert, they must also offer a price for the potential answer. This value is the price the buyer is willing to pay for the answer and can range from $2 to $200. Most of the knowledge requests here can be considered to meet search characteristics, as the buyer must be able to estimate the value. Similarly, on knowledge markets such as BrainBid.com, where projects are exchanged, the knowledge work seller must be able to estimate the value of the work in order to be able to evaluate incoming bids and choose the right price at which to outsource the work.

It is difficult to distinguish between experience and credence knowledge products and services, since the distinction hinges on the buyer's knowledge quotient. If the buyer has expertise in the commodities, they can be characterized as experience goods, or else they will be credence goods. Take the example of an FAQ about computer maintenance: a veteran computer expert reading it will easily determine the value of this document, making it an experience product. However, a computer novice reading the same FAQ would not be able to gauge its full value, making it a credence product. Similar reasoning applies to services. If you are knowledgeable about accounting, especially tax accounting, you will be able to gauge the value of services provided by a tax accountant, making it an experience service. If, however, you do not possess accounting knowledge, you have just used a credence service.

Search products and services are the easiest to manage. Buyers understand the nature of these items and can make informed decisions, provided the market gives them relevant and legitimate information. Experience and credence goods require a bit more effort, since the market needs to provide more information than what is required by search products and services. Detailed information will help lessen the initial anxiety associated with making the purchase by lowering the uncertainty associated with the transaction.

While buyers need to be able to estimate the quality of the product and service offering, they also need information to evaluate the abilities of the knowledge sellers. This information is usually provided by rating systems. These are mechanisms that allow past purchasers to rate how satisfied they were with the knowledge product or service. In addition to providing answers to standardized questions such as: 'Rate how satisfied you were with the purchase,' buyers can also provide detailed comments on what they liked and disliked. The market needs to make such information available to potential purchasers. If buyers are not satisfied with the knowledge they received, the market maker must provide them with recourse. This can be handled via several mechanisms. Answers.Google.com pre-screens knowledge providers. The market provides the knowledge buyer with a satisfaction guarantee, including a refund should the knowledge provided be deemed unsatisfactory. IdeaExchange.com also pre-screens the knowledge products offered for sale, by guaranteeing that the goods provided meet quality standards. Buyers not completely satisfied get a refund.

In addition to rating the knowledge artifact, many markets allow purchasers to rate the knowledge seller. Often, a knowledge seller will offer multiple products and services. While rating systems for products and services capture feedback on the individual goods and services purchased, they do not provide direct feedback on the seller. Knowledge sellers can be rated according to customer service and responsiveness. This information will help buyers of credence products.

In knowledge markets, ratings and feedback provided by the community act as a means of certifying that the seller is capable of creating and delivering a product or service of acceptable quality. Answers.Google.com has an interesting mechanism to provide knowledge sellers with an incentive to deliver high-quality products. Knowledge buyers pay an agreed-upon price for their knowledge request. However, they are also encouraged to pay something extra, as a tip, to show their appreciation. Some knowledge markets ban a knowledge seller if there are repeated complaints of poor service. Others remind knowledge buyers to always check the past comments on and history of the potential knowledge provider before committing to a transaction. This reminder serves as a deterrent to knowledge providers with shady practices.

The information content of the market is hence an important consideration when constructing the knowledge market. As a rule, extra information is almost always better than no information. However, all information must be honest, validated, and trustworthy, or else it will be of no use.

Pricing knowledge

Since knowledge products traded on electronic markets are digital in nature, they are expensive to create but cheap to duplicate.[5] Consider the economics of creating a research paper: writing the first draft is cumbersome and costly, involving research, documenting the results, editing the writing, adding graphs, tables and figures, and so on. However, once it is created, a few mouse clicks can effortlessly generate a duplicate, making the marginal cost of creating an additional copy close to zero. To some extent, the same argument holds for the delivery of knowledge services. The first time you give a presentation to a client you have to invest heavily in terms of time, cost, and effort. The second time things might go a bit smoother, the third time even smoother, and eventually you will be comfortable giving the talk with little effort. The difference between knowledge products and services is that delivery of a knowledge service involves the deliverer, so we must account for the cost of the human who delivers the service.

A knowledge seller can use multiple methods to price a knowledge product or service. The price set for a knowledge product can be determined by the time taken to create it. The cost must be discounted for the projected amount of sales. For example, if a research paper costs us $100 to prepare and we envision selling it to 5 parties, at the minimum we must charge $20 per sale to cover our costs. Knowledge service providers can charge fixed fees or retainers for their expertise. Charging a retainer is common practice in legal knowledge exchanges.

Knowledge goods and services can also be priced as a bundle rather than as individual items. Management consulting firms use bundle pricing to tie various service offerings together, the incentive being that the cost of the bundle is less than the cost of purchasing the services individually. Knowledge products and services can also be provided to sellers on a commission basis. Here, the knowledge buyer will obtain the rights to use the knowledge product or service at no cost. However, if the buyer earns income from the use of the knowledge, the original seller takes a cut of the revenue. Knowledge markets where we have exchanges of sales tips or marketing ideas are ideal for operating on a commission basis, since much of the knowledge here needs to be experienced or has high credence. Deriving value in terms of sales or revenues can help gauge the value of the knowledge.

Following the ways traditional markets operate, there are three price settlement regimes. In the first, private negotiations entail a buyer contacting a seller privately or in isolation from the rest of the community. Private negotiation schemes are common for products and services that are rare, exquisite, or need to be customized. For example, large consulting firms charge clients a fee for services that is based on private negotiations. These negotiations would involve deciding the context of the service delivery, the peculiarities of the organization, past history with the organization, and the potential for future business. Private negotiations are common in knowledge markets when it comes to the exchange of intellectual property such as technology, innovations, and licenses. On markets such as TechEx, private negotiations are used between innovation providers and the commercializing or purchasing organizations. The role of the knowledge market is to facilitate the connection between the buyers and sellers, with price settlement activities conducted outside the market.

In the second regime, posted price mechanisms entail each seller setting the price of their knowledge offering and posting it for sale in the knowledge market. Knowledge markets such as Keen.com and IdeaExchange.com operate on the posted price mechanism. The knowledge providers post the price for their idea (the product) or the delivery of expertise (the service).

There is no negotiation or bargaining. The seller who is willing to pay the stated price will engage in the transaction.

The third regime involves auction mechanisms. The two major auction categories are English and Dutch. In English auctions, bundles of products called 'lots' are sold, rather than individual items. For example, when putting up knowledge objects that represent computer system documentation, individual items such as code, system charts, so on. can be grouped into one lot. In reverse or Dutch auctions, a buyer puts out a request for a quote and multiple sellers bid until the lowest offered price is discovered. Knowledge markets such as BrainBid.com use a sealed-bid Dutch auction mechanism to sell knowledge work. IPMarketPlace.com auctions intellectual property in the form of US patents, copyrights, trademarks, and trade secrets to anyone, domestic or foreign, interested in acquiring and owning such property. Intellectual property auctioned on the site ranges from hi-tech disciplines, business concepts, and business methodologies, to entertainment such as book manuscripts, plays, stories, and recipes.

The importance of pricing knowledge – an illustrative example

We have been studying knowledge markets for some time now. Some of the pricing exercises have been subject to mathematical treatments. We do not want to bore readers or burden them with details of these. However, extrapolating from our mathematical and game-theoretic exercises in pricing knowledge, let us explain why pricing of knowledge is important and how it is conducted.[6] We will discuss the case of trading explicit knowledge within an internal knowledge market. The arguments also apply to exchange of knowledge services.

Consider a simplified scenario. There are two potential knowledge suppliers and multiple knowledge consumers (see Figure 8.1). Suppliers are assumed to be rational and profit-seeking, just as consumers are assumed to be

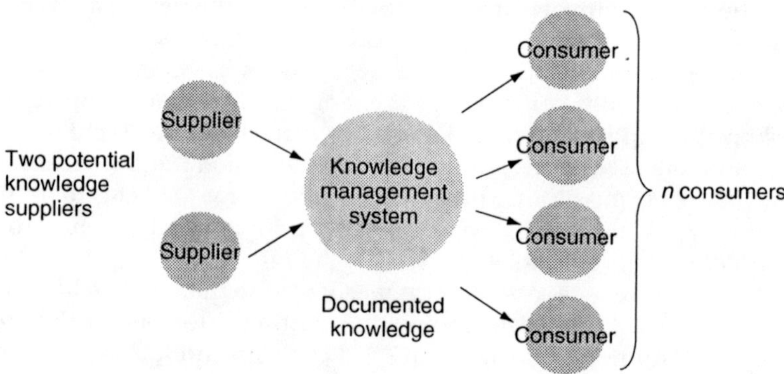

Figure 8.1   The knowledge market model.

rational and willing to acquire relevant knowledge that meets a certain quality standard, for the minimum price.[7]

Each supplier of a knowledge object must go through a two-stage decision process. First, the supplier must evaluate whether they want to enter the market. This will be based on how they evaluate their competitive position in the market. If the supplier feels that there are others in the market that can provide the same knowledge object more economically then they should not enter the market. On the other hand, if they have a competitive edge then entering the market is recommended.

Once the decision to enter the market is made, the supplier must assess how to price the knowledge object. Pricing must be fair and equitable, so as to be higher than the cost of production, but lower than the expected benefit a consumer will get from its consumption. Moreover, the pricing scheme must also be competitive, to prevent other suppliers from entering the market and contributing the same knowledge object.

To summarize, the price set must meet three conditions: (1) it has to be higher than the cost of producing the knowledge, (2) it has to be lower than the utility a buyer will receive from consuming the knowledge, and (3) it should be competitive so as to prevent other sellers from entering the market.

The above pricing scheme will result in only one of the suppliers entering the market. Hence, we do not have the issue of version control. Version control is a problem only when there are two or more knowledge sellers providing nearly similar knowledge objects. This contributes to the problem of having to search through a complicated knowledge repository, rendering the knowledge management program ineffective. Moreover, we can be assured that the supplier who enters the market is going to provide the best available knowledge, since it is their competitive edge, and that it is being delivered at the ideal price.

Now, once the knowledge object is in the market, the question of update becomes relevant. It is common to find outdated knowledge stored in corporate repositories that has not been updated, deleted, or purged. Under the no-pricing schemes pervasive in organizations today, there is no incentive for the producer to go back to the knowledge repository and keep the knowledge current. However, under the pricing regime things are a little different. Let us consider a simple case: assume that the value of a knowledge nugget depreciates over time. In our example, let us assume that supplier number one was the competitive person who entered the market. Three months from the date of entry, the knowledge object has now depreciated. Hence, the value a consumer will get from it will be lower than the original price and so the knowledge object will not attract sales. Supplier number one is now left with three options. First, leave the price as is and take no action. This is not a wise option, as the supplier will earn no profit, since economically rational consumers will not buy a substandard product. Second, retain the same price and update the knowledge object to ensure that consumers will get an updated product. Third, lower the price and leave the knowledge object unchanged. This would ensure that consumers are getting a higher utility than the cost, but would also entice a number of suppliers to enter the market and offer an updated version of the knowledge object.

The pricing of knowledge is an interesting approach to ensure optimal behavior on the part of buyers and sellers in knowledge markets. We have provided a basic illustrative example to show how knowledge products can be priced in the knowledge market. By tweaking variations of this scenario, you can think about how the logic will apply to knowledge services. We reiterate the sole caveat here: with knowledge services, you must account for the cost of service delivery.

Revenue models for knowledge markets

Revenue models for markets are aimed at helping them to be self-sustaining and generate an income. Consider the traditional market. A mall charges each shop owner a fee, normally called rent, to cover the cost of the space. Sellers then take home any monies they earn, less what they have to pay for the fee. This fee insures that the shop owner will have a space to display their products and services and have access to various amenities provided by the mall. For example, most malls will provide tangible benefits such as the electricity needed to run the shop, a telephone for communication purposes, and some kind of security service. There are also intangible benefits. For example, when the mall puts out an advertisement, individual shop owners benefit by more traffic in and around their store, even though they did not pay for the advertisement.

Knowledge markets operate on similar dynamics. Internal knowledge markets do not normally have a revenue model. The market maker, the organization, bears the cost of keeping the market running with the purpose of encouraging its employees to exchange knowledge.

Third-party and consortium markets do have a revenue model. The most common revenue model is charging transaction fees. There is no charge for buyers and sellers to participate in the market. Only when a match is made is a transaction fee charged. The transaction revenue model is ideal if the market is receiving high-volume traffic, with a significant percentage resulting in sales. Transaction fees can be fixed or based on commission. With fixed fees the amount does not change, regardless of the value of the transaction; with commissions the fee is a percentage of the value of the transaction. Answers.Google.com charges a transaction fee for questions posed by the knowledge seeker. The knowledge provider, the expert, takes 75 percent of the fee as remuneration. The remaining 25 percent goes to Answers. Google.com to cover their cost of running the knowledge market.

Another revenue model is charging a subscription fee for access to the knowledge market. This model has the advantage of collecting revenue from buyers and sellers upfront. However, this has a limitation – it may deter individuals who do not want to make a cash commitment right away. Subscription fees can be charged to either buyers or sellers. Knowledge markets such as Experts.com charge knowledge sellers a fee for listing their products and services with the market. Knowledge seekers can freely enter the market, browse the goods and services, and then contact the knowledge seller for the transaction. Websites such as TechEx charge a fee to both the knowledge producers (the scientist and innovators) and the knowledge consumers (the business organizations looking to commercialize the innovation).

The third revenue model is based on advertising fees. While buyers and sellers can participate for free, third parties interested in advertising their products and services are charged a fee that keeps the market running. The advantage of the advertising model is that there is no direct charge for buyers and sellers. However, there is an indirect cost. Anyone who has visited a free internet portal and been annoyed by those pop-ups and ads has paid a fee. Moreover, unless the knowledge market is high-profile, it will not be able to charge advertising fees high enough to cover overheads. It is more common for markets to use the advertising model in combination with another revenue model to run the market.

Choosing the right revenue model is critical to the sustenance of the knowledge market. The revenue model provides a means to cover the costs associated with facilitating the transaction, including the provision of information to buyers and sellers, matching buyers and sellers, devising the contract, exchange of payments and goods, and handling grievances, feedback, and after-sale issues.

Considerations when constructing knowledge markets

So what does it take to set up a knowledge market? In this section we present several considerations to bear in mind. We draw these guidelines from primary and secondary sources. Primary sources include our experience with setting up or experimenting with knowledge markets. Secondary sources include work that has been published in the economic literature on determinants of market structure and behavior. Table 8.1 is an abbreviated list of the knowledge markets we studied.

Market for lemons

A critical concern in devising knowledge markets is addressing the issue of the 'market for lemons' as postulated by the Nobel laureate George Akerlof.[8] Akerlof studied the used cars market, and was curious as to why they sold at a substantial discount compared with the price of new car. He found that

Table 8.1 List of knowledge markets

Knowledge market	Type	Focus
AllExperts.com	Third-party	Exchange of expertise in the areas of social living, personal relationship counseling, and business and general management
Answers.Google.com	Third-party	Exchange of knowledge on a wide assortment of search requests
BrainBid.com	Third-party	Knowledge work exchange
Covisint.com	Consortium	Exchange of knowledge between suppliers, vendors, and manufacturers in the automobile industry
Elance.com	Third-party	Exchange of expertise and knowledge work
Experts.com	Third-party	Exchange of expertise in the areas of business and general management
experts-exchange.com	Third-party	Exchange of expertise in the IT sector
FIND2	Internal	Exchange of software engineering knowledge
Guru.com	Third-party	Exchange of business and general management expertise
HotDispatch.com	Third-party	Exchange of expertise and knowledge work in the IT sector
IdeaExchange.com	Third-party	Exchange of ideas on a wide assortment of topics
Ingenio.com	Third-party	Exchange of expertise in the areas of social living, personal relationship counseling, and business and general management
Intota.com	Third-party	Exchange of expertise in the areas of business and general management
IPMarketplace.com	Third-party	Exchange of innovations and intellectual property
Kasamba.com	Third-party	Exchange of expertise in the areas of social living, personal relationship counseling, and business and general management
Keen.com	Third-party	Exchange of expertise in the areas of social living and personal relationship counseling
Knexa.com	Third-party	Exchange of expertise in the areas of social living, personal relationship counseling, and business and general management
K-Shop	Internal	Exchange of software engineering knowledge
Patentauction.com	Third-party	Exchange of innovations and intellectual property
PatentJunction.com	Third-party	Exchange of innovations and intellectual property

Sharksforum.com	Third-party	Exchange of expertise and knowledge work in the IT sector
Shop.org	Consortium	Exchange of knowledge between online retailers
sycaNet.com	Third-party	Knowledge work exchange
TechEx.com	Third-party	Exchange of biomedical-related innovations
techies.com	Third-party	Knowledge work exchange
Yet2.com	Third-party	Exchange of expertise and knowledge work in the IT sector

the buyers of used cars do not know if their car is a lemon, that is defective. While the buyer can hire a mechanic or conduct a test of the vehicle to ensure its quality this is a tedious and expensive task, the costs outweighing the benefits. Sellers are more informed about the nature and quality of the products offered for sale. This information asymmetry leaves the buyer at the mercy of the seller.

Several concerns are crucial in a market for lemons. First, high-quality products suffer, since they have to be under-priced to compete with lemons in the market. Moreover, sooner or later the market will deteriorate, since adverse selections prompt an imbalance, with the sale of lemons overpowering products chosen at random. The more lemons sold, the less will buyers be willing to pay owing to the perceived low quality of products, and eventually sellers of high-quality products will leave the market as they will not be able to price their products competitively.

The same rules apply in a knowledge market. If knowledge objects sold are defective, fake, or of low quality, the market will eventually crash. There will be no incentives for buyers to purchase high-quality knowledge objects or for sellers to produce them. In addition, what is interesting in a knowledge market is the inverse of the market-for-lemons problem – instead of outdated or second-hand knowledge being defective, we do not know if a new knowledge product is a lemon or not. If we were to purchase a new car we have some assurance as to its quality, but new knowledge objects are riskier to use since they have not been tested, validated, or applied. In terms of quality, knowledge objects that have been used many times are much safer, because a potential buyer can look at the comments posted by previous purchasers of the knowledge artifacts. These comments will help the buyer make an informed decision.

To alleviate some of concerns associated with a market for lemons, mechanisms need to be in place to help buyers evaluate the trustworthiness of sellers. Trust can be defined as the reliance placed by one party on another's ability to fulfill their obligation in the agreed manner. In knowledge markets, trust emerges by each participant monitoring other participants in the market. As mentioned earlier, we can have buyers rate knowledge goods and sellers.

Rating systems are commonplace in most e-marketplaces today. Consider eBay, where there are rather elaborate schemes enabling a potential buyer to receive information not only about the goods or services being exchanged, but also on the abilities and past histories of each participant in the marketplace. AllExperts.com provides ratings on various categories, such as knowledge itself, clarity of response, timeliness, and politeness of the knowledge seller. The rating system serves as a reinforcement tool – the higher the rating, the greater the trust other players in the market have in the vendor and the higher the chance of making a sale. It is important to note that the knowledge participants, especially knowledge buyers, must find the rating system trustworthy for it to be of value.

Chicken-and-egg predicament

In setting up internal knowledge markets, organizations face a common predicament: the 'chicken-and-egg' dilemma. Which comes first? A market is only good if we have enough players participating, but players will not come until the market proves to be a viable avenue for them to seek knowledge objects. So we have a Catch-22. As the number of players participating in the market increases, and more and more users find it valuable, the market increases its overall value.

For internal knowledge markets, the key strategy to getting a market started and avoiding the chicken-and-egg predicament is the provision of incentives. These can be in the form of free give-aways, prizes, and recognition. While this may help to get the market started, it is not sufficient. Employees must start producing knowledge to sell in the market. To this end, specialized incentives can be provided, such as for the top twenty nuggets posted for sale. While incentives can help get the market started, in our opinion nothing works better than getting the senior members of the organization involved. Division managers, project managers, team leaders, so on. need to be enticed to join the bandwagon and lead the knowledge market participation.

Incentives are also important for third-party and consortium markets. Additionally, these markets must also provide information as an advertisement, to attract potential users. For example, the number of questions asked to experts may be a benchmark for potential users about the market size. Providing date and time stamps on knowledge transactions and making them available can be used to gauge whether the market is active or inactive. Information must be provided as a means to advertise the traffic the market draws and how successful the market is in connecting buyers with sellers.

Black markets

Black markets, also called underground or illegal markets, pose several problems for their legitimate counterparts. For instance, for years the entertainment industry faced stiff competition from black markets, which sold pirated copies of its products at significantly lower cost. To a large extent, this problem has been curtailed via new copyright laws and developments in technology protection, such as passwords, digital rights management, and so on.

A knowledge market will fail if people choose to spread knowledge outside it through black markets. For example, if an employee purchases a certain knowledge object from an internal knowledge market, and then shares it with his team members via private email or by printing out copies of it, his team members have no incentive to participate in the market and reward the actual knowledge provider. In rare cases, we can also see a reverse black market, where a knowledge provider sells their knowledge outside the market for a higher price. This happens when employees fear making their knowledge available to all agents in a competitive pricing environment, and choose to share it with a few. Organizations must strive to inhibit such practices, as it will lead to the eventual demise of the market.

Of the many strategies available to curtail the development of black markets, we find the following to be the most successful. First, for an internal knowledge market there must be some kind of an organization-wide declaration or law restricting private one-to-one exchange of knowledge objects during access to the free market. This will be akin to the notion of copyright laws. Obviously, exceptions need to be made. For example, some nuggets of knowledge, such as those held by executives on strategic aspects of the organization, should not be disclosed to all members and will call for private exchanges. Agents must be educated on what constitutes ethical behavior in a knowledge market.

Second, for all types of knowledge markets, the recent advances made in digital rights management technology is proving to be a viable solution to the problem. Knowledge objects can be password-protected, or available as read-only, printing could be disabled, so on. These measures ensure some control over the state of the knowledge object and its use.

Third, we must address the need to have copyrights and patents for knowledge objects. Tough copyright laws and legal ramifications curtail the theft of innovations, with the penalty being high enough to deter a potential thief. Some knowledge markets are beginning to help knowledge sellers protect their ideas and innovations. For instance, IdeaExchange.com has taken major steps towards securing the ideas of its knowledge sellers. Buyers are limited in what they can do with knowledge products, as these are protected by digital rights management technologies. As additional protection, the market has guidelines dealing with statutory and contractual protection issues.

Advertising and packaging of knowledge

Unlike the sale of physical goods such as clothes and shoes, which can be inspected prior to purchase without loss of value, putting knowledge objects on display drastically reduces their value. For example, if a potential buyer can view a working paper, what is the need to purchase it? Probably none, as the value has already been received. To further complicate this problem, in successful and thriving knowledge markets there are not only hundreds but thousands of knowledge objects displayed on offer. In the words of Herbert A. Simon: "A wealth of information creates a poverty of attention." So, how does a seller successfully advertise knowledge objects without killing their value? Some of the common tactics employed for advertising knowledge objects include provision of knowledge abstracts or 'meta knowledge.' Here, a seller compiles a brief yet enticing description that captures the essence of their knowledge object. Buyers can then view the abstract and make a decision about purchasing the nugget. For example, on IdeaExchange.com a buyer can view the price and idea summary, which contains details such as the benefits of the idea, its uniqueness, a value proposition, and the author's experience. Another common strategy to attract attention to valuable knowledge nuggets is by posting access statistics. These can be in the form of: How many times did a person view a certain knowledge object? Or How have others rated this knowledge object? Many organizations have developed internal knowledge portals with elaborate search mechanisms. Thus, when a user-specific search is executed, knowledge objects can be sorted for relevance based on a number of specified criteria.

Future of knowledge markets

In this chapter we have explored the concept of the knowledge market. It is our belief that such markets will grow in prominence and ubiquity. Their future looks exciting, considering the current technologies and protocols that are in research and development phases.

Today, we have a wide assortment of knowledge tools ranging in sophistication from the basic personal digital assistant (PDA) and mobile phones to handheld computers. What is even more interesting is the rate at which these tools have become sophisticated. Consider the basic mobile phone today. It is probably much smaller than it was a couple of years back, has much higher in-built functionality – such as the ability to capture images and videos – and can interact with many other devices such as a computer or a PDA. This increase in connectivity, not only between people but also between people and their devices, and between multiple devices, is a promising budding ground for the growth of knowledge markets. People can have real-time access to the markets and quickly locate the required knowledge.

The maturity of the concept of electronic markets and the internet phenomenon have also made another important contribution – increased acceptance. A few years back, many were still reluctant to conduct transactions on the internet or any other electronic environment. Today, such trepidation would be ridiculed. Time has allowed for increased acceptance of newer technologies, where many people actively embrace electronic media. With the recent development of pervasive, ubiquitous, and mobile computing facilities, we speculate that knowledge markets will become real-time accessible. It will no longer be necessary for individuals to access markets only through their office or home-office sites, but also on the go. This will add more traffic to these markets, making them more valuable.

In addition, research in authentication and trust-building mechanisms, such as higher levels of encryption and advanced rating systems, will contribute positively to the development of knowledge markets. Technologies such as digital rights management and advanced payment methodologies are getting more sophisticated. Today, anyone can purchase a knowledge product, such as a movie, and watch it on their computer for a price that is lower than paying for it at their neighborhood video rental store. The DVD self-destructs after a prescribed viewing period, so there is no need to make an extra trip to return the video. In this kind of arrangement both the video store or more correctly the e-video store! – and the customer gain from lowered costs and increased quality of service. Authentication schemes are going to be critical to ensure that only designated individuals have access to the market. Hackers and other unscrupulous individuals should be kept out of the knowledge market, as the unauthorized leakage of knowledge being traded can be disastrous.

Knowledge markets of the future will be more encompassing and collaborative. We envision an explosion in knowledge markets that will enable multiple organizations to trade expertise and know-how. Consortiums of trading partners will collaboratively develop knowledge markets for the exchange of know-how in the form of process strategies, marketing techniques, customer information, and so on and also to promote the exchange of expertise by allowing for personnel rotations and movement between organizations.

Knowledge markets will also develop to include exchanges both between government organizations and between government and businesses. The whole concept underlying the interest in e-government is to make the provision of public services more accessible, efficient, and effective. E-government initiatives have been very successful in the government-to-consumer arena. Today, many of us can pay our taxes online, get information about our localities via the internet, pay for vehicle registration, and learn about news and activities, all with the click of a button. Efforts in the government-to-business arena have also enjoyed success. Today, organizations wanting to undertake work for the government must bid for projects online, submit invoices online, and so on. The next logical step is to set up knowledge exchanges between government agencies and between the government and businesses. Moreover, setting up a knowledge market will enable each department to charge their peer department for their core knowledge and services.

We will witness a shake-out in the knowledge market industry. The smaller and less successful knowledge markets will be rolled into the more successful ones. This is beginning to take form. Organizations such as UTEK

Corporation have already begun to acquire a number of knowledge markets, such as UVentures.com, TechEx.com, and Pax Technology Transfer, while Keen.com acquired Inforocket.com, among other knowledge markets.

Conclusion

Apart from a few altruistic souls, most of us would like to receive remuneration for our skills, know-how, and abilities. After all, this is how we can put bread on the table. If knowledge is going to be the key resource of the future, people are going to have to pay for it. Knowledge markets provide a worthwhile avenue for the exchange of knowledge. The characteristics of transparency, near perfect information, and competitive offerings of knowledge are enticing. Currently, knowledge markets are in their infancy, but they are growing in prominence, popularity, and sophistication. We expect this trend to continue into the foreseeable future.

9
Engaging to Calibrate Knowledge Management Systems

When the term 'knowledge management' was introduced into the business vocabulary, the first wave of interest was in the development of knowledge management systems (KMSs). We remember our experiences during the late 1990s, when almost every technology vendor had a knowledge management offering in the works or one that was being positioned in the market.

While most early KMS deployments were immature and disastrous, there were exceptions. Successful KMSs were aware, to a certain degree, of the need to strongly consider the human element. Many software engineering firms, for example, focused on building knowledge repositories to help promote code reuse. Medical institutions built KMSs to help employees research ailments, check for medical diagnoses, investigate drug interactions, and help manage patient care. Similarly, the automobile repair sector deployed KMSs to help technicians work with complex machinery and diagnose problems. Another branch of technology used for knowledge management enables individuals to engage in electronic dialogue rather than just person-to-computer interactions. Common examples include email systems, discussion boards, electronic lists, instant messaging tools, and electronic chat rooms.

Most knowledge management technologies can be classified into three categories – *codified*, *personalized*, and *hybrid*. Codified technologies are those that focus on the sharing of explicit knowledge artifacts housed in a central repository. Personalized technologies provide a platform for dialogue between individuals for knowledge sharing. The codified approach entails the separation of knowledge from its creator, since it focuses on gathering individual knowledge in an organization, putting it in a cohesive context, and making it available to its members. The personalized approach is the opposite; here knowledge sharing is fostered through people-to-people interactions and dialogue, and knowledge is not separated from its source, as the knowledge seeker needs to identify the source of the required knowledge to request it. Hybrid technologies aim to bridge both codified and personalized approaches. A KMS normally employs either the codified or the personalized approach as a design base, though some advanced systems use a hybrid approach, as discussed in a later section. Each class of technologies has its associated pros, cons, and management issues.

KMSs can be defined as technology artifacts designed to enable knowledge management. Extrapolating from this definition, in any KMS a set of managerial processes is applied to knowledge. In his studies of human intelligence, Guilford proposed a three-dimensional model of mental processes. We have (1) *products* of mental operations representing units, classes, systems, and so on, (2) *operations* on these products including cognition, memory, divergent thinking, convergent thinking, and evaluation, and (3) *context*, representing the figural, symbolic, and semantic nuances. KMSs include these three components: knowledge represents the product, operations include activities such as transfer, integration and presentation, while context helps in transforming information into knowledge.

KMSs normally focus on the exchange of explicit knowledge – knowledge codified into information documents, such as business plans, software code, marketing presentations, and so on – or knowledge that is highly tacit in nature, with the focus on connecting and enabling communication between human knowledge sources. In more advanced KMSs, both tacit and explicit knowledge can be exchanged simultaneously, such as in instant messaging programs. Using these programs, two or more individuals can communicate through short messages for the exchange of tacit knowledge and also exchange explicit knowledge, such as documents. Moreover, advanced messaging software enables users to share electronic knowledge spaces similar to whiteboards in traditional meeting rooms, where each user can interact with knowledge documents and share ideas to foster constructive knowledge.

In this chapter we will explore the intricacies of the factors governing KMSs and their role in deploying efficient systems. Our goal here is to help managers make wise choices regarding knowledge management technologies and processes, and also help users interact effectively with technology artifacts.

Barriers to effective use of knowledge management systems

We will begin by looking at the factors that enhance or suppress the consumption of knowledge residing in KMSs. It is best to compare this usage decision with a traditional purchase decision, such as purchasing a pair of trousers or going to a pub to buy a pint of ale. In this section, our focus is on looking at KMSs that house explicit knowledge artifacts. Following this, we will look at underlying issues in systems that enable the exchange of tacit knowledge. Finally, we will examine issues involved in getting people to leverage the more advanced KMSs.

Barriers to consumption of explicit knowledge

The adoption of knowledge is heavily dependent on its perceived value. However, knowledge being a special product, its value cannot be assessed before it is adopted, and it can be costly to assess the value even after consumption. This is because, as we discussed in the chapter on knowledge markets, explicit knowledge is either an experience or a credence product or service in most contexts. Both experience and credence goods have a common characteristic: their value cannot be assessed until they are consumed. There is a difference as well: the value of an experience product or service can be assessed without additional cost after consumption, whereas the value of a credence product or service cannot be assessed through normal use, and assessing this value remains costly even after consumption.

As discussed previously, distinguishing between experience and credence goods is complicated, especially in the context of explicit knowledge. For instance, a computer expert reading an article on computer upgrades will easily determine its value, making it an experience product. However, a computer novice reading the same article would not be able to assess its full value, making it a credence product.

Regardless of whether explicit knowledge is credence or experience goods, the value of the knowledge product, prior to consumption, is derived from indicators. Value indicators come from two sources: the knowledge *producer* and the knowledge *product*.[1] If the consumer sees the knowledge as a credence product, the producer is the salient indicator of its value. Owing to the difficulty in estimating the true value of the knowledge product, the knowledge producer's trustworthiness and good reputation will be pivotal in influencing the buying decision. We identify value indicators that affect the assessment of the knowledge producer's influence as *connections*, perceived *proximity*, *competency*, and perceived *credibility*. The consumer can assess the value of explicit knowledge that is an experience product, at least partially, after buying and sampling it. Hence, the knowledge content becomes critical for knowledge adoption. The value indicators we identify here are perceived *complexity*, perceived *compatibility*, and perceived *relative advantage* of the knowledge product.

The above discussion is based on the assumption that the potential knowledge adopter can place it in the correct knowledge category. However, in most cases, it is difficult to clearly identify the category, so we can assume that all factors discussed above will get combined consideration in making knowledge consumption decisions. Moreover, the inability to properly judge a product as credence or experience reveals another indicator – perceived *risk*. Judging perceived risk, as we will discuss later, is an important consideration that will affect decisions about knowledge consumption.

Knowledge producer factors

Let us first look at knowledge producer factors: *connections, proximity, competency* and *credibility*. The relative position and connection between factors embedded in a specific social structure affects the knowledge transfer between them. The strong and weak *connections*, called 'ties' in social studies, complement each other and serve as two modes for knowledge acquisition. Weak connections aid people in special circumstances. Mark Granovetter found that people are more likely to find novel information about future job prospects from weak ties.[2] This is because people with strong connections usually share the same social backgrounds and so, most probably, the same information sources. People with weak connections usually have different social backgrounds, so their information sources may be variegated. The same reason makes the transfer of complex tacit knowledge easier among pairs with strong connections than among those with weak connections.[3] In order to transfer tacit knowledge easily, entities must share contextual information. Without shared context, the meaning of knowledge gets lost and it becomes difficulty to transfer all the subtleties associated with the know-how.

While we can codify knowledge into an explicit form and store it in a repository such as a KMS, the connection between the user and the knowledge producer is probably weak at best. This weak connection has been shown to impact knowledge consumption. We found that software engineers were more inclined to pick up the phone, or walk across to a peer's cubicle to discuss the specifics of knowledge needed, than they were to use the know-ledge in the system.[4] Robert Cross and colleagues found that people are approximately five times more likely to approach friends or colleagues for information than to use a database or other repository.[5] Their research with 40 managers in a consulting firm revealed that 85 percent claimed to receive knowledge critical to the successful completion of projects from other people. They used the knowledge repository only to supplement what they learnt from other contacts. Hence, the *proximity* to the source of knowledge can be viewed as a critical determinant in the intention of knowledge consumption.

Proximity to the knowledge producer needs to be accounted for in terms of both physical distance and also virtual or electronic distance. Physical distance is the simpler measure that we are used to, because it gives us a clear indication of how close two people are – for example, how many cubicles apart one person is from another. However, with the advance in communication technologies we have been able to eradicate some of the constraints of physical distances, making it important to acknowledge and account for virtual distances. For instance, two people located on the same floor might be considered to be in close proximity. However, when two people far apart have a very good telephone connection and can call each other on a regular basis, we see an example of communication technologies helping people eradicate issues of physical distance. Likewise, if two people are on the same floor and never cross paths or return calls and emails, physical distance will still be a problem, despite their proximity. So proximity has much to do with connections with the knowledge producer. Proximity to the knowledge source is a means to build relational trust and credibility. As the frequency of interactions and dependability between two parties increases, positive expectations rise. And therefore one is more willing to consume the knowledge object produced by a source one has positive interactions with on a frequent basis. Proximity is also a means to obtain value indicators about the quality of knowledge objects; if one is closer to the producer, there is a good chance that one will readily receive value indicators from the producer and take them seriously before making a purchasing decision.

Other knowledge producer factors include competency and credibility. *Competency* is the capability to fulfill promises. An agent who seeks to consume knowledge must feel comfortable about the competencies of its producer. *Credibility* can be defined as an entity's predictability, reliability, and honesty in fulfilling obligations. The more one can rely on an entity's credibility, the more inclined one is to trust that entity. We must point out that an entity can have high credibility in one context and lack credibility in another. For our purposes we are concerned with the perceived credibility of the knowledge producer in the domain of expertise.

Credibility fosters internalization, that is the means by which one incorporates the referent's belief structure into one's own. In most cases, the producer's expertise and credibility have been found to be significant determinants of internalization. Accepting knowledge from a producer signifies that one has trust in the producer's know-how and tacit insights. Knowledge residing in systems is not risk-free; unintended results from its usage might incur negative consequences. Hence, it is important that an employee consider the credibility of the knowledge provider before deciding on using the provider's knowledge object. Unless the KMS has a clear and definite way to provide a user with an assessment of the knowledge producer's credibility, knowledge consumption will be hampered.

Knowledge product factors

Let us now look at knowledge product factors: *complexity*, *compatibility*, and *relative advantage*. In most KMSs, we are likely to find a wide assortment of knowledge artifacts, which will likely differ in their degree of *complexity*. Most studies of innovation have found that the more complex an idea is perceived to be, the longer it will take to be adopted. All else being equal, the easier a system is to use, the more likely is the intention to adopt. In the domain of software engineering, the complexity of software is inversely proportional to its usability, and hence lowers the chance of its reuse. Complex knowledge objects like software code entail significant costs to the consumer in terms of effort needed to assess and comprehend the idiosyncrasies of the knowledge object. If knowledge is perceived as complex, the estimated cost for processing it will outweigh the cost of creating a new knowledge object, and hence lower the chance that the original knowledge object will be consumed.

Compatibility is the degree to which using the innovation is perceived as consistent with the existing socio-cultural values, beliefs, needs, and past experiences of potential adopters. The innovation guru Everett Rogers highlights three types of compatibility – with values or beliefs, with previously introduced ideas, and with needs.[6] Employees in organizations are more likely to view knowledge that fits their existing schemas favorably. Festinger's theory of cognitive dissonance posits that decision-makers focus intuitively on information that supports their point of view, owing to the need for self-justification. One reason for this is the ease with which new knowledge can be integrated into established work practices. Accepting knowledge that conflicts with the existing architecture or schema of work will call for more cumbersome integration efforts. Knowledge must also be compatible with the task at hand, otherwise there is no need to consume it. Most users of KMSs have a hard time assessing the compatibility of knowledge artifacts owing to poor explanations and context provided with knowledge objects. For instance, if we find a PowerPoint presentation on a marketing pitch in the KMS, how do we know if it is compatible with our task? Well, we first have to examine where it was used in the past, if it was successful, what issues were pitched, and so on. In most KMSs the PowerPoint file will be found along with minimal information. Such lack of useful information poses a challenge in assessing compatibility and impairs explicit knowledge consumption.

Relative advantage is the gain one receives from accepting a new idea or innovation over a previous one. There are several items that contribute to relative advantage – economic profitability, social prestige, and immediacy of rewards. Economic profitability is the gain one gets from time, cost, and effort savings from using the new innovation. Gains in social prestige are the improvements to one's social status from using the innovation. Immediacy of rewards asks the question: 'Does the innovation provide gains now, or do I have to wait to benefit from it?' Tangibility of results from using technology innovations in many cases contributes positively to usage intention. Extensive research into technology acceptance has found significant support for the perception of relative advantage as a determinant of intention to use.[7]

Similar reasoning can be applied to the consumption of knowledge. Knowledge can be seen as a form of innovation. Its acceptance depends heavily on the perception of benefits by the adopter. If the knowledge artifact fails to yield benefits for the consumer, it will be abandoned. Moreover, unless consuming knowledge is perceived to improve one's position, by aiding in effective and efficient task accomplishment or by providing new insights, a potential consumer will not expend effort attempting to use it. Assessing the relative advantage of a nugget in the KMS is not an easy task, unless the nugget is a superstar, one that has earned a distinguished reputation. Such nuggets may represent only 1 percent of the KMS, and are normally clouded by the other 99 percent, making assessing advantages equivalent to tossing a coin.

Barriers to consumption of tacit knowledge

Systems to facilitate the management of tacit knowledge are normally of two kinds. The first kind are those intended to be pointers to sources of tacit knowledge. These are commonly referred to as knowledge maps, and work in a similar fashion to the yellow pages of a phone directory. Through the use of advanced knowledge maps, a knowledge seeker can locate a person who may have expertise in a given area or areas and find out details such as the projects the person has worked on, their work hours, and their preferred communication mode (email or voice mail). The knowledge seeker can then use this information to connect with the knowledge source and seek out the required knowledge. Systems of the second kind facilitate communication between the seekers and providers of knowledge. Common examples include group support systems, emails, chat rooms, and so on. Here a knowledge seeker may seek to enter into synchronous or asynchronous communication with the knowledge provider. Synchronous communications are conducted through the use of chat software and real-time collaboration tools such as instant messaging or net meetings. Asynchronous communications are traditionally through email.

In the exchange of tacit knowledge, we see a different set of dynamics emerge as barriers. Many of the issues with explicit artifacts are secondary here. For instance, details such as the credibility of a knowledge source are relevant only if the knowledge seeker is engaging in receiving knowledge from a stranger. Other issues such as proximity to the knowledge source are also less important, as long as there is an adequate system in place to facilitate communications. Let us examine some other issues in the exchange of tacit knowledge by personnel.

Fear of being known as an expert

A couple of organizations for whom we consulted are in the information technology and software engineering industry. Software engineering is a highly knowledge-intensive domain, where the keys to success are related to one's experience in design, coding, testing, and implementation. Within each of these domains, we can have many sub-domains; for example in coding, one can categorize expertise based on the different languages or platforms. Owing to the vastness of the field, seldom does one individual have all the resources to complete a project. Furthermore, to keep pace with the developments in computer science, one has to remain constantly up to date with the latest developments to prevent becoming obsolete.

Contrary to popular opinion, software engineers fear being dubbed experts. Branded experts find themselves being assigned to projects based on their past experiences, rather than projects which may be more intellectually challenging and offer scope for learning. This fear, found to be pervasive across all organizations, explains why software engineers are reluctant to share their expertise and contribute to the knowledge bases.

The access statistics on individual records that KMSs store in the database reveal details such as how often a particular document was accessed, by whom, and the user's opinion of its relevance or quality. This transparency makes it easy to identify the experts whose opinions matter. One engineer went on to say: "If I contribute nuggets of know-how on how to run applications on the Unix box, soon I will be dubbed the "Unix Guru" and that is all I will end up being in charge of."

Software engineering is a continuously evolving field in which survival is dependent on keeping abreast with new developments and experimenting with the latest technologies. Hence being stereotyped as an expert, though flattering for the employee, works to one's disadvantage and hampers rather than advances one's career. This concern over how access statistics were going to be used by management was common to employees we spoke to, in almost all organizations. Knowledge workers do not want their expertise in a particular language or aspect of design to be the key determinant of stunted intellectual growth. Organizations must respect this and allocate people to projects not only according to what they know, but also on their potential to learn and explore. Executives need to do more to eradicate this fear factor by outlining the scope of the KMS clearly enough to address it.

Language and communication issues

Another reason why it is difficult to communicate tacit knowledge is the lack of common agreements on language protocols, standards on how to respond to knowledge requests, and issues of context management. When consulting with software project teams, we have seen these issues plague most distributed development teams, where people from different countries, organizations, and functions collaborate on an endeavor. Consider the following misunderstandings that occurred within a distributed development team.[8] The initial meeting between the staff based in the USA and in India never occurred for a simple reason – no one specified the time! An excerpt from the US project manager's email reads: 'Let us schedule a meeting for 4 – OK?' The response came from the team leader in India: 'Sure…see you then'. Never was it clearly specified whether it was to be 4 a.m. or 4 p.m., or in what time zone. During the postmortem, the root cause analysis for this problem was established to be no clear agreement on communication conventions. One of the takeaways from the project postmortem was to clearly post communication conventions such as the use of the metric or the non-metric system, the 24-hour or the 12-hour clock, the time zone reference, and so on.

Misunderstandings also occurred with disparate interpretations given to issue sensitivity. The two teams had problems signifying items such as urgency, the need for punctuality, explanation facilities, and responses to emails. For example, if an Indian developer wanted clarification on an item, they would almost never use the word 'urgent' but would frame the email: 'I would appreciate it if you could answer this at your earliest convenience.' The American interpreted 'earliest convenience' to mean that it was not urgent and a delayed response would suffice.

These irritants, among others, are owing to lack of appreciation for contextual details. The knowledge sender is not diligent in the evaluation of the context and how the knowledge might be interpreted, while the knowledge seeker does not appropriately frame the knowledge request and explicate the contextual subtleties. Hence, while information transfer may occur, its interpretation will be ad-hoc and incomplete.

Advanced knowledge management systems

Advanced KMSs, as we have mentioned, are those that combine the codified and personalized approaches within an integrated framework using a hybrid approach. Common examples of these include instant messaging software such as ICQ or MSN. Through the use of such tools, knowledge seekers can find relevant knowledge providers by looking up their contact list. They can then set up a synchronous communication session via chat. The software permits the exchange of text, images, voice, and even videos. If they have cameras attached to their computers they can also see each other's reactions while engaging in the discussion. They can even drop an email if the person is not online. In addition, advanced KMSs come with electronic whiteboards and other collaboration tools that help users engage in creative thinking, thus facilitating the creation and sharing of knowledge.

These systems are going to be the KMSs of the future and will continue to increase in prominence. One of the growth drivers is their loose design, making them largely future-proof. Advanced KMSs allow users to customize their usage of the technologies, and hence entail minimal cost. In addition, they allow for the appreciation of emergence in knowledge work, provide a good representation of context, and also manage the distributed nature of communications by providing adequate support. We discuss these concepts next.

Appreciating emergence

One of the critical components of KMSs that must be appreciated is the notion of emergence and, more specifically, emergent behavior of their users. KMSs are difficult to calibrate under deterministic conditions, that is the design assumes that all knowledge about how the system will be used, what components are needed, and other particulars can be specified a priori. Knowledge workers, especially high-end workers, most often work on unstructured problems. Hence, their knowledge needs are also emergent and depend on the current task they are handling. Since their needs may change and evolve in the future, it is difficult to forecast how best to design a system for such unstructured work practices.

The good news is that there is no need to design a comprehensive system for such nuances. Knowledge workers, by self-definition, are highly capable of learning and tackling new knowledge. Accordingly, they are innovators and can figure out how best to engage with a technology artifact. We examined the practices of a group of knowledge workers who were introduced to a new technology artifact. We studied how these users engaged with the technology, how they increased their stock of knowledge about it, and how this knowledge affected their interaction with the technology artifact.[9] In this case, the technology artifact was an integrated development environment (IDE) used by software engineers to calibrate the software programs and applications. Most of the software engineers we studied came not from traditional programming or computer science backgrounds, but were originally in the business and management domains of the organization, including areas such as marketing, consulting services, operations management, and even accounting and financial functions. This salient point makes our findings more interesting, as our sample of software engineers truly represented 'customers' of technology. We gathered data from software engineers who were relatively new to the organization or who had been programming for no more than two years. Most of our interviewees had transitioned into their new roles owing to organizational downsizing. The organization decided that it was in its best interest to have individuals who possessed business knowledge conduct the design functions as well, so that there would be less ambiguity and risks in understanding client needs. Hence, what we present below can be seen as a study of how knowledge emerges in users of technology, helping them move from novice to expert status.

When a user is first introduced to a given technology artifact, they must learn the bare essentials needed to get the technology into a state of operation – the *operability* stage. The operability stage is influenced by whether the user has had prior exposure to the technology (such as using a past version of the software) or to similar technology artifacts (that is familiarity with Notepad or WordPad will help a user gain operational knowledge in working with Microsoft Word). The operability stage is also present when users take it upon themselves to experiment with new technologies without organizational mandate. For instance, the diffusion of instant messaging systems in organizations commonly has a bottom-up approach. A select group of users may begin to use them to enable easy communication and the usage may then spread to other members of the organization. When users first begin to explore new technologies, they are left on their own to figure things out, hence they must rely on their personal knowledge or access to personal knowledge resources such as friends who may be familiar with the technology.

Over time, and through continued exposure and interaction with the technology artifact, the user will begin to modify the original artifact – this is the *flexibility* stage. Modifications for flexibility can be defined as personalizing the technology parameters to meet the specificities of the user. Drawing on the usage of the term 'flexibility' in industrial engineering, we can define being flexible as the ability to work within a given range. For instance, a flexible manufacturing system is one that can produce products within a given range of quantities. In the context of technology, flexibility calls for changing the established parameters of the technology. For example, changing the appearance of a toolbar by moving one or more icons, or changing the background of the display screen are modifications for flexibility. The user is not creating anything new here, but is personalizing an existing option of the technology within the bounds set by the technology creator. In our discussions with software engineers, we found a wide assortment of modifications for flexibility. These included changing the default directory pointers, customizing the appearance of the screens, customizing drop-down menus, and so on.

Modifications for flexibility are the most basic and simple in nature. A user's individual requirements drive the need to customize the technology. Based on mental models and task peculiarities, each user will decide the nature and scope of the customization. The more tech-savvy a user is and the more often they interact with the technology, the greater is the propensity towards modifications for flexibility. Economics dictates that a user is better off personalizing the technology artifact once, rather than attempting to modify it on a repeated per-use basis.

As the technology diffuses through the organization and its usage increases, standards will emerge for organized work to take place in an efficient and effective manner. At this point users will be forced to customize the technology to meet these requirements – the *adaptability* stage. Modifications for adaptability can be defined as customizing the technology parameters to meet the specifics of the user's environment. Adaptability is the accumulation of small changes over time in response to the changing environment. Modifications for adaptability differ from the modifications for flexibility on one salient point – here, the user is adapting to the external environment. Modifications for adaptability are not driven by the individual needs of the user, but are a result of the user's involvement in an environment. The environment can be the user's work team or group, or even the organization.

In our discussions with software engineers, we deduced that the need to adapt is governed by one's workgroup and projects. Since the use of technology is socially constructed, it is influenced by the social context. In the context of software engineering, customizations occur to meet standards. Standards can be categorized based on the dimensions of purpose (reference point or compatibility) and enforcement (voluntary or mandatory).[10] Software engineers must customize their technology for all combinations of this 2×2 matrix of standards. In the context of working in a group, software engineers have to customize their directory parameters to point to the common repositories in order to jointly work on the code; these represent mandatory standards that seek to enhance compatibility. As most software engineering is now conducted on a global basis, IDEs must be synchronized in terms of language, date, time, and so on. These are mandatory standards that seek to enforce clear reference points. Two or more individuals working at close quarters might create their own standards to facilitate better work practices. In our discussions, we learnt of a case where three software engineers decided voluntarily to customize their IDE desktops for uniformity, so that each of them could access anyone else's PC in case one of them was away and the work called for this. This represents a voluntary standard intended to increase compatibility and serve as a reference point between the engineers.

As users continue to innovate with the technology after adaptation to organizational standards, these innovations lead to the development of novel functionalities, the *exaptability* stage. While *ad*aptability entails small changes over time to improve an existing function, *ex*aptability is defined as the ability to develop new functions, or the utilization of a structure or feature for a function other than that for which it was developed through natural selection.[11] Gould offers the following definition of exaptation: "[A] feature, now useful to an organism that did not arise as an adaptation for its present role, but was subsequently co-opted for its current function." Modifications for exaptability can be defined as inventing additions to the existing technology artifact and/or discovering new functions for existing components of the artifact. Modifications for exaptability include creating add-ins, scripts, modules, and so on to enhance the productivity of the technology. These modifications add on to the existing technology and are to be used in conjunction with the original technology. In the case of IDEs, add-ins are used to increase the efficiency of programming assignments. For instance, a developer working on a financial trading module was frustrated with the limitations of the default setup of the IDE when conducting testing. This led him to compose a macro that read his test data, ran his program, and generated results. Results were then fed through a statistical package for analysis and the final output was visually displayed using a graphics editor. Exaptations such as these may be considered inventions.

In addition to building new components, exaptation is also the use of existing functions in novel ways, most commonly referred to as 'work-arounds.' Owing to the limitations of the technology artifact, users find new ways to use existing functions in order to meet their needs. The simplest example is found in the use of statistical packages. Most statistical packages are highly restrictive in terms of the number of variables, types of variables, parameter requirements, and so on. To counter these restrictions, users create schemes such as 'dummy coding of variables' to work around them. In the context of IDEs, we found software engineers also create workarounds to increase the effectiveness of tasks, mostly in the testing and debugging phases of writing code. For instance, workarounds were commonly used to tweak the input and output of test data. In one case, a software engineer was frustrated with the lack of effective integration between output files of Microsoft's Excel and Project software. He took it upon himself to build a workaround using Visual Basic that would integrate the two output files, so that a project manager could easily move data between the costing tool using a spreadsheet interface and the administration tool that used a project management/Gantt chart layout.

Exaptations, the most complex form of modifications performed upon technology artifacts, can occur to meet the needs of the individual or a group. As in the case described above, individuals may get frustrated with the existing functionality of the technology and develop their own inventions. Similarly, team members working on a project may spend time and effort to innovate a new feature because of the benefits it poses to their project and work. Individuals might collectively pool resources in order to build a new technology feature or add-in. As can be witnessed from the proliferations of altruistic software communities, users have a tendency to contribute resources when there is hope for a better and more robust solution than what is currently available.

As a user continues to innovate with the technology, they will ascend to the status of an expert or super-user where they are knowledgeable enough about the intricacies of the technology artifact to make changes to it under time and resource constraints, that is to work agilely with the technology artifact. The *agility* stage is characterized by high proficiency in the use of the artifact, when a user is not just using the technology but is exploiting it to the maximum, and figuring out enhancements to the artifact.

The process model (operability–flexibility–adaptability–exaptability–agility) discussed above is interesting because it appreciates the roles played by the individual technology user, their group, and the organization as a whole. When the technology is first introduced to users, or when they decide to experiment with new technology, most often they are left on their own to figure out how to get it operational enough to meet immediate needs. Once operational, we see the emergence of flexibility to tailor the technology to the user. The stages of operability and flexibility are largely dominated by individual user decisions and preferences. The involvement of the users' local group or the organization is minimal. This is because, like the user, the rest of the organization is still grappling with learning to use the technology. Over time and with experience, as individual users become sophisticated and comfortable with the technology, it is used increasingly in the organization. Soon, conflicts will arise, through lack of compatibility and synchronization in how the technology is used. Economics dictate that it is in everyone's best interest to develop standards. The development of standards can be top-down or emergent. We postulate that in highly distributed organizations, standards are likely to emerge from the bottom up, owing to the lack of a dominating authority and the differences in technology usage across the various centers.

Rationally, standards are not updated in real time or on a regular basis and are slow to change, as maintaining standards a costly and resource-intensive effort. Therefore, users seldom stop at the adaptability stage, but continue using the technology, which leads them to discover shortcomings. Some users will then engage in acts of exaptation to meet their needs. The exaptation level is where the difference between experts and regular users starts to emerge. At the exaptability stage it is critical that an organization have mechanisms to connect regular users, their groups, and the organization at large with the experts who modify the technology. Unless this occurs, the organization's experience with the technology may not grow effectively – the experts will increase their personal stock of experience and may use the technology more effectively, while the rest of the organization will be struggling with shortcomings and will attempt to reinvent the wheel. In the best-case scenario, the organization is able to tap into the exaptations conducted by the experts. These can be evaluated by user communities such as the expert's local group or organizational members. If the modifications are found to be suitable, they can be diffused throughout the organization and existing standards can be updated. This results in the greatest benefits for both the individual user and the organization.

Given enough time, usage, and exposure to the technology, the individual or the organization is bound to reach a stage of agility. Organizations that are successful in knowledge sharing and innovation diffusions will become agile owing to innovations by individual users and their associated adoption, assimilation, and diffusion throughout the organization. Less successful organizations may find differences between their users in the knowledge they possess about the technology artifact. There will be 'the experts,' who can work with the technology with agility, and 'the rest,' who have limited knowledge about the technology and its capabilities. This situation will not be ideal for the organization, as conflicts in the use of the technology are bound to occur between the two sets of users. A software organization designated one day as 'Show Me Day'. This half-day event took place once every six weeks and consisted of presentations made by software engineers to their peers. Engineers who had customized, modified, or invented add-ins to the IDE were asked to make brief presentations to showcase their work. These presentations worked as a means to infuse new knowledge into the software engineering community and to help stimulate further discussions, critiques, and collaborations on modifying the IDE for effective work.

Appreciating emergence will require us to build more flexible and customizable KMSs. Consider using the analogy of how traditional knowledge work gets done. The reader may care to visualize their own office space. There are some workers, perhaps a blackboard, a projector, and some papers and pens. These devices are employed during the meeting where knowledge is exchanged, created, and leveraged, but they do not determine the nature of the meeting. Two or more groups can use the same devices in different forms, depending on their meeting. In traditional technology systems, like transaction processing systems, technologies were built in pre-defined structures and were rigid. A report came out a certain way, and it was not easy to customize or modify it. The programmer had to be called in to make changes. As technologies increased in sophistication, decision support tools emerged that were amenable to basic customizations. Users could change the type of reports, the layouts, the type of analyses, and so on. However, all changes were restricted to working with pre-defined objects. For instance, using a traditional spreadsheet tool you could choose a set of graphs from a set of pre-defined options. KMSs, however, need to provide users with one stride forward. In addition to providing users with pre-defined sets of options and devices to be used, it is also important to allow them to build their own tools and customize the technology, especially the interface, to meet their needs.

Appreciating context

Knowledge artifacts are created in context. As pointed out by Nonaka, the *ba* is what gives knowledge its context.[12] According to Nonaka and Konno, knowledge is embedded in the ba. The ba is a shared space that provides a platform for advancing individual and/or collective knowledge creation. As a workspace, the ba can be *physical* (such as an office location), *virtual* (such as net conferencing), or *mental* (such as shared experiences). If knowledge is taken out of the ba it becomes information.

There are four types of ba. *Originating ba* is where socialization occurs and members share their tacit frames and mental models, thereby establishing a context for knowledge sharing and exchanges. *Interacting ba* is where tacit insights are made explicit. Metaphors are used here to help capture tacit knowledge in codified formats. *Cyber ba* represents the virtual shared space and is used mainly to facilitate the exchange of explicit knowledge via the use of technological solutions such as knowledge repositories, communication technologies, or a combination of the two. *Exercising ba* is the space where explicit knowledge is internalized into the mental frames of individuals, such as training programs, self-learning schemes, and learning via job rotations.

Context includes the social, cultural, historical, and personal perspectives for one to evaluate information, and can be defined as the situational factors that surround the knowledge work. For example, a software engineer writing a piece of code will do so in the context of a project. The project requirements, system designs, work schedules and other intricacies all affect the outcome of the software engineer's task. If the engineer has to create the code on an unrealistic and overly tight schedule, the quality of the code might be affected. If the project is terminated before completion, the software code may not be put through testing and quality assurance efforts. Context is the way to include the tacit dimension of explicit knowledge. Explicit and tacit knowledge are not opposite ends of the spectrum. The same knowledge might be explicit for some people but tacit for others. This is where context comes in, to help in the explication of tacit insights. Such contextual factors are important in evaluating the output of the work, the knowledge artifact.

To date, most KMSs capture the knowledge artifact without adequate appreciation for its context. If we detach the context component from a knowledge *artifact*, we are left with an information *object*. As a result, most KMSs get populated with information objects, 'useless documents' rather than valuable knowledge artifacts. Information *objects* should be stored in a database, where we have logical relationships between data items. A KMS must house *knowledge*, that is information in context. When a potential consumer of knowledge searches the KMS for an artifact, they are likely to find a document that is a close match. On examination of the document, however, one is not likely to gain any appreciation for the document's credibility, value, problems, and so on. As such, the potential consumer of the knowledge artifact is reluctant to use it. This will lead to constant reinvention of the wheel. Over time, the KMS will house multiple versions of the same knowledge artifacts, many of which will never be used by members of the organization. Eventually, users will abandon the KMS as it will be too time-consuming to search the large repository and too cognitively expensive to understand the intricacies of the various variants of knowledge artifacts.

We must remember that knowledge artifacts are intimately tied to the creator or producer. No knowledge is created in a vacuum. In organizations, besides the knowledge creator we must also be concerned with the task or project that led to the creation of the knowledge. We must also account for the knowledge document having its own context.

A user of a knowledge artifact must be able to examine it by evaluating the producer. Hence, it is important to state clearly the producer's know-how and level of expertise. It is even more important to document if the producer was a novice or had less than adequate knowledge in the subject matter. Consider an example from the medical field: a patient diagnosis entered by medical resident needs to be weighted differently from that of a specialist or a doctor. Details such as the producer's past experience in the subject-matter are helpful for a future consumer who is looking to adapt or reuse the artifact. In daily life, we constantly ask for references from professionals before hiring them on projects. These references help us evaluate the skill of the professional and make judgments as to their caliber. The same rules apply for knowledge producers in the organization. We must also allow the producers to document their confidence in the artifact. It is not uncommon to find that a professional has created an artifact that they are not completely satisfied with. The context of the project, as we will discuss next, may play a role here. When the producer is not completely sure about the solution or product captured in the artifact, such reservations must be documented. It is only fair that a knowledge consumer be made aware of these caveats before spending time and effort in attempting to use the artifact.

Work in organizations is mostly executed in the context of projects. It is rare to find individuals working in isolation. Consequently, knowledge artifacts, which are the outcomes of project assignments, are affected by the dynamics of the project. Software organizations are notorious for having artifacts residing in KMSs without appropriate context. With the high rate of IT project failures, it is common to have artifacts from incomplete, suspended, or cancelled projects. These are stored in code libraries and other KMSs. Very often, a potential user may begin to incorporate the knowledge artifact without knowing whether it was ever put through rigorous testing measures. Thus the user will be building new software code using a potentially defective component, resulting in wasted effort. The dynamics of the project need to be captured and documented, including such details as the answers to the questions: Was the project completed? Did the project meet client requirements? How did the client perceive the knowledge artifact? Information that answers such project-specific questions enables future knowledge users to understand the *background* of the knowledge artifact.

We also need to be concerned with the *context* of the artifact, usually called metadata, that is knowledge about the knowledge. Here, we are interested in how the artifact in question relates to the other artifacts residing in the KMS. Was the artifact recycled or built using existing knowledge artifacts? If so, does the new artifact replace the old ones? It is important for a consumer to have such details in order to be able to trace the history of the artifact. Metadata must also contain other relevant details: How can a potential customer use the knowledge artifact? Are there dimensions and/or components that can be customized? Are there specific bounds within which customization will work? More important, are there peculiarities under which the knowledge artifact cannot be used? Adding these details will help in building an integrated KMS. Documenting the context is vital for building a knowledge artifact. We suggest that KMSs and knowledge artifacts have 'comments' features, akin to those allowing the use of comments in software programs. Comments should cover the three dimensions of context – the *producer*, the *project*, and the *artifact*.

Currently there are automated tools to handle some of the specificities of documenting the context of the artifact. Integrating project management systems with KMSs may be one way to automate the capture of project contextual details. Manual effort is still needed to document the details of the producers, especially details such as their confidence in their knowledge artifact. Similar intervention is needed in current knowledge management practices for us to successfully capture context. Technological interventions such as automated reminders, control boxes, and other validation tools, may help remind the knowledge worker to explicate the context of the artifact. For instance, if an employee begins to post a knowledge nugget to the system, the input program could ask the user to answer a series of questions, all of which are geared towards explaining the context. Another option would be to provide the user with a 'comments' field, which needs to be filled out prior to posting the nugget to the system. While technology interventions may enforce the need to explicate context, they will not be sufficient. Knowledge workers must be trained in the importance of context. Only when they are made aware of the high cost of not describing the context will they be willing to spend time and effort to document it. Project managers should also be more cognizant of the need to budget cost and time for such efforts. Failure to do so will lead employees to do a haphazard job in capturing and storing knowledge.

Imagine the case of a patient visiting a doctor, who must capture the contextual nature of the patient's symptoms along with the diagnosis and prescriptions. Failure to do so will make it very difficult for any doctor to treat the patient effectively in future. Without adequate context, another doctor might wrongly infer why a certain prescription was given, may not appreciate the sensitivity of drug interactions, or may misdiagnose the problem, any of which could even prove fatal to the patient. Medical professionals, especially physicians, are model knowledge workers. Much of their interest in managing knowledge is because if they do not they may simply lose their ability to practice medicine. Hence, almost all of their tasks, routines, decisions, and thinking are guided by knowledge management principles. Consider this: when a doctor is unable to diagnose a patient's peculiar ailment, they do not just propose an arbitrary prescription. Instead, the doctor spends time diagnosing the problem using the existing knowledge base; if unsuccessful they are more than willing to collaborate with a peer.

It is important to note a significant aspect of the medical professional: they spend time and effort documenting the context of their findings, more for the good of the medical community than for themselves. If the community cannot adequately share the patient's context, its members will not be able to treat the patient and, even worse, they may treat them incorrectly. All of this will result in disrepute for the profession.

In the medical community, knowledge is exchanged and discussed openly in order to get to the crux of the problem and solve it. We can only wish this were a routine process in business organizations. While most organizations do not have the medical community's sensitivity to knowledge context, there are correspondingly huge potential losses if the context is not adequately captured.

Appreciating distributed natures

Knowledge exchanges using technology occur when two or more individuals are *distributed*. Two or more people do not necessarily have to be distributed in the context of geographical space. They could be distributed across time, that is not available at the same time, or even in terms of office locations, for example separated by twenty floors. If the knowledge seekers and providers were in the same space, chances are high they would not use technology to communicate and could engage in a face-to-face conversation for exchanges of information and knowledge.

Given that technology helps in communicating in the distributed context, the technology used must help support the concept of distributedness, and must reflect this in the infrastructure of the technology artifact. In order to appreciate the distributed nature of knowledge communications, a technology artifact must appreciate the three salient elements of any communication – *actors*, *interpretations*, and *actions*.[13] *Actors* are the individuals involved in the communication, *interpretations* are the meanings they ascribe to knowledge and information being transferred, and *actions* represent their possible behavior, such as sending or receiving a knowledge item, storing it, and so on.

In distributed communications, ownership of knowledge and communications must be clearly defined. For instance, it is important to identify who is sending a piece of communication or who has posted a given document to the repository. Additionally, each actor is responsible for their own interpretation of the knowledge. It is important that the system have a way to assign ownership to interpretations and not make an individual interpretation equal to a group interpretation. Interpretations may not be cogent or in convergence with one another, and during such times each owner must be allowed to hold on to their own interpretation and not have to compromise on it.

Owing to the distributed nature, the technology artifact must allow the user to travel across and within knowledge spaces. One may think of this in the context of visiting a website. Visitors to the site should be able to access it in a top-down fashion, drilling down to finer granularities of information as needed. They must also be able to move laterally and visit sites that complement or refute the present context, so as to increase their exposure to knowledge and to easily navigate distributed knowledge spaces to seek out requisite knowledge. Similarly, actors must also be allowed to engage in a multitude of conversations at any one time. The real thrust of current advanced KMSs is that they allow this functionality. For instance, through the use of messaging tools it is possible to engage in multiple chat sessions on different topics simultaneously. The only limiting factor is the cognitive and attention capacity of the individual participating in the conversations and the speed at which they can type or speak their thoughts – the actor's capabilities in interpretation and action.

In addition, the system must appreciate the concepts of emergence addressed above, and also allow users to specify their contextual details. For instance, through the use of instant messaging tools, users (actors) can send emoticons that indicate their feelings when a piece of information is transmitted. They can also signify if they are away from their desk or on the phone by changing their status messages. This enables a knowledge seeker to gauge how busy one might be and get a better sense of time pressures and other contextual elements, thereby improving interpretation and action during the exchange.

Knowledge management systems in varying environments

Most organizations operate in different environments and face varying pressures. The environmental pressures a government agency faces are different from those a technology startup or a healthcare enterprise experiences. An organization must be cognizant of the environment characteristics and how these affect the type of KMS it might successfully deploy.

Here, let us recall the *codified* and *personalized* approaches we discussed at the beginning of this chapter. For static environments that can withstand delayed changes to actions, it may be best to pursue a codified strategy, since knowledge captured is not going to be quickly outdated. Dynamic and continuously changing environments, however, will not be able to use systems that rely on codification, since by the time knowledge gets codified it may be outdated. Managing the costs and benefits of the codified and personalized strategies is critical. Moreover, in environments that are simple and easily decomposable we may be able to deploy automated, rules-based KMSs. In complex and dynamic environments, the KMS should ideally focus on creating an environment that fosters creative work, by facilitating the sharing of ideas and the combination of these ideas into possible innovations. It will not be possible to run automated routines here, as it will be difficult to decompose the problem in a reasonable timeframe and, once it is decomposed, the environmental conditions will most likely change.

KMSs need to align closely with conditions faced by the organization. Lack of proper alignment will result in an excellent KMS not attaining its objectives. Knowledge that needs to be generated and managed in organizations is heavily dependent on the environmental and organizational realities. The KMS should reflect this dependency and be cognizant of and attentive to relevant details.

Deploying knowledge management systems

There are three main strategies for deploying KMSs (see Figure 9.1). Each strategy has pros and cons; identifying them will help you choose the right strategy, depending on your organizational peculiarities. Each organization

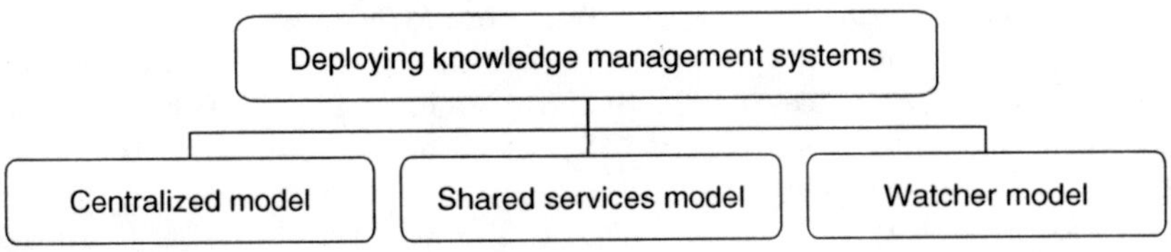

Figure 9.1   Deploying knowledge management systems.

normally has a unit that oversees the technology construction and management duties that normally fall under the umbrella of information systems departments. We will now present the different options, ranked according to how much control the technology department wields in deploying the KMSs.

The *centralized model* calls for the technology department to be responsible for the construction, deployment, and management of KMSs and for setting and implementing standards. The technology unit houses the expertise needed to calibrate the KMS and also the management expertise needed to oversee its successful deployment. This model gives the technology department maximal control over KMS deployments, but at the cost of maintaining a significant calibration staff.

The *shared service* or *consulting model* calls for the technology department to serve as expert consultants to other units considering KMS deployments. They help other units by conducting searches for possible solutions, helping them design and calibrate solutions that will integrate appropriately with the existing infrastructure, and also provide support if operational issues arise. The technology department needs also to be a repository of best practices that can be used to guide the future technology choices for each unit, by compiling and storing best practices from organization-wide implementations. Best practices are used to make global decisions on the technology architecture of the organization. In this model the technology unit does not have the same level of control as with the centralized model, since it can advise what each unit should do but cannot demand it. The lack of control is compensated for by the lack of requirement for heavy investment in technology staff. The technology department needs only to have project managers and business consultants who can advise on technology matters and does not need calibration staff. System calibration or purchases are handled by the individual units and charged to their budgets.

The *watcher model* calls for the technology department to keep a watchful eye over KMS deployments. Unlike the shared service model, this model does not require the technology department to serve as consultants. Rather, the technology department is responsible for ensuring that the KMS calibrated and designed by the individual units fits the global technology architecture of the organization. In doing so the technology unit provides the rest of the organization with a list of accepted tools, interfaces, preferred applications, vendors, and any other authorized information. Each department can consult the list to see what choices they have in implementing KMSs. The technology department aims to promote reuse of existing technology across the organization by adhering to standardized choices. Doing so minimizes compatibility issues associated with disparate systems. The watcher model lies between the centralized and shared services models in terms of coordination. While the technology department exerts no direct control over each unit, it restricts its choice of what technology solutions can be implemented. However, it does allow each unit the freedom to customize a given technology solution to its own needs. As in the shared services model, the watcher model also calls for the technology department to assemble best practices of technology implementations and use them to decide changes to the global technology architecture, which will then be reflected in the approved technology solutions lists to be used by other units.

Knowledge management systems and decision-making

KMSs help individuals, teams or groups, departments, and even the whole organization engage in effective and efficient decision-making. One KMS might be aimed at efficiency for its primary focus, another be more focused on being effective, even at the cost of efficiency. Consider a KMS in the medical sector, one that provides support in prescribing medicines. It is important that such a KMS check adequately for the various drug-to-drug and drug-to-patient interactions – among other caveats and constraints – before suggesting possible medication. While timeliness is a concern, getting quick suggestions that are inaccurate will not do much good, and may come back to haunt the medical organization in the form of lawsuits. Effectiveness is clearly the dominant criterion for evaluating such a KMS. Now, consider a KMS that is helping a financial trader decide which stocks to purchase or sell. Here, it is important that the trader be provided with timely knowledge, that is which stocks to purchase or sell. No system will be 100 percent effective or accurate in this domain, as we have a large number of variables – accounting measures, market reactions, government news, and so on – that must be evaluated and taken into account for decision-making. Hence, striving for near-perfect effectiveness will remain an elusive goal. Moreover, timeliness is crucial in this domain. It is no use getting accurate knowledge on stocks purchases after the close of trading, since timeliness and relevance have been compromised.

A KMS's role in decision-making can be examined using a process perspective. The decision-making process is: (1) problem identification, (2) alternative generation and evaluation, (3) decision execution, and (4) feedback monitoring. Feedback received will most likely trigger new problem identification. KMSs can focus on any one or more of the stages of the decision process.

Some comprehensive KMSs may actually provide support for the entire cycle of activities. We will now explore each stage of the decision-making process.

Decisions are triggered when we realize that there are *gaps*. Gaps can be differences between our current state and our desired state. For instance, if you have $100 and would like to have $101, there is a gap and decisions are required on how this gap can be closed by achieving or revising the desired state. Gaps can also be between what is expected and the unexpected. For instance, if while driving from Amsterdam to Vienna, quite a scenic route, we encounter a landslide or other damage along one of our intended roads, we must then revise our plans and seek alternative routes. Organizations are inundated with information from internal entities and also the external world. It is through parsing such information that the organization identifies gaps. KMSs that help in problem identification normally belong to one of two types. First, we have KMSs that scan the given environments. For example, an externally oriented KMS might scan competitor moves by examining news and press releases, along with other publicly available information. It would then organize such information in a readily accessible format. Next, it would either push it to knowledge workers (through mechanisms such as emails or electronic messages or via devices such as mobile phones) or announce the availability of the knowledge and wait for it to be pulled by the worker (by making the knowledge available in a centrally accessible location like a website, and leaving it up to workers to retrieve it in their own time). Understandably, the push mechanisms are used for sending knowledge that is highly urgent, as it will interrupt the recipient's work and, most often, claim instant attention, while pull mechanisms are suitable for making less urgent knowledge available.

Second, we have KMSs that are 'auto-detectors' for problem identification. The best analogy might be that of baggage or passenger screening devices at airports. If one of these beeps, indicating the possible presence of explosives, metals, or other unauthorized substances, the airport officials (the knowledge workers) are alerted and check the person or item and make a decision to either pass or quarantine. In organizations, we have KMSs that work on similar premises. They routinely take in assorted inputs, akin to putting baggage through the x-ray device. Once the information item is entered, they conduct basic operations on it, much like the algorithms used to scan the baggage. If the rules signify no abnormalities the information item is passed, but if triggers are activated then manual intervention becomes essential. As an example, consider rudimentary customer support systems that provide basic information such as shipping and delivery dates, or which allow passengers to get troubleshooting help in automated formats. These are for the most part rule-based, that is they deliver knowledge through parsing of simple rules, most of them in the format IF–THEN: 'IF the customer says the problem is with the screen, THEN ask the customer to check if the power is being delivered to the monitor,' and so on. As long as information items pass through without abnormalities then automated tools can solve the problem; if not, a human customer service operator may be required.

Recently, we have seen advance in identification technologies such as RFID (radio frequency identification devices). These can be attached to items of interest and have the ability to emit real-time information. For instance, a retail store may want to tag their expensive items with them, using the information they emit to monitor where such items are being moved to in the store, or whether a customer needs to be attended to – someone holding three tagged items may be a highly lucrative purchaser. ID tags can also help stores manage theft by detecting the movement of material in and around their premises. As computing knowledge advances, we can expect ID technology to be combined with automated detecting routines to help organizations with real-time identification of problem areas.

Once the need for decision-making is identified, the next step is to generate alternatives of possible solutions. KMSs used to generate alternatives are normally referred to as decision support systems (DSSs), which can be classified as being either model-based or data-based. The traditional DSSs were model-based, the programmer or system designer specifying a mathematical model to be used to generate alternatives. Common approaches include linear programming models. As information systems and computer processing advanced, it became evident that there was a lot of data on events that was not being used effectively. Owing to advancements in computer processing power, the power of analyses could be increased and these databases could be mined. The data-based approaches focus more on generation of alternatives from data analysis rather than specifying models a priori. The entire field of knowledge discovery from databases (KDD) has emerged around this concept. Common approaches include the application of machine learning, advanced statistical analyses, and classification procedures. The key difference between the model-based and data-based approach is between the respective problem domains. Under the model-based approach, the designer is confident about their understanding of the environment, can specify a model a priori, and also is confident that the model will not change too rapidly to render the effort of specifying it a waste. In the data-driven approach, the designer is normally working in a more complex and less completely understood environment. Besides, there are too many variables and interactions to clearly specify a mathematical model, and the designer is seeking to discover latent relationships along with known ones from the data. By 'data,' we do not necessarily mean rudimentary data like numbers. Today, we have KDD endeavors that are mining collections of text (for example, scanning corporate emails), images (for example, mining criminal databases), and also videos (for example, scanning airport cameras for potential terrorists in and around terminals). The speed and accuracy of KDD approaches also continue to increase, both in the time taken to generate knowledge and the preciseness of such knowledge. The focus of KDD researchers is most often on reducing the numbers of false positives and false negatives associated with predictions and pattern detection.

After enumerating the alternatives, we must select the ones we would like to implement in the execution phase. KMSs that help in the execution phase are normally engaged in simple, static environments. As we have discussed earlier, these environments are easy to work with as they do not change that frequently and are easily decomposable into finite and manageable components. The use of artificial intelligence techniques, such as rules-based expert systems technologies, is common here. For instance, most financial institutions have deployed sophisticated credit scoring and loan application systems that are automated. They take input from users, process it, generate alternatives, and then choose the right alternative as the decision. For example, a system for housing loan applications might take in details (such as current earnings, financial history, asset portfolios, demographic information, and collateral or guarantee information), process the information, and tell the customer the amount of loan that is going to be provided and its interest rate. It is difficult to calibrate KMSs for decision execution in environments that are highly complex and dynamic, owing to the constant need to refine and redefine decision-making rules used to generate decisions. It makes little economic sense, because by the time rules are calibrated, they need to be refined to comply with changes in the environment.

Once a decision is made we must carefully monitor the environment for feedback. Sometimes a decision may bring about desired outcomes, resulting in positive feedback. At other times, it may result in unintended consequences, generating negative feedback. Regardless of whether feedback is positive or negative, it is important to monitor the environment so that we may be able to better plan future decisions. With positive feedback we may want to see if the outcomes are a function of our decision, and examine the possibility of using good decisions in future situations, instead of incurring costs by going through the entire process of decision-making. With negative feedback, we realize that we have to rethink the decision and try to resolve inconsistencies.

Feedback is an important concept in any system design. One might argue that feedback has been one of the salient driving forces behind advances in technology. One of the goals of technology artifacts is to increase the depth and quality of feedback received and the speed at which the feedback is delivered. If we look at current voice and video technologies, which are forms of KMS used to engage in dialogues and knowledge sharing, we see that the way we communicate has not changed, but the feedback has become sharper and quicker. In the past, if we had to communicate with people in geographically distributed areas, we had to write and mail a letter. The feedback – reply – we received sometimes came weeks or months later. Also, being restricted to non-verbal cues and communication, it would be of low quality. We then advanced to the telephone, where the feedback could be instantaneous and verbal. Today, we have a whole arsenal of communication technologies at our disposal that have fairly advanced feedback mechanisms, and we can combine the technologies to get a wider assortment of feedback. Thus we can be talking to someone on the phone while sending them a document via email or instant messaging software, and also watching their facial reactions via a web camera. KMSs that help in feedback monitoring include all these communication technologies, as they help in the sharing of tacit insights and know-how. Communication technologies can also be used for the other decision stages such as problem identification, alternative generations, and even execution of decisions. We have addressed them here because they are very prominent in the feedback stage.

We must also include the traditional feedback mechanisms such as report generation tools. Report generation tools generate batch or real-time outcomes on items of interest that give us feedback on how the item is performing. For example, if we devise a new incentive system we can study employee work hours and productivity reports to get feedback on the incentive structures. On the internet we have feedback systems that are social and public in nature, where one entity shares feedback with other entities. The individual does not necessarily gain from their own feedback, but other users do. Consider rating systems on the internet: at Amazon.com, for instance, books are rated by readers who want to share their feedback with other potential readers. Since the rater has most likely purchased the book, their own ratings do not necessarily provide them with any direct benefit, but other potential purchasers can gain from such insights. Rating systems, as we saw in Chapter 8 on knowledge markets, are an important component of feedback on knowledge exchange.

We have discussed KMSs sequentially according to the various decision stages. There are KMSs that are integrative and comprehensive in nature and can help in the complete process of decision-making. Let us consider two examples: in most organizations, we see the usage of group support systems such as Lotus Notes that, if integrated properly with the various corporate databases and operational systems, can alert knowledge workers to problems in real time, suggest alternatives, help employees debate and discuss alternatives with their peers to work out the right decision, and even execute the decision via the sending of communications. The feedback received can be fed into standardized reports and be pushed to or pulled by workers. Similarly, advanced mobile phones have capabilities to receive messages (text, voice, and image) that can be used to alert the receiver about a problem, enable them to connect up to databases or corporate systems to seek alternatives, communicate with peers on the right alternative to employ, and even execute such instructions via a communication with peers or, in especially advanced cases, by sending instructions from the mobile phone directly to computerized systems.

Conclusion

When introduced, the term 'knowledge management' generated a surge of interest from consulting houses, both large and small. The general idea was: "Let's make a few quick bucks out of this new buzzword." It was not uncommon to find some opportunistic consultants trying to sell knowledge management on a CD, claiming: "This CD contains the answers to all your knowledge management problems!" Unsurprisingly, this did not last long. Those who had jumped on to the knowledge management bandwagon for the short run lost their assets and reputation, and eventually exited. Much to their dismay, no one wanted to invest the sums they wanted! Why? Well, the truth is that they never stood a chance.

Knowledge management, as we have described it so far, is more than a technology solution. Knowledge management is conducted *by* people and *with* people; technology serves the role of support. Technology helps make the practice of knowledge management more effective and efficient – or ineffective and inefficient, as the case may be. However, technology alone is not the answer to an organization's knowledge management problems.

The most notable advance in KMSs will be in the quality and intensity of feedback. In addition, the interconnectivity between knowledge appliances will increase, promoting greater mobility. Finally, such devices will become non-intrusive and invisible. They will exist and work in the background but will not interfere or place additional burdens on humans as an imposing foreground presence. Correspondingly, KMSs are going to increase in prominence, sophistication, and pervasiveness as we advance.

10

The Future of Engaged Knowledge Management

Thus far we have shown how knowledge management must be engaged with to get suitable results for investments in the effort. In doing so, we have outlined eight topics that call for a renewed effort to realign current knowledge management practices in order for an organization to be poised for success. We began by highlighting tensions when trying to exert centralized versus decentralized control over knowledge management programs. Following this, we highlighted the three missing capabilities that will need due attention as knowledge management programs advance. Next came the intricacies of four senior-level knowledge personnel, the need to pay attention to the concept of distributedness and its impacts on knowledge management, how to garner and leverage knowledge from external sources, how best to engage in the management of customer knowledge, and the intricacies of knowledge markets. Finally, we surveyed the design of knowledge management systems.

Figure 10.1 depicts the key concepts presented in the book. While it is difficult to tie all the concepts together with one piece of string, there are connections that we would like to point out. First, unless an organization appreciates the realities presented in each chapter it will lack an engaged knowledge management program. Second, each concept presented has bearings on the effectiveness of the other concepts. For instance, if an organization does not take the protection capability seriously then the chances are high that it will not create a CSO position or, if such a position exists, that it will lack sufficient authority and credibility. By the same token, a lack of appreciation for the protection capability will cost the organization dearly in terms of knowledge management in strategic alliances and will also lead to the calibration of KMSs with poor security procedures. We can make similar arguments for the concepts of centralized and decentralized control regimes or distributed knowledge management. Finally, having an engaged knowledge program will in fact act as a source of energy for the organization, hence the sun-like depiction in the figure. Not only will the engaged knowledge program help each aspect of knowledge creation, storage, distribution, and application,

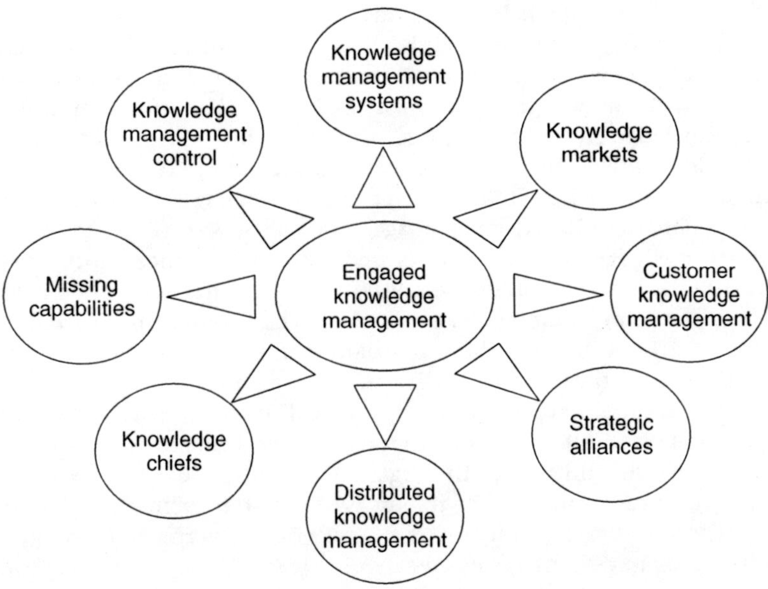

Figure 10.1　Engaged knowledge management.

but this will in turn help the organization better achieve its overall objectives and goals.

In order to appreciate the materials presented here, from a pragmatic perspective, we suggest the following procedure. An organization should first conduct a basic "inventory analysis." By this we mean it should compare its current knowledge program with the concepts presented here. Does the organization have a CSO? Are there knowledge destruction capabilities? This done, the next step is to conduct a gap analysis. Here the question of interest is how much attention is being paid to concepts, and whether the current capacities are sufficient for the organization. An outcome of conducting a thorough gap analysis will be the identification of areas of improvement for the organization. The next logical step is then to prioritize these areas for improvement. We know that an organization will have more areas for improvement than resources exist. Our instincts tell us that the first area where resources need to be expelled is in the area of senior personnel – the knowledge chiefs. These chiefs, if they exist, should be given the due means to improve knowledge programs in the organization. If the chiefs do not exist, they need to; it is that simple. We cannot have an organization without a CEO, and a knowledge chief is similarly vital. The second area of focus should be in the area of customer knowledge management. Customers are the lifeblood of the enterprise and hence we are likely to see speedy and tangible results if knowledge programs improve customer experiences. For instance, if management of customer support knowledge helps us increase repeat purchases and sales, these will bolster the credibility and seriousness associated with knowledge management, and this will benefit other initiatives of the knowledge chiefs. After the customers, we must focus on the areas of missing capabilities and the centralized and decentralized regimes of knowledge control. These need to be put in place and managed in order to lay the right foundation for knowledge management efforts. Next comes the management of knowledge in distributed contexts, strategic alliances, and the setup of knowledge markets. These elements are important, but can be held off until the preceding components are in place. The deployment of technology artifacts will then emerge, these normally being of use only if the other, non-technology aspects of a knowledge-based organization are in place.

The above sequential process is only an idealized one; the chances are that the organization will need to focus on multiple aspects sequentially. Under this condition, we still think that the organization should use the above depiction to decide the proportion of resources to invest in each effort. An organization cannot expect to succeed if they devote 90 percent of resources to knowledge management system development (much as consultants would love this) and only 10 percent to efforts in understanding and improving customer knowledge management. The steps involved in building an engaged knowledge program will need to be refined on a regular basis corresponding to changes in the organization's internal and external realities – the future.

The future

The world is not static, and time is dynamic. Change is the only constant. We must, hence, be prepared to be forward-looking and futuristic. By the time this book makes it to bookshelves, some of the material we have covered in it will already have been improved upon by others. Some of these may refute some of the ideas presented here. While it is common to have criticisms outweigh praises in most efforts, we feel that this book has provided a thorough grounding in eight salient realities that we thought needed the attention of managers and scholars. In this concluding chapter, we would like to share our opinions on what the future may hold for knowledge management, and what emergent realities an organization should engage itself with, if and when they materialize.

Customer-focused knowledge management

One of the many realities we are convinced of is the growing need for organizations to better manage their customers, and, more importantly, to listen to them so that management efforts can be geared towards making sure they have pleasurable experiences with products and services. As discussed in Chapter 6, customer knowledge management is a vital capability because it serves as an antecedent to other organizational processes. In our opinion, the future will call for greater work in this area. In particular, we feel that an organization will be forced to redesign or realign its knowledge management processes to make them *customer-focused*.

To understand the meaning of being customer-focused, one may want to examine the practices in the various the defense sectors of governments. Who are the customers of the defense departments? While some may say it is the citizens of a country or the politicians, there is a more important customer segment – the soldiers on the battlefields. These are the true customers of the offerings of the defense departments, especially the information and knowledge resources. Information and knowledge generated in and around these installations is geared towards helping soldiers perform their jobs better and come home alive. Soldiers represent the customers for information on battlefield layouts and knowledge of enemy tactics and strategies. Their ultimate success or failure will often depend on how well the organization is able to process information and knowledge and make this available to them in a timely manner. It would be a shame were the soldiers in the field to get attacked while downloading knowledge about enemy positions – timeliness of knowledge delivery is essential.

In organizations we seldom see the drive to be customer-focused in terms of knowledge management. We have practices in place that help us attain customer objectives or listen to customers, but seldom is this taken seriously enough to redesign existing processes and procedures to make them customer-centric. Knowledge management is no exception to this norm. While many organizations manage the various types of customer knowledge, and a select few are even successful at integrating them, only a handful are customer-focused in their knowledge management efforts.

Having customer-focused knowledge management practices is going to differentiate between competitors for the next few years; after this, it will become a necessity for competition in the marketplace. In order to transform current practices to make them customer-focused, an organization must now reverse its current knowledge management practices. Knowledge management efforts grew inside-out. The first instances of knowledge programs were to help employees to better share ideas, know-how, and solutions to improve their processes. Only recently, principally owing to technology and communication advances such as the internet, has the customer been included in the knowledge management practices of the organization. Now the inside-out thinking must be reversed, to one that is outside-in. In doing so, the organization must ask: How can we make the lives of our customers better in terms of the goods and services provided by the organization? Once articulated, these objectives need to drive changes to processes and practices so that they better reflect a customer focus.

In order to be customer-focused, the organization will need to conduct some back-end work. The first effort that will be called for is one of paying attention to the sources of knowledge. Organizations are laden with sources of knowledge, ranging from automated machines to individuals and teams. Each source emits knowledge and information that is used by others in the organization for work, which ultimately has some bearing on products and services delivered to the customer. Management efforts need to be more cognizant of the sources of knowledge to ensure that we do not get in a situation of "garbage in, garbage out." We must make certain that the knowledge emitted from sources meets basic quality standards. In doing so, we must ensure that sources perform quality control procedures to validate and test their knowledge before it is passed on to other entities in the organization. Too often myth or bad knowledge is passed on from source to source, being amplified with every passing, and in the end bad decisions are made which effect the customer. Lessons must be adapted from the literatures of quality management and information quality practices to make it clear how knowledge is to be moved from source to destination (the customer).

Second, we need to strive for interoperability and portability between the various knowledge generating entities in the organization. Knowledge, knowledge processes, and knowledge systems need to be connected and integrated. During the first wave of the information systems revolution, it was not uncommon to find unintegrated and disparate systems residing in organizations. Today, we have technologies such as enterprise resource planning (ERP) that help to integrate the flow of information across the enterprise, and even between the enterprise and the external environment. Similar movements must occur in terms of knowledge movement within and around the organization. For this, we must focus on "interoperability." Interoperability calls for building links between the knowledge generated in different environments (teams, departments, groups, locations, and so on), so that it can be accessed, visualized, and integrated and used effectively and efficiently. In addition to interoperability we have also to pay attention to portability. Portability will call for making sure there is mobility between the various knowledge nuggets generated and the processes that govern them. Knowledge generated in one location should be able to be ported into another, and used towards ends, rather than having to be recreated. Dell has a policy where software applications (knowledge) generated in one location should be implemented in any other locations within six months, without the need for recreation of the software. Failure to work towards the goals of interoperability and portability will result in an organization that is not customer-focused, and hence will soon be out of business. As an example of a success story in terms of being engaged with the process dimension of knowledge management, one can consider the case of Siemens. Siemens's E-logistic Virtual Information Center is an example of an attempt to coordinate and integrate knowledge management. Through the use of this technology, the various members of the Siemens medical sales team, technical support staff, and even their customers, can share information and knowledge to reduce the cost and effort involved in the sales and installation of complex medical equipment. In the past there were significant delays between the time at which an order was taken and that when the equipment was installed, because details such as the dimensions of the hospital's doors and rooms were not shared with technical installation staff in a timely manner. This resulted in the reworking of equipments, the reordering of parts, and other costly errors that could have been avoided had the knowledge been shared at the right time.

Third, being customer-focused means understanding how the customer is going to change in the future. Changes in customer behavior, especially those already prompted by increasing sophistication in technology, can be described as dynamic. Most customers can be considered as "thin clients," to borrow a terminology from computer hardware, meaning they want to have the capability to plug-and-play. That is, they want not to be bogged down with large upfront investments, but instead to be mobile, adaptative, and agile, and they require the organization to be the same. An organization lacking a mature policy that allows the customer to plug in, receive their products and services in a timely manner, and leave with pleasurable experiences, is going to lose out in tomorrow's marketplace. Take the example of internet cafés. A few years back, most of these had computer stations that required a customer to sign on, fill in their details, enter credit card information, accept permission policies, and so on – all before they access the internet – by which time their coffee was already cold! Those days were the old ones of having "thick clients," and were characterized by the customer having to make an upfront investment to use the service. Today, such cafés are rare if not obsolete; instead they have been replaced by wireless centers. Here, the customer brings in their own computing equipment, gets connected on their own, uses the services as they choose and then leaves, all of this without direct intervention from anyone or being forced to used the equipment of the organization. There are two subtle points here. First, the customer is more mobile and can get their services in the manner or manners of their own choosing. Second, the customer can bring their own resources and use them in conjunction with the organization's infrastructure. The customer can bring their laptop, containing their applications and data, and then use the infrastructure of the organization for the internet connection. One reason why plug-and-play is an important characteristic is that no customer will be able to tell a priori what they need from an organization, nor will an organization know exactly how best to predict it. Hence it is important that an organization possesses an open architecture where a customer can come in to try products and services; then, if the customer decides to stay on, steps can be taken to customize and personalize knowledge delivery to meet their needs.

Changes from "thick" to "thin" clients are on the rise. We can see many instances of these in and around technology innovations. The whole drive is to make technology more accessible, mobile, ubiquitous, and pervasive to the customer. In this, the customer is empowered by the availability of information and knowledge, and the technologies do not interfere with their work. Technology is moving to the background, and information and knowledge to the fore. Customers in future are going to require knowledge not only greater depths and breadths, but also that organizations present these in a clear, cogent, and easy-to-use manner. Take the mobile phone: in the recent past, it weighed twice as much as today and performed only a tenth of the current functionalities. In our opinion, customers are going to put similar demands on organizations. Organizations are going to be forced to lay out architectures and spaces that their customers can utilize in emergent manners. Having thin clients calls for the organization to demonstrate agility. Agile organizations are going to win over those who are adaptative or just flexible. Agile organizations are able to create or reshape products and services in a time-constrained environment. This will require foresight with regard to customer behaviors and needs, which comes only from being customer-focused.

Involved knowledge management

An organization consists of various groups, each of these made up of individuals. Groups range in composition from manual workers such as plumbers and mail delivery personnel to strategists and abstract thinkers like senior managers. Groups differ in their knowledge bases, for example engineering and accounting, and also in their problem-solving orientation and skills. The strength of any organization lies in the underlying mechanism of integration that brings these disparate and distinct entities together to work in a cohesive fashion. Imagine the chaos that would result if the accounting department worked independently of the engineering or marketing group. Each group needs to be engaged with the realities of the other entities in the organization, and all must work in an interdependent fashion for success.

The success of knowledge management efforts calls for no less serious efforts towards integration. Each group can and should contribute to the knowledge management efforts in the organization. And by contribute, we do not mean simply take part in the implementation of knowledge management. For example, it is one thing to use a knowledge management system, and quite another to help design it. The former is what many mean by participating in knowledge management efforts. Unfortunately, however, participating after the fact, that is after the system has been designed, has limited value. We would like to challenge the organization to get all the various groups and sectors involved in the design of the knowledge management policies, procedures, mechanisms, and systems. Each group must be engaged to do their bit to contribute their know-how to help the organization to leverage knowledge better.

A case in point: industrial engineers

Two years back, one of us was challenged on this very point: Can each group contribute to the organization's knowledge management program? Over a few pints of beer and a heated debate, a bet was set: write an article that demonstrated how industrial engineers (IEs) could contribute to knowledge management efforts.[1] Let us share with the reader some of the material from that article.

What does knowledge management have to do with industrial management? At first glance, many people would dismiss an association and claim the ideas are at opposite ends of the spectrum. Industrial management is a well-defined science to a great degree, while knowledge management is still an undefined art and an emerging science. We will assert, however, that industrial engineers are the optimal group to enable the systematization of knowledge management efforts in organizations. The know-how and experiences of IEs can be brought to bear on solving the difficult problem of managing knowledge in organizations.

IEs are involved with the design, construction, installation, and advancement of complex systems. The central tenet is to design operational and reliable complex systems while being efficient through minimization of resource consumption. Complex systems can be broadly defined as entities in which two or more components interact in non-linear and highly dynamic ways. Much as with the problems faced by IEs, the knowledge management problem in organizations is one of managing a complex system.

The knowledge IEs possess is varied, ranging from the highly quantitative (such as mathematics and physics) to the qualitative (such as the social sciences and management). The focus areas in which an IE needs to possess skills are manufacturing or materials engineering, production engineering, system engineering, and safety engineering. Each of these areas has bearings on how knowledge management problems can be addressed. Certain knowledge management issues trouble virtually all managers to some degree:

- How to organize a knowledge repository (a layout problem).
- The best mechanism for knowledge transfer from employee to employee and from system to employee (a transportation problem).
- Maintaining a knowledge management system (a maintenance problem).
- Making a knowledge management system user-friendly (a human factors problem).

The key to having a robust knowledge management system is to tackle all these systematically. Each of them helps an organization better engage the knowledge management program to meet the strategic, process, and people issues. Industrial engineers are well positioned to help tackle these issues.

Before we can manage, we must organize. It is difficult but not impossible to manage things that are in a constant state of unpredictable flux. Take a macroscopic view of an organization and you will find that some sectors generate a lot of knowledge, while others consume and apply such knowledge, and others still take in knowledge without generating appropriate actions. It is rare to find an organization that thoroughly and systematically lays out knowledge; however, some have come very close. We have highlighted the saliency of this issue in our discussion of the segmentation capability. Think about a factory floor, where raw materials evolve into finished goods. Machinery, raw materials, and personnel are organized to achieve goals with the least amount of resource consumption. Things are also organized for the efficient transportation and movement of goods. Similar thinking can be applied to knowledge in organizations. For illustrative purposes, consider a knowledge repository like an intranet portal. Today, such a portal is passive, simply displaying knowledge. It could be compared to a factory with piles of raw materials in one room one, tools in another, and a manual on how to use them in yet another. An employee would have to expend a lot of effort to consume knowledge found in the manual. Were the intranet portal to be redesigned using the principles of workflow and layout design, employees would be able to consume the knowledge in raw form and build a finished product. Advancements in virtual-reality-based engineering can also be imported to help manage and consume explicit knowledge. Some organizations have complex intranet portals that use a workflow model.

Similarly, tacit knowledge is in a constant state of flux in the organization. This is not a bad thing in itself. However, when an organization does not have protocols to manage the dynamic tacit knowledge, things get troublesome. Let's examine how things are managed on a traditional factory floor. In most cases, senior personnel make the rounds, supervising personnel and machines at appropriate internals. Because the layout of the factory is adequately mapped, people know where any given item will be at any point in time. Therefore, people who seek knowledge from personnel or machines on the factory floor can locate information easily. Similarly, efforts must be undertaken to map tacit knowledge in an organization. This is akin to taking an inventory of who knows what, which prevents an organization from losing knowledge through downsizing. Moreover, it will enable the organization to plan for redundancy and failures. IEs can help by devising formulations that detail the fragility of an organization's knowledge base. This can ensure that appropriate backups are in place and tacit insights are captured. Many organizations realize the knowledge drain only after downsizing, sometimes having to hire back old employees at inflated salaries to fill gaps.

When mapping is complete, the next item should be to detail the communication mechanisms people have access to. This will enable the organization to devise primary, secondary, and tertiary communication protocols and will ease knowledge transportation. The ultimate goal of laying out knowledge is to avoid gaps that force groups in the organization to operate in a vacuum that doesn't allow them to consider information that exists in their midst. This leads to costly duplication of efforts.

Knowledge is abundant in almost every organization. The main issue is how to get it from producer to consumer. Ad-hoc and inconsistent knowledge communication (transportation) approaches are pervasive in organizations. Some knowledge gets transferred using computerized systems, some is transferred via formal personal mechanisms such as training and job rotation, and some gets across through informal personal mechanisms such as the grapevine. Most people are at a loss when it comes to deciding which path to request knowledge from and which path should be used for transmitting their own knowledge. The cost of confusion makes knowledge management inefficient and highly unsuccessful in organizations. An additional issue is that of timing. Should knowledge be pushed to individuals, or should they pull it from central sources? Disagreements or lack of clear protocols will result in either famine or abundance, neither of which is optimal. In every organization, some knowledge is ignored because there is no agreement on the path, medium, and timing of transfer.

IEs have training in logistic and scheduling problems; much of it is applied to the movement of digital goods and the scheduling of jobs on factory floors. These insights can be brought to bear on the knowledge transportation problem. IEs can aid an organization by studying the routing and movement of knowledge to determine the efficient mechanisms for connecting people. While striving for efficiency, we can't forget effectiveness, which is critical in designing for redundancy. What happens if a knowledge communication path breaks? What will be the alternative route? Knowledge about scheduling will also be salient. The IE literature is abundant in scheduling algorithms based on the characteristics of goods and the environment. It is unwise to transport perishable goods by land or sea unless the source of such produce is in close proximity. Similarly, certain types of knowledge need to be transported quickly, while others can wait. The study of these dynamics will uncover useful suggestions about how to design appropriate mediums and timing schemes for knowledge transfer.

Most knowledge management systems (KMSs) lack adequate maintenance. The lack of maintenance makes these systems unusable, obsolete, and costly for organizations to manage. When a corporate intranet portal is commissioned, for example, knowledge nuggets are properly classified, efficient search mechanisms are put in place, and the system is usable. As time passes, the system degrades into a state of disorganization. Knowledge nuggets get thrown into the wrong places and are classified improperly. Several versions of the same knowledge object reside in the repository. If the material captured is factually sound and relevant, no rigorous checking takes place on information posted to the system. As a result, there is continuous error correcting and knowledge updating. Like explicit knowledge, tacit knowledge needs maintenance. Consider a start-up organization. Few individuals run the organization, so everyone knows who has knowledge in a given domain. Over time, the organization grows, and things become less clear.

IEs can help resolve such problems in multiple ways. Their knowledge in the design of adaptive and self-repairing systems is pivotal. Consider the design of a printer: Well before the printer stops working, there are signs that, if measured properly, can call attention to the problem. These signs can be used as gauges for proactive repair, which would eliminate the downtime and expensive of reactive maintenance.

Similarly, IEs are well advised to aid organizations in devising appropriate measures that gauge the quality of knowledge management systems. Items such as search and seek times and the amount of duplication can be used as surrogates to predict when a system will become unusable. Proactive maintenance such as organizing and cleaning can make systems more usable and manageable. IEs can also aid an organization in the difficult task of tacit knowledge maintenance. As discussed earlier, the knowledge map of the organization will be crucial. Before an organization contemplates downsizing or mergers it should check how the new organization fits into the existing knowledge map. If it cannot be placed adequately on the map, are there avenues to expand the map? Which knowledge sectors will be lost? Which will be gained? These are important questions to consider in order for knowledge, processes, and people to be aligned for optimal functioning of the organization.

In addition, IEs can aid in the design of flexible systems that will enable growth and evolution. Any knowledge management system in an organization should accommodate modifications and updates that account for changes in the organization. For instance, if more people need to use the system, it should allow for multiple points of access. It should be flexible enough to allow for varying read and write privileges on various knowledge bases. It should be customizable for additions and deletions of knowledge without disruption to the core architecture.

A knowledge management system is useful only if it is accepted throughout an organization. Most knowledge management systems are designed adequately in the aesthetic sense, but they have not been designed appropriately to account for human work factors. To use a knowledge management system, people usually have to leave what they are doing, consult a remote system, and then return to the work. This approach is inefficient and makes it less user-friendly. Moreover, it results in lower usage of the system.

IEs have been working on human factors and safety engineering issues for decades. This knowledge can be used to aid knowledge system design. The goal should be to make knowledge management part of the work processes. Assimilating them into daily work will lead to a true knowledge-based organization. Without this, knowledge management will still be viewed as an ancillary task. IEs have been working on problems that are closely related, such as efforts to "industrialize" work environments. It will be beneficial to apply the same thinking to make knowledge management ubiquitous and pervasive in organizations. IEs can aid in the design and development of real-time "knowledge gadgets." These devices can be used by members of the organization to receive real-time knowledge about products and processes without having to be bogged down by either carrying a laptop or going to a desktop. They are already in circulation through the use of PDAs and cell-phones. Much work still needs to be done to optimize their designs. One of the key areas of research is how to make heterogeneous forms of knowledge transferable adequately among disparate devices. The aim will be to make knowledge management a seamless part of every tasks for every individual in the organization.

As the above discussion illustrates, the skills of IEs are valuable and salient for making knowledge management a reality in organizations. In fact, this may well be the new agenda for IEs. For decades, IEs have optimized, industrialized, and engineered physical components of organizations. The knowledge manager should use the talents of industrial engineers to apply the same skills to the non-physical components of the organization. The case of IEs is only an illustration of the gains knowledge management programs can receive by including the various disparate sectors in the planning, managing, maintaining, and redesigning efforts. Failure to engage the various sectors will call for building knowledge programs that do not resonate with user realities, and hence are subject to being abandoned.

Knowledge management process improvements

The concept of engagement calls for one to be continuously connected. In order to do so, one must constantly seek ways to improve oneself and continuously improve one's processes. Knowledge generated and applied in organizations must be used to *improve* the knowledge management process of the organization. Put another way, knowledge must be used to improve knowledge management.

The discipline of knowledge management currently suffers from lack of reliable metrics, scales, or indicators for gauging how well an organization conducts knowledge management. Gauging the maturity of knowledge management is important for several reasons. First, metrics can help us identify areas of strength and weakness, which can be reinforced and improved respectively. The concept of gap analysis is salient here. Through the use of a maturity model an organization can clearly measure the "gaps" between where it currently stands and where it needs to be. Second, if maturity metrics are used by multiple organizations, we will have an opportunity to engage in benchmarking activities. Through benchmarking, best practices in industries can be identified and can be used to improve the process of knowledge management in organizations. Third, an effective maturity model will clearly elaborate and describe the process of knowledge management. Without this, it will not be possible to come up with clear maturity indicators. An outcome of clear descriptions of the knowledge process is the fact that we can view the trajectory of knowledge management, and hopefully control the process in an effective manner. Maturity models are being calibrated by scholars today; we hope that in the future these will receive the intended reception from organizations so that we may more clearly measure the success or failure of knowledge management efforts. The field of software engineering has embraced the capability maturity model; similar models exist in quality management, and in other disciplines. These models have helped to standardize some of terminology in their disciplines and have also forced a renewed interest in measuring processes and outcomes.

In order to improve knowledge processes, we must use the measures to audit each process and hold individuals accountable. Just as an organization's acid-test of performance is found in the release of quarterly and annual financial statements, so we must have statements to show the progress of knowledge processes. Knowledge processes are seldom audited or accounted for in current organizations, which leaves an impression that they are not important.

One avenue where we must make efforts in future is trying to link knowledge management efforts to success (or failure) in organizations. We all know that failure to conduct optimal financial management will come back to haunt an organization and result in poor performance. However, the discipline has yet to establish links between knowledge management and firm performance. We think it is a matter of time before this happens.[2] Can we find a link between successful knowledge management practices and better organizational performance or increases in productivity? It may be difficult to show direct links between knowledge management and organizational outcomes, and we may need to use mediating variables to get the job done. Knowledge management efforts, to be worthwile, should contribute to the strategic potency of the organization. Organizations should lead the effort by devising appropriate scorecards, report cards, or performance measures that link the conduct of knowledge management processes (for example knowledge sharing) to the process outcomes (for example increased employee morale and quicker task completion), and finally to financial outcomes (for example lower cost of goods and services). Work in this area is a must to move the field of knowledge management ahead and build engaged knowledge management programs that earn the respect of all executives.

The sciences of measurement and estimation are home to some of the most contested scholarly debates. Unless we can sufficiently measure a phenomenon we are not capable of describing it effectively. However, we must remember that not everything that can be counted, counts! Measuring the number of documents in a knowledge repository should not be viewed as the sole indicator of system success; it may however be one of many indicators.

Measuring knowledge processes has long been thought to be tricky proposition. This should not however stop us from trying to come up with adequate measures. Measuring and auditing knowledge processes provides us an avenue to pinpoint weaknesses, holes, and gaps. These can then be improved upon resulting in an optimized knowledge processes. An organization that is not engaged with continual improvement efforts will have a knowledge program that is a few steps behind its competitor, and this will result in poor performance in the marketplace.

The engagement imperative

In closing, it is our hope that we have provided a look at the vitality of the engagement concept in knowledge management. The knowledge management efforts of any organization must be engaged with the organizational realities. If this is done properly, an engaged knowledge management program can provide an opportunity for the organization to redefine itself, be more agile, definitely more competitive, and ultimately successful.

It has been our pleasure to put this text in order. We hope that readers have found it useful and insightful. Our project, like any other, has limitations, the most critical being our scarce resources. While we have tried to be thorough, comprehensive, and diligent, we know that this book is far from perfect. Any errors and omissions are our responsibility and should not be attributed to our research sources, our respondents, or our publisher. We hope to hear from our readers regarding any of these shortcomings. Moreover, we also hope that they will share with us their thoughts on matters that have intrigued them, or spiked their curiosities, or challenged their assumptions. We thank them for reading the book, and wish them all continued success in their efforts in engaged knowledge management.

Appendix: Two Commentaries on Knowledge Security Issues

These two commentaries cover knowledge protection, highlighted in Chapter 3, in further detail.[1] As mentioned before, having adequate knowledge protection capabilities will differentiate winners from losers in the competitive environments of today and the future.

Commentary I: Managing security risks in outsourcing engagements

While the increase in offshore outsourcing endeavors will continue in the foreseeable future, we must caution organizations to be cognizant of the security issues involved in these dealings. Most organizations are naive in their efforts to secure the outsourcing deal. We continue to hear horror stories of events that transpired owing to lack of care for security protocols in an outsourcing engagement. Owing to the abundance of attractive benefits, many of the innate security risks often tend to get overlooked or simply ignored. When viewed at an individual level, security risks are summarily dismissed owing to their low probability, but in today's world a breach in information technology could bring down an organization in seconds. Moreover, depending on the organization that sends work offshore, such a breach could be considered as an act of cyberterrorism and undermine national security.

While security risks are inherent regardless of where an information system is created or maintained, the risks are greater when a system is out of one's control both physically and logically. In an outsourcing engagement (especially those that are conducted offshore), the commissioning organization has little if any control over the IS vendor. Geographical distance, costs, time, and resources prevent the client organization from exerting appropriate control over the vendor.

The first security issue that one must contend with is the lack of adherence to security and quality standards. As more software code gets written by offshore development companies, the lack of supervision over how exactly the code is written could be a concern. Since the competitive positions of the offshore developers depend on providing information systems at the lowest possible cost for the highest achievable quality in the quickest delivery time, much of the software development integrity may be violated. Corners may be cut and sacrifices made to ensure a "product" is delivered, which may not be the most reliable or complete one. Many of these offshore development companies have multiple clients; there is no guarantee that a contracting organization's data, programs, and applications will not be duplicated for other clients. Duplication and reuse of code is one of the easiest ways to ensure increased productivity of code writing, which helps to keep costs low. We must be careful of the environment in which the knowledge assets (software code, system designs) are created, and how the process of knowledge asset creation is governed and regulated.

Second, if cost savings are what motivate the offshore contracts, organizations are less likely to spend time and effort on a thorough validation and testing of the code when a finished product is developed. This increases the possibility of malicious code being placed and going undetected, which may be a source of information or data leaks. This is a concern especially when we are dealing with sensitive organizations such as defense departments or national research labs and critical innovation factories. For example, malicious code placed in an IS sponsored by a defense ministry could do serious and profound damage to that country. We are living in a time of international turmoil, when there is no telling how the next war will be fought, but we may be assured the use of technology will be among the deciding factors in the battle. If humans can be taken hostage, there is no reason why technology systems should not be either.

Third, physical control over security regarding systems and facilities is limited when work is done offshore. It is nearly impossible to guarantee that security measures will ensure the data and systems are not compromised. Since outsourcing companies are concerned primarily about perimeter and host security (that is the technical solutions), the people aspects of security are often ignored (we discuss this point in Commentary II). Moreover the necessity to keep costs low and remain competitive may provide a motive for unlawful practices such as password sharing for joint access to copyrighted material, multiple users per system, and so on. These can lead to data leaks and system damage, which in many cases could bring an organization to a halt.

Fourth, intellectual property (IP) theft is on the rise today. Recently we have seen episodes of espionage involving the most prestigious national research laboratories such as Los Alamos in the USA. While the occurrence of these within the country can be prevented or discouraged through the local legal system, the laws of other countries are less hostile to such thefts. When an employee leaves a company or project, experience and knowledge are lost. And while in the USA legal agreements between employees and employers are typically put in place in order to prevent intellectual property (IP) from being placed into the hands of a competitor, protecting intellectual property rights in foreign countries can be difficult. Even in countries where the government feels that it is in their own long-term interest to protect the IP of a foreign investor, this is often not easily done for legal, cultural, or political reasons, and/or because of particular business practices. At Los Alamos, computer hard drives containing information about US and Russian nuclear weapons could not be accounted for. While no evidence of espionage was found by the FBI, it was revealed that nuclear emergency officers were allowed to remove and replace secret classified hard drives from a secure vault without signing for them. This weakness in security control demonstrates that intellectual property representing national security can be mishandled at a domestic level. If such a thing can happen in an institution where security controls and their maintenance should be handled at an extreme level, it can undoubtedly occur in an offshore organization where security controls are not maintained under a watchful eye.

In addition to the physical theft of IP, one must contend with issues of copyright infringement. For instance, while China does have copyright laws in place they tend to favor Chinese companies. The facts show that IP laws in offshore countries are difficult to deal with, which creates a risk for US firms that outsource to these countries. We have witnessed cases where an employee of an offshore vendor attempted to sell proprietary software to a competitor. The deal would have gone through had it not been for some unusual local law enforcement professionals who detested the norm of keeping quiet in return for taking bribes. Another salient issue is the notion of tacit IP. In order for an offshore vendor to produce a piece of software for a domestic firm it must possess some level of knowledge about the domestic's firms business and systems. What guarantees exist to ensure that this will not be shared with other clients or left exposed? In short, none. In acts of international industrial espionage, the greatest losses are sustained by companies in the form of information regarding manufacturing processes and R&D. The way foreign companies acquire such information is partly through foreign research facilities and software development companies working on commercial programs. One must be careful what knowledge one shares with an external vendor, and must be cognizant about how that knowledge is used by the vendor.

Finally, while considering where to outsource, one must consider the geopolitical stability of the environment. In many otherwise conducive offshore environments, political instability is common. This, coupled with the fact that employees working on the projects are often underpaid, culturally different, and even in some cases hostile towards the home countries of their clients, makes a disastrous mix. Let us hypothesize a situation. A disgruntled employee working in Pakistan is approached by a terrorist group. This group offers him a hundred times what he earns in exchange for dropping a worm in the server that secretly leaks information and eventually controls a government organization's server. This situation is not too far from reality and could lead to grave and serious consequences. In fact, in December 2002 the US Customs raided the offices of the Ptech Corporation, a Boston-based company, which handled sensitive military and national security information, including software development on products used by the FBI counter-terrorism unit. It was then reported that Yassin Al Qadi, a Saudi millionaire with possible ties to Bin Laden, underwrote that company. Political unrest and war could have a devastating effect on an organization, were a large portion of its client data and operations to reside in the region affected. Countries currently leading in offshore developing efforts have ironically the highest ranking on the geopolitical risk meter; consider the case of India, where the heated tensions between it and Pakistan continue to mount, with talk even of a nuclear conflict.

Steps towards securing outsourcing engagements

The security risks associated with sending work offshore are grave and need to be accounted for. The success of offshore endeavors will depend on how an organization addresses and navigates these security risks. Organizations need to know two things intimately: who they are selecting as an offshore developer, and their own needs for security. For example, a company that manufactures wire coat hangers and a company that builds rocket delivery systems for the US military will probably have different security needs. Once the security needs are recognized and the offshore developer has been researched a service level agreement (SLA) can be prepared. The SLA is the first step in ensuring success, as it offers a contractual agreement that will measure performance, while also covering legal concerns regarding intellectual property and national or international security laws. As well as having a strong SLA put together, we propose the following simple steps. Taken in isolation many may seem trivial, but executed as a set they can produce a successful offshore campaign:

1. Engage with offshore vendors that have a local (onshore) development facility that can take over operations in case of catastrophe, thereby reducing risk. Make sure monthly backups are done of all programs and data. Upon completion, ship these backups and store them in a locally housed repository for safe keeping.
2. In devising the SLA, make provision for termination clauses in respect of acts of terrorism, national security, and domestic unrest. It is important to contemplate an exit strategy before entering into the engagement. Successful organizations always have a viable exit strategy to manage the engagement, should things go sour.

Devise pre-emptive measures for getting data, systems, and people to a more secure location if the situation demands this. If in-house resources are not available to evaluate the security levels of the offshore vendor, hire an outside firm to perform an initial security assessment in addition to follow-up security audits. This will ensure that security measures are maintained at the levels outlined in the SLA.

3. Backup and documentation have always been critical aspects of system design. They become even more critical as one moves work offshore. The quality of backup and documentation will determine whether an organization will survive and recoup after the damage caused by exogenous forces such as war. For instance, the more recently a backup of the system was taken, the quicker can one reload data with minimum data loss or delay, while on the other hand if the backup was taken a month back, depending on the data the organization could be out of business. It is important that an organization take the necessary steps to ensure that knowledge processes and practices are documented. An organization should not leave these issues to chance. If a contract goes sour, an organization must have the necessary knowledge to be able to manage the work independently of the outsourcer. This will be impossible if the knowledge is not captured in an explicit format.

4. Management must devise a liaison or a project manager who works in closely with the offshore vendor. Their task would involve ensuring compliance to SLA and monitoring performance. In addition, this person must have deep knowledge of the offshore culture and climate so as to proactively advise management on how to deal with issues such as political unrest, worker strikes, and so on. An organization should not rely blindly on certifications and assurances provided by a vendor. Just as nobody ever hires someone simply because they possess a bachelor's degree from a prestigious institution, we cannot rely blindly on certifications. If an organization possesses a certification, such as capability maturity level for software development, it is a good start and may be used as a criterion in pre-screening vendors for contract negotiations. However, before signing on the dotted line, the organization must physically inspect the security protocols in place to ensure that what is documented on paper is actually practiced.

5. Do not rely exclusively on one vendor. The more an outsourcing vendor knows about your organization, the more they can gain. Moreover, relying exclusively on one vendor could result in the organization being taken hostage by the vendor. It is better to work with many vendors and manage the coordination between these entities, so that no single vendor knows all about your organization. In addition, should one vendor not perform to par, work can be shifted to other parties with relative ease, while if an organization relies exclusively on one vendor, it will be difficult for a new vendor to take over operations, as the newcomer will have to begin by learning from scratch.

6. Offshore outsourcing should not be used for developing systems that are highly confidential and strategic to the organization. Management must realize and appreciate the fact that these systems are critical assets for the organization, and as such they must be respected and given due attention both in terms of cost and governance. Systems where privacy, security, and secrecy are prominent ingredients need to be built in-house or in rare cases by external vendors that can be strictly and easily monitored for compliance.

7. Lastly, an organization would be always better off, by maintaining a small local IS staff and keeping their skills up to date. Even if an organization outsourcers all facets of systems development, the local IS staff can help in governance of the outsourcing projects and also serve as a backup to pull work back into the organization, should

there be issues with the vendor. The local staff can also ensure that appropriate security protocols are being met and can communicate changes in protocol between the vendor and the management staff.

In conclusion, we hope we have put offshore security risks in a perspective. The challenge, now, is for you to frame your perspective on the particular risks faced by your own organization and to put that perspective into practice. Remember: offshore outsourcing is here to stay, and as management we must recognize this and do our best to conduct our engagements with it in a secure manner.

Commentary II: Do not let us catch you sleeping – guard your fortress

We have been inundated with issues of technological security. Technology systems are increasingly at risk from attacks by unscrupulous individuals. While we would take nothing away from this point, we do however feel that businesses have gotten so caught up in technology security that they have sometimes forgotten the more basic, yet salient, notion of physical security. By physical security, we mean securing your office buildings and other physical assets from unauthorized access, usage, movement, and destruction. Physical security has lost its glamour, in recent times, and has taken a back seat to issues of technology security. However, an organization can be brought to the ground in seconds if the right perpetrator is able to breach physical security and gain access to sensitive areas in an office building.

To cite a recent example, one of us had just wrapped up a consulting project for a large financial institution (let us call it Gamma) based in the USA. The project was simple and straightforward. Gamma had just finished a review of its security procedures, protocols, and practices. Confident about the strengths of its security regiment, Gamma asked us to see if we could gain access to one its office suites. There was only one condition: we had to gain access using unauthorized mechanisms, that is they did not provide us with any information (such as blueprints of the office layout) or access mechanisms (such as ID cards). Gamma's security protocols were breached in under "ten" minutes! To put this in perspective, the company's budget for security issues ran in the millions of dollars. Here is how it happened. Kevin got dressed in a pair of jeans and a T-shirt and grabbed a FedEx envelope from his office. He then rode the subway to the bank's location and went to the reception desk. The reception desk was a common one for all of the tenants of the office building. He introduced himself as "Kevin," using his real name, and the receptionist said "Hello Kevin, how are you? Whom do you have to deliver the mail too?" (Kevin never said he had mail to deliver, actually he was just there to get a sense of the building premises, but an opportunity for a security breach opened, that could not be wasted.) Kevin replied, "Yes, it sure is a nice day today, can you please let me know how I get to the reception desk of Gamma Bank." The receptionist gave out the floor number of the reception desk, and also informed Kevin that the mailroom was on a different floor. Then, without checking identification or even calling up Gamma's receptionist, she directed him to the elevator. Kevin went to the floor that housed the mailroom, and was greeted by another employee. She advised him that the package (a blank FedEx envelope!) could be left with her and he could leave. Kevin was persistent and insisted that the package had to be hand-delivered to the chief operating officer. The mailroom attendant was eventually convinced, and decided to escort Kevin to the main office floor. She helped Kevin pass the main receptionist desk, once again without any check for identification, and then directed him towards where the chief operating officer's suite was located. Kevin now had access to the main office floor, and by asking two more employees eventually reached the designated office suite. This security breach led the executives of Gamma to rethink a major component of their security plans – protecting the physical organization from intruders.

Gamma's measures to ensure protection of their fortress were simply inadequate; Gamma is not alone in this deficiency. Most organizations are vulnerable to physical security breaches – they are caught sleeping. A lot of money and resources have been diverted to ensuring technological security, many times at the cost of physical security. This is unfortunate and will cost the organization dearly. Ensuring physical security is much easier than protecting one's technology from vulnerabilities. However, organizations have become careless in this area and many have the misconception that ensuring technology security is a much more serious effort than those involved with physical security. To conduct the break-in described above, there was absolutely no technology involved! It was a human penetration of an organization's office space!

Failure to protect the fortress

A large percentage of the personnel who are thrown into a "security" role do not have the necessary knowledge, experience, or skills. We spoke to over 60 different private security personnel who were charged with protecting office buildings in downtown Chicago. Over 85 percent of them had never attended a university or had training in any aspect of crisis management, security, or law enforcement. Of the 15 percent that did attend university, most were college dropouts and had minimal training in security management. Moreover, most of the job descriptions for security personnel were vague in their description as to minimal requirements for hiring. As one of our respondents put it: "In the interview . . . the most important question was if I knew how to use a walkie-talkie." If we do not hire personnel of the right caliber, we should not expect much in terms of protection. To be effective, security personnel must have the requisite knowledge in the areas of security, crisis management, and law enforcement. Without these skills, we might as well leave our doors open to intruders, as the security guard will not know how to effectively detect an intruder, or if they do how to deal with them.

Most organizations view their physical security measures as an expense, not an asset. As such the first line of thinking is: How I can reduce this expense? In the current times of shrinking budgets and difficult growth periods for organizations, any way to reduce expense is looked upon favorably by management. Most organizations outsource their security management functions, many times to the lowest bidder, and without executing due diligence in evaluating the capabilities of the security vendor. In the Chicago downtown area, most security guards barely earn $8 to $12 an hour in wages, with minimal fringe benefits. With such salaries, we cannot expect to attract the best and brightest to take up security positions. What is more critical is that with such low pay, the security personnel can be easily subject to manipulation by scrupulous individuals. For example, if we wanted to get access to an office space and found a security guard who was having a hard time making ends meet on his salary, the chances are high that we could get access to the space after a bit of convincing and upon offering some extra income. Organizations put themselves at risk by creating such environments, where allegiance to the organization may be compromised. Would you pay your best software programmer or salesperson a minimal wage? Of course not! If you did that, they would probably leave for another organization or if they stayed with you they would perform below their true potential. We need to start thinking in a similar fashion when it comes to security personnel.

Security personnel are like puppets in uniforms. In the majority of organizations they lack significant authority or accountability. Put another way, there are always ways to get around them, if someone wants to. Consider the following case. In one organization a security guard was fired after not allowing a person without an ID card into the office building. The security guard did his job; he was hired to prevent unauthorized individuals from entering the building. However, the person he stopped was a senior member of the organization's management team. Because he questioned the senior official of the organization and delayed him for a few moments, the vigilant and innocent-minded guard was relieved from his post. Why? Because he inconvenienced a senior manager. After this incident, do you think any security guard at this organization will stop a person who looks like a senior manager? Security guards have a hard time enforcing "security rules." For example, in most organizations there is a rule stating that you must display your ID at all times. Well, try this for an exercise: walk around your office premises for a day without your ID and see if you are questioned by a security guard. Unless we give security personnel requisite authority they will not be successful in protecting our assets. Just as the police have authority to ensure that all citizens abide by the laws, so security personnel must have authority to enforce security policies.

Securing the fortress

We can now share some guidelines drawn from examination of security practices at various government organizations in the defense and intelligence sectors (DIS).

First, it is not surprising that most DIS organizations do not view security as a cost item. To the contrary, such organizations go to great steps to ensure that their assets are protected from unauthorized access, sabotage, and vandalism. DIS organizations, in most cases, have their own internal security personnel and resist outsourcing this responsibility to a third party. To be in charge of security matters at a DIS organization, one must have a proven track record, possess the necessary knowledge and skills, and be tested for allegiance to the organization. There are extensive training modules provided for security personnel to ensure that they have the knowledge needed to perform their duties.

Second, security personnel at DIS organizations have the authority to take actions for security breaches. In the most general sense, they can reprimand or quarantine a staff member for alleged security breaches. An investigation into failure to adhere to security protocol can significantly impact one's chances of promotion in the organization, or in some cases can even lead to loss of one's job and suspension of security clearances. Private sector enterprises can take serious actions such as termination of employment. There must be a seriousness displayed towards security measures; unfortunately, human nature dictates that sometimes harsh penalties be imposed to show the gravity of the offence.

Third, train, retrain, and retrain. Security policies and practices are not static. They are dynamic and need to be updated on a regular basis as new information on threats becomes available, new security protection measures are implemented, and changes take place in one's operating environment. It is hence important that employees are kept abreast of changes to security policies and practices. This will call for keeping in place a viable training program so that employees and security personnel can be educated on new issues in terms of asset protection. It is a shame to have an updated security policy on paper but no one trained in it, so that the knowledge on paper is not incorporated into practice.

Fourth, it is critical that we have an appropriate asset management system. Security policies are in place to protect against the destruction of assets. We must hence know what assets that we are protecting. An organization must have a way to tag its assets, for example with serial numbers on the computer system, and also have ways to gather information from sensitive assets in real time. This is possible through monitoring the logs of ID card swipes and also by viewing a video camera feed. Highly sensitive assets should have tags in place to detect movement when they are moved, touched, or manipulated in any other way. The use of radio-frequency identity (RFID) tags is helpful here. If attached to an asset of interest, they can be used to track its movements, any tampering with it, and so on.

Fifth, it is important to centralize the security function. One way to achieve this is to appoint a person as the chief security officer. Someone needs to be held responsible for security issues. Unless we have a central unit in place, we will lack thorough accountability. The centralized security unit will be responsible for crafting securing policies, enforcing them, and maintaining them. The unit must have links to the financial, information system, and human resource functions of the organization. These links will be critical in ensuring that they are successful in taking the measures required to protect the organization.

In conclusion, the management of security is a strategic matter for organizations. It must be given the same attention, resources, and care as any other strategic management activity. Failure to do this will compromise the longevity of the organization.

Notes

1 Introduction

1. See *Webster's New Collegiate Dictionary*. Springfield, MA: Merriam-Webster.

2 Engaging Tensions of Knowledge Management Control

1. *Webster's New Collegiate Dictionary*. Springfield, MA: Merriam-Webster.
2. Schumpeter, J.A. (1934). *The Theory of Economic Development*. Cambridge, MA: Harvard University Press.
3. Brown, J.S. and Duguid, P. (2001). "Creativity Versus Structure: A Useful Tension," *Sloan Management Review*, 42 (4), 93–4.
4. Coase, R.H. (1937). "The Nature of the Firm." *Economica*, 4 (16), 386–405; Williamson, O.E. (1981). "The Economics of Organization: The Transaction Cost Approach," *American Journal of Sociology*, 87 (3), 548–77.
5. Davenport, T.H., Thomas, R.J. and Cantrell, S. (2002). "The Mysterious Art and Science of Knowledge-Worker Performance." *Sloan Management Review*, 44 (1), 23–30.
6. Awazu, Y. and Desouza, K.C. (2004). "Open Knowledge Management: Lessons from the Open Source Revolution," *Journal of the American Society for Information Science and Technology*, 55 (11), 1016–19.
7. von Hippel, E. and von Krogh, G. (2003). "Open Source Software and the 'Private-Collective,' Innovation Model: Issues for Organization Science," *Organization Science*, 14 (2), 209–23.
8. Williamson, O.E. (1975). *Markets and Hierarchies: Analysis and Antitrust Implications*. New York: Free Press.
9. Desouza, K.C. and Awazu, Y. (2004). "Need-to-Know: Organizational Knowledge and Management Perspective," *Information Knowledge Systems Management*, 4 (1), 1–14.

3 Engaging with Missing Knowledge Management Capabilities

1. Teece, D.J., Pisano, G. and Shuen, A. (1997). "Dynamic Capabilities and Strategic Management," *Strategic Management Journal*, 18 (7), 509–33.
2. Barney, J. (1991). "Firm Resources and Sustained Competitive Advantage," *Journal of Management*, 17 (1), 99–120.
3. De Holan, P.M., Phillips, N. and Lawrence, T.B. (2004). "Managing Organizational Forgetting," *Sloan Management Review*, 45 (2), 45–51.
4. Liebeskind, J.P. (1996). "Knowledge, Strategy, and The Theory of The Firm," *Strategic Management Journal*, 17 (Special Issue), 93–107.
5. Hamel, G. (1994). *Competing for the Future*. Boston, MA: Harvard Business School.
6. Desouza, K.C. and Vanapalli, G.K. (2005). "Securing Knowledge in Organizations: Lessons from the Defense and Intelligence Sectors," *International Journal of Information Management*, 25 (1), 85–98.
7. French, S. (2003). *Code of the Warrior: Exploring Warrior Values Past and Present*. Lanham, MD: Rowman & Littlefield.

4 Engaging the Knowledge Chiefs

1. Rockart, J.E. (1982). "The Changing Role of the Information Systems Executive: A Critical Success Factors Perspective," *Sloan Management Review*, 23 (1), 3–13; Earl, M. J. and Feeny, D.F. (1994). "Is Your CIO Adding Value?" *Sloan Management Review*, 35 (3), 11–20.
2. Tushman, M.L. and Katz, R. (1980). "External Communication and Project Performance: An Investigation into the Role of Gatekeepers," *Management Science*, 26 (11), 1071–85.
3. Cross, R. and Prusak, L. (2002). "The People Who Make Organizations Go – Or Stop," *Harvard Business Review*, 80 (6): 105–12; Cross, R., Nohria, N. and Parker, N. (2002). "Six Myths About Networks – and How to Overcome Them," *Sloan Management Review*, 43 (3), 67–75.
4. Cross, R. and Parker, A. (2004). *The Hidden Power of Social Networks: Understanding How Work Really Gets Done in Organizations*. Boston, MA: Harvard Business School.
5. Adler, P.S. and Kwon, S. (2002). "Social Capital: Prospects for a New Concept," *Academy of Management Review*, 27 (1), 17–40.
6. Nahapiet, J. and Ghoshal, S. (1998). "Social Capital, Intellectual Capital, and the Organizational Advantage," *Academy of Management Review*, 23 (2), 242–66.
7. Hollis, E. (2003). "J. C. Penney: Fashioning Workforce Development," *Chief Learning Officer*, January, 2003.
8. Markus, M.L. and Benjamin, R.I. (1996). "Change Agentry: The Next IS Frontier," *MIS Quarterly*, 20 (4), 385–407.
9. Desouza, K.C. and Raider, J.J. (2005). "Cutting Corners: CKO & Knowledge Management," *Business Process Management Journal*, forthcoming.

5 Engaging with Distributed Knowledge Management

1. Grant, R. (1996). "Toward a Knowledge-Based theory of the Firm," *Strategic Management Journal*, 17 (Special Issue), 109–22; Tsoukas, H. (1996). "The Firm as a Distributed Knowledge System: A Constructionist Approach," *Strategic Management Journal*, 17, 11–25.
2. Hayek, F. (1945). "The Use of Knowledge in Society," *American Economic Review*, 35 (4), 519–30, p. 520.
3. Ghoshal, S. and Bartlett, C. (1998). *Managing across Borders*. Boston, MA: Harvard Business School.
4. On a personal note we would like to acknowledge the many great contributions made by Sumantra Ghoshal to the field of management. Sumantra Ghoshal was born in 1948 in Calcutta, India. He wrote two PhD dissertations at MIT's Sloan School of Management and at the Harvard Business School. Dr Ghoshal was a vivid, eclectic, and renowned management scholar, mentor, adviser, and friend to many of us in the management field. Professor Ghoshal died of a brain hemorrhage on March, 2004, at Hampstead, UK. Kevin Desouza would like to personally acknowledge his guidance in thoughts and words on his paper, "Global Knowledge Management Strategies" published in the *European Management Journal* in 2003, 21 (1), 62–7.
5. Gupta, A.K. and Govindarajan, V. (1991). "Knowledge Flows and The Structure of Control within Multinational Corporations," *Academy of Management Journal*, 16 (4), 768–92; Gupta, A.K. and Govindarajan, V. (2000). "Knowledge Flows within Multinational Corporations," *Strategic Management Journal*, 21 (4), 473–96.

6. Desouza, K.C. and Evaristo, J.R. (2003). "Global Knowledge Management Strategies," *European Management Journal*, 21 (1), 62–7; Desouza, K.C. and Evaristo, J.R. (2004). "Managing Knowledge in Distributed Projects," *Communications of the ACM*, 47 (4), 87–91.

7. Zeigler, C.A. (1985). "Innovation and the Imitative Entrepreneur," *Journal of Economic Behavior and Organization*, 6 (2), 103–21.

8. Katz, R. and Allen, T.J. (1982). "Investigating the Not Invented Here (NIH) Syndrome: A Look at the Performance, Tenure and Communication Patterns of 50 R&D Projects Groups," *R&D Management*, 12 (1), 7–19.

9. Michailova, S. and Husted, K. (2003). "Knowledge-Sharing Hostility in Russian Firms," *California Management Review*, 45 (3), 59–77.

10. Evaristo, J.R. and Fenema, P.C.V. (1999). "A Typology of Project Management: Emergence and Evolution of New Forms," *International Journal of Project Management*, 17 (5), 275–81.

11. Evaristo, J.R. Scudder, R., Desouza, K.C. and Sato, O. (2004). "A Dimensional Analysis of Geographically Distributed Project Teams: A case study," *Journal of Engineering and Technology Management*, 21 (3), 175–89.

12. Desouza, K.C. and Evaristo, J.R. (2004). "Managing Knowledge in Distributed Projects," *Communications of the ACM*, 47 (4), 87–91.

13. Awazu, Y., Desouza, K.C. and Evaristo, J.R. (2004). "Stopping Runaway Information Technology Projects," *Business Horizons*, 47 (1), 73–80.

14. Hargadon, A. (1998). "Firms as Knowledge Brokers: Lessons in Pursuing Continuous Innovation," *California Management Review*, 40 (3), 209–27; Hargadon, A. and Sutton, R. (1997). "Technology Brokering and Innovation in a Product Development Firm," *Administrative Science Quarterly*, 42 (4), 716–49.

15. Hoopes, D.G. and Postrel, S. (1999) "Shared Knowledge 'Glitches' and Product Development Performance," *Strategic Management Journal*, 20 (9), 837–65.

16. Hargadon, op. cit.

17. Desouza, K.C., Dingsøyr, T. and Awazu, Y. (2005). "Experiences with Conducting Project Postmortems: Reports vs. Stories and Practitioner Perspective," in *Proceedings of the Thirty-Eighth Hawaii International Conference on System Sciences* (HICSS-38), Big Island, HI, Jan. 3–6, 2005. Los Alamos, CA: IEEE.

18. Birk, A., Dingsøyr, T., and Stålhane, T. (2002). "Postmortem: Never Leave a Project Without It," *IEEE Software*, 19 (3), 43–5.

19. Collier, B., DeMarco, T. and Fearey, P. (1996). "A Defined Process for Project Post-mortem Review," *IEEE Software*, 13 (4), 65–72.

6 Engaging Knowledge Management in Strategic Alliances

1. Prahalad, C.K. and Ramaswamy, V. (2004). *The Future of Competition: Co-Creating Unique Value with Customers*. Boston, MA: Harvard Business School Publishing.

2. Kogut, B. (1988). "Joint Ventures: Theoretical and Empirical Perspectives," *Strategic Management Journal*, 9 (4), 319–32; Gulati, R. (1998). "Social Structure and Alliance Formation Patterns: A Longitudinal Analysis," *Administrative Science Quarterly*, 40 (4), 619–52; Gulati, R. and Singh, H. (1997). "The Architecture of Cooperation: Managing Coordination Costs and Appropriation Concerns in Strategic Alliances," *Administrative Science Quarterly*, 43 (4), 781–814; Gulati, R. (1998). "Alliances and Networks," *Strategic Management Journal*, 19 (4), 293–317; Simonin, B.L. (1990). "Ambiguity and the Process of Knowledge Transfer in Strategic Alliances," *Strategic Management Journal*, 20 (7), 595–623.

3. Williamson, O.E. (1979). "Transaction-Cost Economics: The Governance of Contractual Relations," *Journal of Law and Economics*, 22 (2), 233–61.
4. Teece, D.J. (1986). "Profiting from Technology Innovation: Implications for Integration, Collaboration, Licensing and Public Policy," *Research Policy*, 15 (6), 285–305.
5. Dyer, J.H. and Nobeoka, K. (2000). "Creating and Managing A High-Performance Knowledge-Sharing Network: The Toyota Case," *Strategic Management Journal*, 21 (3), 345–67.
6. von Stamm, B. (2004). "Collaboration with Other Firms and Customers: Innovation's Secret Weapon," *Strategy + Leadership*, 32 (3), 16–20.
7. Fine, C.H. (1998). *Clockspeed: Winning Industry Control in the Age of Temporary Advantage*. Reading, MA: Perseus.
8. Bleekel, J. and Ernst, D. (1991). "The Way to Win in Cross-Borders Alliances," *Harvard Business Review*, 69 (6), 127–35.
9. Nanda, A. and Williamson, P. (1995). "Use Joint Ventures to Ease the Pain of Restructuring," *Harvard Business Review*, 73 (6), 119–28.
10. Dyer, J.H., Kale, P. and Singh, H. (2001). "How to Make Strategic Alliances Work," *Sloan Management Review*, 42 (4), 37–43.

7 Engaging with Customer Knowledge Management

1. Prahalad, C.K. and Ramaswamy, V. (2004). *The Future of Competition: Co-Creating Unique Value with Customers*. Boston, MA: Harvard Business School.
2. Levinson, M. (2004). "Data Mining for Carbs," *CIO*, April 15.
3. Davenport, T.H., Harris, J.K. and Kohli, A. (2001). "How Do They Know Their Customers So Well?" *Sloan Management Review*, 42 (2), 63–73.
4. von Hippel, E. (1991). "'Sticky Information' and the Locus of Problem Solving: Implications for Innovation," *Management Science*, 40 (4), 429–39.
5. von Hippel, E. and Katz, R. (2002). "Shifting Innovation to Users via Toolkits," *Management Science*, 48 (7), 821–34.
6. Thomke, S. and von Hippel, E. (2002). "Customers as Innovators: A New Way to Create Value," *Harvard Business Review*, 80 (4), 74–81.
7. von Hippel, E. (1989). "New Product Ideas from 'Lead Users'," *Research Management*, 32 (3), 24–7.
8. Davenport *et al.*, op. cit.
9. Reichheld, F.F. (1994). "Loyalty and the Renaissance of Marketing," *Marketing Management*, 2 (4), 10–20.
10. Levinson, M. "Getting to Know Them," *CIO Magazine*, February 15, 2004.
11. Culnan, M.J. and Armstrong, P.K. (1999). "Information Privacy Concerns, Procedural Fairness, and Impersonal Trust: An Empirical Investigation," *Organization Science*, 10 (1), 104–15.
12. Mittal, B. and Lassar, W.M. (1996). "The Role of Personalization in Service Encounters," *Journal of Retailing*, 72 (1), 95–109.
13. Day, G. (1990). *Market-Driven Strategy: Process for Creating Value*. New York: Free Press.
14. Bettencourt, L.A., Ostrom, A.L., and Brown, S.W. and Roundtree, R.I. (2002). "Client Co-Production in Knowledge Intensive Business Services," *California Management Review*, 44 (4), 100–28.

8 Engaging to Construct Knowledge Markets

1. Biggart, N.W. and Delbridge, R. (2004). "Systems of Exchange," *Academy of Management Review*, 29 (1), 28–50.

2. Desouza, K.C. and Awazu, Y. (2003). "Constructing Internal Knowledge Markets: Considerations from Mini-Cases," *International Journal of Information Management*, 23 (4), 345–53.
3. Yoshimura, K. (1996). *Network Renaissance*. Tokyo: JMAM.
4. Kambil, A. and van Heck, E. (2002). *Making Markets*. Boston, MA: Harvard Business School.
5. Varian, H. and Shapiro, C. (1999). *Information Rules*. Boston, MA: Harvard Business School.
6. Desouza, K.C., Yamakawa, S. and Awazu, Y. (2004). "Pricing Organizational Knowledge: An Imperative," *Ivey Business Journal*, 67 (7), 1–5.
7. The reason for choosing two suppliers is for brevity and clarity in discussion; all matter discussed below can very easily be adapted to an *n*-supplier model.
8. Akerlof, G. (1970). "The Market for Lemons;" *Quarterly Journal of Economics*, 84 (3), 488–500.

9 Engaging to Calibrate Knowledge Management Systems

1. Desouza, K.C., Awazu, Y., and Wan, Y. (2005). "Factors Governing The Consumption of Explicit Knowledge," *Journal of the American Society for Information Science and Technology*, forthcoming.
2. Granovetter, M. (1973). "The Strength of Weak Ties," *American Journal of Sociology*, 78 (6), 1360–80.
3. Hansen, M.T. (1999). "The Search-Transfer Problem: The Role of Weak Ties in Sharing Knowledge across Organization Subunits," *Administrative Science Quarterly*, 44 (1), 82–111.
4. Desouza, K.C. (2003). "Barriers to Effective Use of Knowledge Management Systems in Software Engineering," *Communications of the ACM*, 46 (1), 99–101.
5. Cross, R., Parker, A., Prusak, L. and Borgatti, S.P. (2001). "Knowing What We Know: Supporting Knowledge Creation and Sharing in Social Networks," *Organizational Dynamics*, 30 (2), 100–20.
6. Rogers, E. (1983). *Diffusion of Innovations*, 3rd ed. New York: Free Press.
7. Venkatesh, V. and Davis, F.D. (2000). "Theoretical Extension of The Technology Acceptance Model: Four Longitudinal Field Studies," *Management Science*, 46 (2), 186–204.
8. Desouza, K.C., Dingsøyr, T. and Awazu, Y. (2005). "Experiences with Conducting Project Postmortems: Reports vs. Stories and Practitioner Perspective," in *Proceedings of the Thirty-Eighth Hawaii International Conference on System Sciences* (*HICSS-38*), Big Island, HI (Jan. 3–6, 2005). Los Alamos, CA: IEEE.
9. Desouza, K., Awazu, Y. and Ramaprasad, A. (2004). "Modifications and Innovations to Technology Artifacts," *Diffusion Interest Group in Information Technology* (*DIGIT*) *Workshop*, Washington, DC (Dec. 12, 2004).
10. Antonelli, C. (1994). "Localized Technological Change and the Evolution of Standards as Economic Institutions," *Information Economics and Policy*, 6 (4), 195–216.
11. Gould, S.J. (1991). "Exaptation: A Crucial Tool for Evolutionary Psychology," *Journal of Social Issues*, 47 (3), 43–65.
12. Nonaka, I. and Konno, N. (1998). "The Concept of 'Ba': Building a Foundation for Knowledge Creation," *California Management Review*, 40 (3), 40–54.
13. Boland, R. and Tenkasi, R. (1995). "Perspective Making and Perspective Taking in Communities of Knowing," *Organization Science*, 6 (4), 350–72.

10   The Future of Engaged Knowledge Management

1. Desouza, K.C. (2004). "Knowledge Management: A New Commission for Industrial Engineers," *Industrial Management*, 46 (1), 26–30.
2. Desouza, K.C. (2004). "My Two Cents on Knowledge Management," *Journal of Information Science and Technology*, 1 (2), 1–6.

Appendix: Two Commentaries on Knowledge Security Issues

1. The first commentary is adapted from Desouza, K.C., Awazu, Y. and Mehling, J. (2004). "The Risks of Outsourcing," *J@pan.Inc*, 60 (October) 32–7. The second one is adapted from Desouza, K.C. and Awazu, Y. (2004). "Do Not Let Us Catch You Sleeping: Guard Your Fortress," *J@pan.Inc*, 61 (November), 20–3.

Index